Visual perception: An introduction

Visual perception:
An introduction

2nd edition

Nicholas J. Wade and Michael T. Swanston

Published in 2001 by Psychology Press Ltd
27 Church Road, Hove, East Sussex, BN3 2FA

www.psypress.co.uk

Simultaneously published in the USA and Canada
by Taylor & Francis Inc
325 Chestnut Street, Suite 800, Philadelphia, PA 19106

Psychology Press is part of the Taylor & Francis Group

British Library Cataloguing in Publication Data
A catalogue record for this book is available from the British Library

Library of Congress Cataloging-in-Publication Data
Wade, Nicholas
   Visual perception: an introduction / Nicholas J. Wade and Michael
Swanston.–2nd ed.
      p. cm.
   Includes bibliographical references and index.
   ISBN 1–84169–203–4 (hbk) – ISBN 1–84169–204–2 (pbk.)
      1. Visual perception.   2. Visual discrimination.   3. Motion
perception (Vision)   4. Vision–History. I. Swanston, Michael, 1947-
II. Title.
BF241.W32 2001
152.14–dc21   2001016093

ISBN 1–84169–203–4 (hbk)
ISBN 1–84169–204–2 (pbk)

Cover design by Jim Wilkie
Typeset in the UK by RefineCatch Limited, Bungay, Suffolk
Printed and bound in the UK by Biddles Limited,
Guildford and King's Lynn

To our families

Contents

Preface to first edition

Vision is our dominant sense. We derive most of our information about the world—about where things are, how they move, and what they are—from the light that enters the eyes and the processing in the brain that follows. These functions are performed by all sighted animals, including ourselves, and yet we still do not understand how. Vision is also the sense about which we know the most, because of the vast amount of empirical research that has been undertaken over the years. This large body of knowledge is celebrated in most of the textbooks that have been written on visual perception; indeed, it can act as a shroud that obscures the purpose of vision from many of those who study it. We feel that textbooks tend to focus too closely on the plethora of phenomena of vision rather than on its function: They frequently reduce vision to a series of headings such as brightness, colour, shape, movement, depth, illusions, and so forth, while remaining blind to the uses to which it is put. We have tried to redress the balance a little in this book The principal focus is the function that vision serves for an active observer in a three-dimensional environment—we must be able to see where objects are if we are going to behave with respect to them. Thus the perception of location, motion, and object recognition provides the core to the book, and our intention is to make the ideas involved in their study accessible to the reader with no background in psychology. With this in mind we decided deliberately to avoid citing references in the text. This strategy might prove trying for the instructor, but it is hoped that it has the effect of making the book more readable. If it is necessary to qualify every minor point regarding the experimental base of a scientific discipline then it can not be very securely founded. Another feature we have tried to stress is the historical context in which our present studies are conducted. The history of the study of vision is as long as that of science itself, and many forces have fashioned the conceptual framework in which it operates today—our ideas have been shaped by art, optics, biology, and philosophy as well as by psychology. We need to appreciate these influences if we are to learn from, and avoid repeating, errors from the past.

The other framework that has structured this book is that of three-dimensional space: All our behaviour takes place with respect to it, and since behaviour is guided by perception it is logical that they share the same coordinate systems. In the course of our joint research on space and motion perception we have developed a scheme for examining the logical stages through which we believe perception passes. This scheme, which involves specifying the frames of reference for extracting visual information, has guided the description of vision presented here. It has involved the introduction of some novel terms in the text, but we believe that this is a small price to pay for maintaining a degree of coherence when dealing with widely disparate topics in vision. It has also resulted in some selectivity of subject matter, but this can be remedied by referring to the general references cited at the end of each chapter.

Science is a social endeavour, and we have benefited from collaboration with many colleagues most particularly with Ross Day, Walter Gogel, Ian Howard, Hiroshi Ono, and Charles de Weert. We also wish to express our thanks to Mark Georgeson who read the manuscript with great care; we have profited from the many insightful comments he made on it. The errors that remain are, of course, our own.

Vision is a subject of enquiry that has fascinated students for centuries and continues to hold our attention. We hope that some of those who read this book will be encouraged to join in the endeavour of broadening our understanding of it.

Nicholas J. Wade and Michael T. Swanston
Dundee

Preface to second edition

When we began the task of preparing a second edition of this book, we were unsure how much of the original structure and content should be retained. After all, there have been far-reaching developments in visual science during the last decade. Also, we now have experience of students' responses to the book, and the benefit of views from many colleagues. As a result there have been considerable changes, and many sections have been rewritten. However, the essential structure of the book is unchanged. It is still based on a functional approach to vision as a basis for action, and the core chapters are those concerned with perceiving the location, motion, and identity of objects in the environment. The introductory chapter has been rewritten and expanded, as has the following chapter on the historical roots of modern concepts about how we see. The chapters on location and motion retain the same emphasis on defining the frames of reference within which object characteristics are represented, but we have sought to make the development of the ideas clearer and more accessible to students. The conceptual model that informed our analysis of space and motion has itself evolved in the last decade, and shadows of these developments are cast in the core of the book and in the Summary and Conclusions. The chapter on recognition (Chapter 6) has been radically revised, and we have included sections on the major theoretical approaches to this topic. Nevertheless, we have retained the original basis for this account, which is the definition of the representations on which object recognition can be based and how this can be derived from visual and other sensory stimulation. A new chapter on the perception of visual representations such as pictures has been added (Chapter 7). This includes a section concerned with the perception of computer-generated images, which is an increasingly pervasive aspect of visual experience.

Much of what was said in the Preface to the first edition is still entirely relevant to the second edition. However, we have decided to introduce a limited number of references in the body of the text, and we hope that this will help students with the critical transition to learning from a wider range of sources. We hope that the book will normally be read as a whole, but it is also possible to use various chapters independently or in groups. Chapter 2, "The Heritage", can be read on its own, or omitted if historical issues are not of particular concern. Clearly, we would argue that this is not a strategy likely to lead to a balanced perspective on modern achievements, but if time is short this may be a sensible strategy. Chapters 1, 4, 5, and 6 are the core of the book, and these constitute a minimal selection. Our experience, no doubt shared by others, is that students will probably be drawn to read just those chapters that they have been told to omit, and that this often leads to the most useful subsequent discussion. We have tried throughout the book to reflect the intrinsic fascination of the subject matter, and its relevance for everyday activity and experience. Although there are many illustrations, there are very few of the pedagogical devices of modern textbooks, such as discussion boxes, quizzes, and the like. We have eschewed these for the sake of narrative continuity and because we are unsure of their real worth. We hope that the book will demand effort to achieve understanding. This effort will be repaid if it facilitates analysis and discussion in the tutorial setting and a desire to learn more about vision.

We are grateful to a number of people for helpful comments on the first edition, and to the very careful and thoughtful readers of a draft of this second edition, including Johan Wagemans, John Harris, Tom Troscianko, and Iain Gilchrist. Any errors and infelicities that remain are of course our own responsibility, but they are certainly fewer than would otherwise have been the case. Our families have continued to show the unqualified support and tolerance of our collaboration on this and other endeavours that has made the work possible, and we are glad to have this opportunity to say how grateful we are.

Nicholas J. Wade and Michael T. Swanston
Dundee

1 Understanding visual perception

The world around us seems concrete and immediate, and our ability to perceive it is easily taken for granted. Objects have positions, shapes, and colours that seem to be perceived instantly, and we can reach for them or move to where they are, without any apparent effort. Clearly, there must be some process that gives rise to visual experience, and it is not surprising that throughout history people have found it fascinating. If what we perceive is what we take to be true or factual about the world, are everyone's experiences the same? What is the perceptual world of animals, or infants, like? What sorts of errors do we make in perceiving? Can perceptual experience be communicated to others? Philosophers, artists, physicians, and, more recently, psychologists have tried to find ways to answer such questions, which are among the most fundamental that can be posed about the human mind.

Although we perceive the world around us, we have no direct knowledge of how this experience comes about. In fact, it can often be hard to believe that there is any mechanism involved in perception at all; for most people, most of the time, perceptions are simply "given" as facts about the world that are obviously correct. Perception is indeed a fundamental psychological process, and a very remarkable one. Its success in providing us with accurate information about the characteristics of the world around us is an index of its power, because there are relatively few situations in which it is seriously in error. A perceptual process that gave rise to subjective experiences grossly different from physical reality would make survival virtually impossible.

This chapter provides an overview of central issues in the study of visual perception, many of which will be discussed in more detail in later chapters. It is important to understand the functions that any visual system must perform if there is to be coordinated, effective action, and the problems of devising explanations for how this comes about. If perception is to be explained, appropriate measurements of its characteristics must be obtained, and related to the information potentially available from the physical environment. Each of these issues contributes to the general framework of ideas that guides the investigation of vision.

FUNCTIONS OF VISUAL PERCEPTION

We all enjoy contemplating the experiences provided by our senses, and much of our language is associated with describing them. In human cultures considerable effort is devoted to enhancing perceptual experiences by decorating our bodies and our surroundings and by producing artefacts (like pictures) to stimulate the senses and to channel our contemplations. With so much emphasis on extending our perceptual experiences it is tempting to think of their function as enabling us to enjoy and describe them. In evolutionary terms the function of perception is much more mundane—it is to enable us to interact with the objects in the world surrounding us. More specifically, we use our perceptions to guide our behaviour. We use vision to determine the location of objects with respect to us, so that we can approach them, grasp them, cast them aside, or avoid them as appropriate for our survival. Some objects, like food, will be particularly significant for our sustenance, and we learn how to recognise them from all sorts of positions. Perceiving the location of objects and recognising them is achieved when we are still or moving, or if the objects themselves move. Accordingly, we need to be able to distinguish between static and moving objects whether we ourselves are static or moving.

Action and recognition

The distinction between action and recognition can be illustrated with an everyday example of their operation that we have all engaged in successfully many times—crossing the road. We walk up to the kerbside, look in both directions and cross the road if it looks safe to do so. But what does this seemingly simple sequence entail, and how can it be explained? Crossing the road itself requires coordinated activities in many muscle groups that control balance and locomotion. However, before the walking is initiated a whole series of decisions have to be made on the basis of perceptual information. How far away is the kerb and in what direction is it? How wide is the road and how much time will be required to cross it? Is there a vehicle approaching? What size is it? How far away is it? How fast is it travelling? How long will it take to reach here? What type of vehicle is it? Each of these questions is directed to some aspect of the three-dimensional environment and our relation to it.

How far away is the kerb and in what direction is it? To answer these questions it is necessary to determine where the pavement stops and where the road starts. It could be on the basis of some markings (e.g., white lines) that we have learned to associate with roads, or on a difference in the perceived level of the two surfaces. Some theorists consider that we can derive information regarding the orientations of surfaces in the environment without recourse to knowledge about the nature and purpose of objects. That is, the information available in the pattern of stimulation is sufficient to specify the layout of space with respect to the viewpoint of the observer, and assumptions about the nature of the world are not necessary. On the other hand, perception can be likened to thinking and other high-level cognitive processes such as reasoning and problem solving. Such cognitive theorists argue that we use our knowledge of roads and their features to recognise the kerbside, and that we make use of a "knowledge-base" to find and identify objects in the visual scene. Thus what we see is a logical, rational interpretation of sensory information on the basis of stored knowledge, in terms of possible real events. It is certainly not necessary to have verbal labels like "pavement" and "road" to perceive the positions and sizes of the actual objects, as guide dogs for blind people carry out such discriminations with remarkable skill. In the discussion that follows, we will contrast the capabilities of a human and a guide dog in crossing a road, as this helps to indicate how far the perceptual processes involved depend on verbal knowledge.

How wide is the road and how much time will be required to cross it? When the edges of the road have been isolated, by whatever means, some estimate of the distances of both from the observer is required. Distance information can be with respect to the observer or between objects in the visual scene. For example, the near kerb could be perceived as 2 metres away and the far kerb 20 metres distant, then the width of the road could be determined from the difference between the two estimates. Alternatively, the distance between the two kerbs could be perceived in some relative way, such as "three cars wide". The time required to cross the road could then be computed as long as there is some value of walking speed available.

Is there a vehicle approaching? Before this question can be addressed it is necessary to define what a vehicle is. An abstract definition in terms of, say, a metal body with windows supported by four wheels, would not suffice visually, as we rarely see all the wheels on a vehicle at the same time; often we do not see any wheels at all. Moreover, some vehicles have two wheels, others ten, and so on, making any definition either very abstract or very long-winded. It is more fruitful to pursue the aspect of motion, as the vehicles of importance will be moving rather than stationary. Is some moving object on the road? The perceptual problems involved here are those associated with the principles of grouping, for example the perceptual separation of an object from its background. Such perceptual segregation can be difficult for line drawings, and so it may be all the more difficult for a real scene in which the light intensity differences between an object and its background (which may be other objects) can be minimal or nonexistent. Assuming an object is segregated from its background how is its movement perceived? This might be particularly difficult if the background (other objects) also moves.

How fast is the vehicle travelling? A decision as to whether to cross the road is critically dependent on accurate judgement of the velocity of an approaching vehicle. There are differences of interpretation by theorists depending upon the extent to which perception is thought of as "data driven" or "hypothesis driven". In the former case other perceptual information about the distance of landmarks and size of the vehicle might be used to obtain an

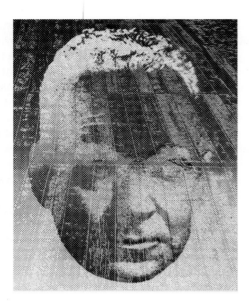

Figure 1.1 James J. Gibson (1904–1979), as represented in Wade (1995).

estimate of velocity. In the latter, knowledge about the likely velocity and acceleration of familiar vehicles could be accessed. The American psychologist J.J. Gibson (Figure 1.1) rejected the equation of the eye with a camera, and the consequent analysis of vision in terms of processing static images. He replaced the concept of a static projection to the eye in favour of transformations of the pattern of stimulation over time. He referred to the total pattern of light entering the eye as the optic array, and the transformations of it, often as a consequence of the observer's own movements, as the optic flow. That is, he incorporated the time dimension in perception, so that all perception becomes motion perception. Optic flows can be produced by motions of objects with respect to the background or by motions of the perceiver, the projective consequences of which will be different. If a vehicle is moving then there will be specific transformations in the optic array: It will occlude parts of the road in the direction it is pointing and disclose other parts behind it. This situation only occurs with object motion. Observer motion would result in simultaneous displacements of all parts of the optic array. An alternative approach would determine that the vehicle was moving by comparing the information available in successive time frames. Speed would then be estimated by computing distance divided by time, in the manner of a physicist. The problem with this is that the moving object needs to be identified in successive instants, before its movement can be obtained. This requirement for matching different sources of information about the same object is known as a correspondence problem, and it is a feature of many theoretical accounts that rely on analysis of a series of static images. The guide dog can respond appropriately to vehicles travelling at different speeds, so its perceptual system, like ours, can either solve the correspondence problem for movement, or, if Gibson is right, never has to face it.

How long will the vehicle take to reach here? This question is based on the assumption that we have determined how long we require to cross the road. The answer is dependent upon the information gathered from the earlier questions: If we have determined the location of the vehicle, as well as its direction and velocity, we can estimate the time available for crossing the road. Here the guide dog is far superior to humans, for it could cross the road far more quickly than the person it is guiding. However, it has been trained to estimate the parameters that apply to humans rather than to dogs. Moreover, guide dogs are more likely to use pedestrian crossings than are normally sighted humans! If the approaching vehicle is very close to the observer then the time before contact can be determined from the optic flow pattern. This changes in a characteristic way that provides information about the time before a collision takes place.

What type of vehicle is it? This is a question of object recognition. A vehicle can be specified as having a certain size, shape, and motion at a given distance, but it might not be identified as belonging to a particular category. The categories can be general like "motor car" or specific like "red 2000 Ford Focus". Object recognition involves two aspects, discrimination and naming. The first is essential whereas the second is not: The guide dog will perform the first but not the second. We perform many discriminations for which we have no verbal categories. For example, many people can differentiate between species of fish without being able to name them, although some are able to do both. It is the naming aspect that is characteristically human, and so tends to be investigated at the expense of discrimination. It also creates the impression of some implicit discrimination—some comparison of the presently available instance with a mental model of other instances. Here we have entered the cognitive domain, and we are dealing with processes that need not directly influence behaviour. The guide dog can discriminate between a Geo Prism and a Ford Focus, and its behaviour can be suitably influenced, for instance if the Focus belonged to its former trainer. Discriminations can be made on the basis of the perceived surface characteristics (size, orientation, and texture) of objects, and that can be sufficient to guide our actions.

The approaching vehicle could be a toy bus nearby or a normal bus at a distance. According to their sizes and distances from the observer it would be possible for them both to fill equivalent areas of the visual field, that is, to subtend the same angle at the eye. This comparison seems ludicrous in the context of buses on roads, and so it is, because of the vast amount of other information that would distinguish between the two in the real world. Normally we can see other objects too, and most particularly we can usually see the surfaces supporting the objects. Along with other sources of information, called cues to distance, this would allow the ambiguity to be resolved.

Alternatively, knowledge about roads, and the likely objects to be seen on them, could bias the observer towards seeing full-sized vehicles; this would constitute a high-level cognitive explanation. Gibson argued that there is no problem of ambiguity in the real world; rather the pattern of stimulation specifies the sizes and distances of objects. For example the amount of surface texture obscured by an object in contact with it remains constant at differing distances, and this invariant feature could determine the perception of constant size despite variations in optical projection. The guide dog can respond appropriately to vehicles of different sizes and at different distances, but this does not rule out any particular explanation. The dog would be capable of using either size and distance information, or optical expansion, and would have extensive experience of vehicles on roads.

Species differences

Guide dogs are selected because of their temperament, their susceptibility to training, and their vision. The fact that they are successful in guiding visually impaired people indicates that they can detect and discriminate aspects of the world in a similar way to sighted humans. However, there are differences in the vision of humans and dogs as well as similarities. One of the major dimensions is in colour discrimination; this is related to the receptors in the retina and will be described in more detail on pages 126–127.

The senses which respond to external events play the major role in perception, and species of animals differ greatly in the types of physical energy that they can detect. For example, high-frequency sound waves are employed by bats and dolphins for recognising objects and for navigation. Certain species of snakes are responsive to the infra-red emissions of warm-blooded prey, and bees to ultra-violet, so that the appearance of flowers to them is very different from that which we experience.

Spatial vision, the ability to discriminate detail in patterns, also differs considerably across species. Various tests are used to determine the limits of spatial vision (see pages 96–102), and visual acuity in humans is about 10 times better than that for cats. Certain primates (like macaque monkeys) have very similar spatial and colour vision to humans, and so they are increasingly employed as subjects in perceptual experiments, particularly when aspects of the underlying physiology of vision are investigated.

MODELS OF VISUAL PERCEPTION

Our understanding of perceptual processes like those outlined in the previous section has very often been shaped by concepts and models drawn from other fields of scientific enquiry. These have provided ways of describing and explaining the processes that give rise to perceptual experience. At the present time, many of the terms that are used to describe perception, as well as other psychological processes, are drawn from the vocabulary of computer science. This has been a feature of psychology since the 1940s, and it has resulted in new approaches to long-standing problems. Perhaps the most significant concept is that of information processing, which refers to the logical operations performed by a machine like a computer (see pages 80–84). Such operations can be described and analysed independently of the particular physical device that carries them out. This was made clear by Marr (Figure 1.2) whose contributions to visual science have been amongst the most important of recent years. His work brought together knowledge in computer science, psychology, and physiology, and his ideas have had a great influence on the development of the field of machine vision.

Marr defined three levels at which any information processing system, including the visual system, can be understood. At the top level is the description of computational theory. This involves stating the purpose and goal of the process, why it is appropriate in the context of other functions, and the general logic of the strategy needed to carry it out. Below this is the algorithmic level of representation. This level requires statements about the actual sequence of processes that take place, so that the computation is achieved. As an example, consider the process of multiplication. If you wish to multiply two numbers, then the goal of your computation is to generate a third number which is the product of the two. To achieve this, various logical procedures, called algorithms, could be employed. You could repetitively add one number to itself, as often as specified by the second number. Alternatively,

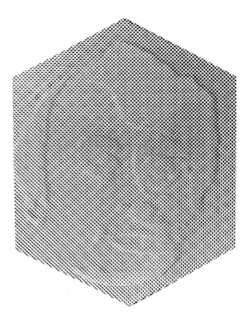

Figure 1.2 David Marr (1945–1980), as represented in Wade (1995).

you could make use of remembered information about the results of such additions, in the form of multiplication tables. Either procedure would in principle produce the correct answer. There will generally be a number of algorithms for any given computation. That is, the computational theory doesn't specify a particular means of achieving a goal, which must be determined independently. Marr referred to the first level as the "what" and "why" of the computation, and to the second as the "how" of it. Independent of both computational theory and representation is the level of hardware implementation. Just as a given computational function can be carried out by a number of algorithms, so a given algorithm can be instantiated by various alternative physical devices. An algorithm for multiplication can be implemented in an electronic computer, a mechanical calculator, a brain, or even an abacus. In terms of visual perception, Marr's analysis suggests that we should be careful not to confuse the different levels of explanation. In addition, the starting point must be a proper description at the level of computational theory, because only this can provide a framework for understanding the operations at lower levels. If we lack a good general description of the purpose of a perceptual process, we are unlikely to understand its underlying logic, or the physiological hardware in which it takes place.

The computer provides a useful metaphor for the brain because both can perform many different functions with the same structures. Despite these similarities we have to be careful not to take the metaphor too far. It has in fact proved very difficult to create anything resembling perception in a machine, despite the advances of recent years. Computer-based machine vision is a goal of many research groups, not least because of the considerable practical and economic advantages that it would give in industry, commerce and administration. However, it has proved exceptionally difficult to achieve, despite a world-wide effort. There are probably several reasons for this, one of which may be the unsuitability of current computer architectures for the simulation of biological information processing. Human vision relies on an extremely large number of relatively simple computations, occurring in parallel. Many of the computing elements are interconnected in a complex manner, which can alter as the result of experience. Since nerve impulses travel slowly compared to electronic signals, and nerve cells take time to recover from activity, biological computation is also slow. A typical electronic computer uses serial processing, in which only one computation at a time can be performed, but at very high speed. There are rapid developments both in parallel computing and in the organisation of processes in the form of connected networks, but the scale of these is at present very far from that of even quite simple organisms. In addition, it is possible that we simply do not have a clear enough idea about the way in which perceptual processes operate to be able to recreate them in a computer. In terms of crossing a road, the output of a video camera would have to be used to find out, amongst other things, how wide the road is, if there are vehicles and how long they will take to arrive. While solutions to some aspects of these problems can be achieved, an effective machine vision system would have to solve them all, and with a very high probability of success. It is certainly true that neither we, nor many animals, are wholly expert at road-crossing, as accident statistics sadly demonstrate. However, we do not know to what extent this reflects a failure of perception, rather than cognition; that is, the individual may see the environment correctly, but may make an inappropriate decision about the riskiness of an action due to memory failure or errors of judgement. Nevertheless most people would be happier to trust their safety to a trained guide dog rather than to the most advanced of machine vision systems.

The lesson from history is that our understanding of the brain has been very dependent on the use of analogies drawn from the current state of physical science. At the time these analogies may have been widely believed, but their inadequacy has become apparent before long. Clockwork automata of great ingenuity were built in the seventeenth and eighteenth centuries, and these seemed to indicate that living organisms might be thought of in terms of similar types of device, although of much greater complexity. Before the electrochemical nature of the nerve impulse was understood, communication in the nervous system was explained by analogy with pneumatic or hydraulic devices, which were in common use. Later, in the nineteenth century, analogies with power and force were widely employed. In the early twentieth century the brain was described in terms of the functions of a telephone exchange, switching messages from one point to another. No doubt all such metaphors are useful at the time they are proposed, but it is important to be aware that they are just metaphors, and that this applies as much to the computer as it does to clockwork. It is simply a measure of our ignorance that we do not know how to characterise the operation of the brain in terms that are independent of analogy with other sorts of mechanism. This situation is not uncommon in science, where an unknown process is described in terms of others that are understood. A good example is the controversy over whether light consists of waves or of discrete particles. Evidence can be produced to support either point of view, depending on the type of experiment carried out. In fact light consists neither of waves nor of particles, since these are metaphors drawn from everyday experience, and both are inadequate characterisations.

Textbooks on perception tend to concentrate on two-dimensional stimuli and the effects that they generate. Accordingly, they have chapters concerned with phenomena like contrast and colour, size and shape, constancies and illusions. The function that perception serves is often hidden amidst the plethora of experimental detail that has accumulated in these areas. This trend has been opposed by the two principals discussed in this chapter. Gibson (1950, 1966, 1979) has written three monographs on perception; in these books he has stressed the importance of vision in guiding action, and also that vision cannot be divorced from the dimension of time. David Marr's book *Vision* was published posthumously in 1982. Marr emphasised that understanding vision can only be achieved by first appreciating the purpose that perception serves. He contended that this purpose will not be discovered by confining our enquiries to particular levels of functioning, like those of physiology or psychophysics or artificial intelligence, rather it should involve all three.

Despite this appreciation of a common goal, the paths proposed to reach it are radically different. Gibson analysed vision in terms of an informationally rich stimulus—the optic flow—that rendered redundant any requirement for internal representations of the world. Marr's whole approach is based upon levels of internal representation, starting from distributions of light and ending in some description of the objects that would have generated the distributions. These contrasts can perhaps best be followed not in the writings of Gibson and Marr themselves, but of their students and supporters. Their theories have not remained static but have been extended and modified by subsequent students. Gibson's approach has been called Direct Perception, and a book with that title summarising his work has been written by Michaels and Carello (1981). The term direct perception refers to the perception of objects in three-dimensional space; indirect perception is concerned with pictures of objects rather than the objects themselves (see Cutting, 1986; Rock, 1997). More detached and critical assessments of both Gibson's and Marr's theories can be found in Bruce, Green, and Georgeson (1996), Gordon (1997), and Palmer (1999). Gordon's book is one of the few concerned primarily with theories of vision rather than data, and it provides an excellent introduction to the problems any theory requires to address.

Early vision

Marr's computational approach to vision has concentrated experimental attention on the various representational levels proposed in his model. A major distinction he drew was between representations dependent upon the viewpoint of the observer and those that are independent of it. For example, the book you are reading is seen at a particular direction and distance from you, and the open pages can be seen but the cover cannot. This would correspond to a viewer-centred representation. On the other hand, you can imagine characteristics of the book (like its cover or whether it is open or closed) that are not tied to a specific viewpoint. Marr called this an object-centred representation, since it uses the object as a frame of reference rather than the observer. Although there are many problems with this distinction, it has led to a division of visual processing between viewer-centred phenomena and those that are dependent on memory. The former is called early vision, and the latter late vision. Another theoretical aspect of this dichotomy is that early vision is considered to be a data-driven (or bottom-up) process. That is, the phenomena are based on the pattern of stimulation at the receptor surface; they occur rapidly, and they are computationally tractable; those usually included under this umbrella are colour, texture, and motion as well as binocular vision (see Papathomas, Chubb, Gorea, & Kowler 1995).

Late vision

Late vision (a term which is not used as frequently) involves the operation of stored knowledge of the world; it would be called top-down in computer terminology. It also encompasses the area referred to as high-level vision (see Farah & Ratcliff, 1994; Ullman, 1996), and one of its principal concerns is with object recognition. Cognitive theories of vision incorporate top-down concepts, because they argue that the pattern of stimulation at the receptor level is impoverished or inadequate to determine our perception; knowledge of past occurrences are required to serve useful perception. Such theories are based in philosophical empiricism (see pages 80–84), and they emphasise the influence of learning in perception. Accordingly, the traditional aspects of space perception, such as perceptual constancies and object recognition, are often subsumed under this heading. Surprisingly, studies of early and late vision share a common concern with two dimensional stimuli; pictures, usually presented on computer screens, are the stimuli used to investigate aspects of vision that are clearly nonpictorial, as is the case for object recognition. The cognitive approach to vision has been advocated in several very readable books by Rock (1984, 1997).

One feature of pictures is that they can readily traduce perception. Even simple line figures can induce errors in our judgements of length or orientation, and these visual illusions have been taken to provide ample evidence of late vision. Gregory (1997) has developed a theory of vision as an hypothesis testing process in which visual illusions are treated as the epitome of late vision. Visual illusions reflect instances where perception is not veridical (not in accord with physical measurements) and further discussion of them can be found on pages 25–29.

MEASURING VISUAL PERCEPTION

Although all of us experience perception of the world, obtaining useful measurements of this experience can be very difficult. The attempt to communicate subjective experience to other people has fascinated and frustrated writers, painters, and other artists for centuries. It is only through communication that we can convey what we see, hear, taste, smell, and feel. Our language is replete with words relating to the senses, but this abundance can provide problems for understanding perception, and alternative procedures have been developed that rely less on language and more on other responses.

One of the standard procedures developed for scientific enquiry into complex natural phenomena is to reduce them to simplified situations in which relevant features can be isolated and controlled. In the case of colour vision, we would want to ensure that a stimulus produced light of a known wavelength and intensity. We might wish to control the size of the stimulus, and perhaps its shape. Other sources of light would need to be eliminated, unless the effect of these was to be specifically studied. Such control over stimulation would generally require laboratory conditions, and usually special apparatus as well. Experiments carried out in this way can provide unambiguous and detailed measurements of visual performance. This approach has been very influential in studies of perception, which often involve visual environments so restricted as to be far removed from natural visual experience. Measurements of perception are obviously easier to obtain when the perceptual experience is itself very simple; for example, sitting in a dark room and pressing a button if and when a single faint light source is seen. The measurements obtained in an experiment are used to infer the nature of perceptual processes, since we can never measure perception directly. It might be thought that this makes the study of perception subjective and indirect, but the situation is not fundamentally different from, for example, an investigation of biochemical processes. Here, too, measurements are used to infer the underlying chemical reactions, which cannot be directly observed. Probably the opportunity for error due to uncontrolled factors is greater with perception, since the system being studied is a good deal more complex, and responsive to a wider range of influences.

Verbal description

The simplest approach is to ask someone to describe their experience, and to draw conclusions from their reports. Descriptions of the same scene or event can be compared across observers, and it may be possible to classify the verbal reports to give some degree of quantification. In principle, free description of experience offers potentially the richest source of information, since language is the most flexible means of communication we have. For many centuries, philosophers and others interested in perception, relied upon verbal description as the only means of obtaining data for analysis (see pages 66–67). Although perceptual experience is subjective, we are able to communicate quite effectively with other people regarding the nature of the world around us; disagreements about experience are much less likely than agreement. Although language is a powerful means of communication, it is nevertheless restrictive; in the limit, only those experiences for which we have words can be described.

Reliance on verbal descriptions has not always clarified our understanding of perception, and this can be illustrated in the context of colour vision. Suppose two people look at a piece of coloured paper: One says that it is red and the other that it is black. Can the same object have two different colours simultaneously? It does not seem likely for a piece of paper, so why are different colours reported? One possibility is that the two people are having the same visual experience, but they are describing it differently—the verbal labels attached to the same experience differ. This could be tested by asking them to describe two other coloured papers; suppose they agree in calling them green and blue, respectively. The problem becomes complicated by this because some colour names correspond and others do not. It would be odd to say that they were each having the same experience for all three colours but only one was described differently. Another possibility is that one of the two individuals is colour defective, that is, one does not have colour experiences like the majority of the population. If so, which one is colour defective? A straightforward way of determining this would be to ask a number of other people—a sample of the population—to describe the same coloured papers, and to note their descriptions. If most of the sample say that the initial paper is red, then it would indicate which of the two people is colour defective. It seems more reasonable to account for individual differences in perception in terms of variations in the mechanisms of perception rather than changes in the world.

Some perceptual experiences vary in intensity rather like the variations in stimulus intensity, so that the question "How much?" can be applied to them. For example, length is such a dimension: Variations in length can be measured physically (say in centimetres) and its perceived intensity can be given a value—we can apply a number (often in similar units) to the length of an object. There are many such dimensions of sensations, like loudness, brightness, duration, and temperature. They are distinguished from other experiences for which the dimension of intensity is inappropriate, even though there is a systematic change in the underlying stimulus dimension. For example, variations in the wavelength of light do not result in variations in intensity, but in colour. Changing the wavelength of light from, say, 550 to 650 nm produces a change in experience from green to red. The appropriate question here is "What kind?" rather than "How much?".

Psychophysical methods

The general characteristics of perception can be determined by verbal description, which provides a qualitative index of what we perceive. In order to study perception in more detail, quantitative measures are required; that is, measures to which numbers can be assigned. With quantitative measures experimental manipulations become possible and hypotheses about the nature of phenomena can be tested. For example, the phenomenology of colour has been very successful in highlighting the aspects of colour vision that require explanation, like colour naming, primary colours, and contrasts between colours. However, in order to study any of these phenomena in more detail it is necessary to relate aspects of the stimulus (like its wavelength) to features of the response. Stimulus definition is in the domain of physics and the response to stimulation is the province of psychology—so relating one to the other was called psychophysics by Fechner in his book with this title published in 1860 (see page 72). For colour many possible response measures could be taken: Detecting the presence of one colour amongst other similar ones; matching the colour of one stimulus to that of another; judging whether pairs of coloured stimuli are the same or different. The physical aspect of psychophysics is the measurement and control of the stimulus, and the psychological feature is the measurement and control of the response. It is generally the case that very simple responses are required, like Yes/No, rather than detailed descriptions of experience.

Psychophysical procedures have been employed to determine the limits or thresholds of perception. Detection thresholds are concerned with detecting the presence of a stimulus of low intensity—e.g., is a light on or off? Difference thresholds are of much greater use: they concern discrimination (the detection of a difference) between two stimuli—e.g., is one light brighter or dimmer than another? Typically, a standard stimulus is presented against which a comparison is judged. The observer indicates whether the comparison is greater or less than the standard on some dimension (e.g., brightness). When they are of similar intensity the judgements can be very difficult, and the observer can make different decisions when the same stimuli are presented on separate trials. Because there is some uncertainty in the observer's decision, and therefore variability in the response, it is essential to measure the same conditions many times. Accordingly, the threshold is a statistical concept; it does not signify an abrupt change between not detecting then detecting a difference between two stimuli. Rather it is an arbitrarily defined point in the gradual transition between these states.

There are various psychophysical methods that can be applied to measure perception. Most are based on the methods developed in the nineteenth century by Weber and Fechner in Leipzig. The classical methods are now called: the method of limits, the method of constant stimulus presentation, and the method of adjustment. The method of limits involves presenting stimuli in an ascending or descending sequence; the sequence stops when the subject's response changes—e.g., from Yes to No, or vice versa. The stimuli change in intensity by fixed steps and they start from a value that is either easily detectable or impossible to detect. Another classical psychophysical method, which has many similarities, is the method of constant stimulus presentation. In both methods stimuli are presented discretely; that is, the stimulus is presented at a single value and a judgement of it is required. Typically a forced-choice judgement is required—either Yes or No. In the method of limits the next stimulus value depends on the last response, whereas in the method of constant stimulus presentation the sequence of stimuli is random. The range of stimuli to be examined is determined in advance, and each stimulus value is presented many times, so that a probability of detection or discrimination can be calculated. In order to prevent the subject from responding Yes to every trial, catch trials (in which no stimulus is presented) are also given. If subjects respond Yes to these then they are probably guessing rather than detecting the stimulus. The method of constant stimulus presentation provides data that can be represented graphically; the graphs can be either in terms of the obtained values or of some smoothed function derived from statistical curve-fitting procedures. The curve-fitting procedure produces an S-shaped relationship which is called the psychometric function (see Figure

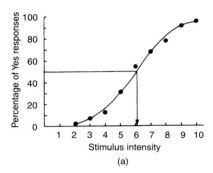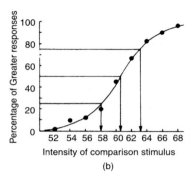

Figure 1.3 Schematic representation of psychometric functions (a) for detection and (b) for discrimination thresholds.

1.3). For detection, where subjects indicate only Yes or No, the 50% point on the psychometric function defines the threshold. For discrimination, where subjects state whether the comparison stimulus is greater than or less than the standard stimulus, the 50% point defines the point of subjective equality (PSE); for some tasks (like visual illusions) this can differ systematically from the point of objective equality (POE). The stimulus range between the 25% and 75% points on the function are referred to as the interval of uncertainty (IU), and the difference threshold is IU/2; the difference threshold is also called the just noticeable difference (jnd).

Both the method of constant stimulus presentation and the method of limits have certain disadvantages. The former is very time consuming, and involves presenting many stimuli that are not difficult to judge; it also requires prior knowledge of the likely threshold so that a suitable range of values can be predetermined. The latter can take many presentations to reach the area of uncertainty (where judgements are difficult to make); there are errors of anticipation and errors of habituation; only one point from a sequence (where there is a change in response) is used in computing the threshold or PSE. The method of adjustment generally provides a more efficient means of measuring thresholds. It consists of the observer adjusting the stimulus to find the threshold. Any single adjustment will have an error of measurement associated with it and this can be reduced by taking the average of many judgements rather than one.

Most information can be derived from judgements that are difficult, i.e., those in the area of uncertainty. Modern modifications of the classical methods have tried to find the area of uncertainty with greater efficiency. Staircase methods have been particularly successful in this regard (see Sekuler & Blake, 1994).

The original concept of threshold, in the nineteenth century, was an abrupt change from nondetection to detection or vice versa. As we have seen, it is now considered as a statistical concept, but is the 50% point on the psychometric function a constant value? In the first half of the twentieth century laboratory experiments to determine absolute thresholds were found not to correspond to the performance of operators in practical situations where the threshold measured depended on the importance of detecting a stimulus. That is, the threshold measured depended upon the motivational state of the observer. Accordingly, a greater appreciation of the decision processes involved in psychophysical judgements led to a novel approach to psychophysics. Green and Swets (1966) named this Signal Detection Theory and they described the procedures that could be employed to distinguish between the detectability of a stimulus and the criteria that affect the subject's responses. Signal Detection Theory can be applied when there are considered to be two states of the world for which there are two possible responses. In the context of detection thresholds the two states of the world are referred to as noise (N), which is variable in intensity and always present, and signal + noise (SN); the responses are Yes (there is a signal) and No (there is not). SN and N are presented many times with the stimulus intensity (signal) set at one level. Factors influencing the observer's decision are the signal probability (the proportion of trials on which a signal is present) and the payoff (the rewards and/or punishments associated with a given outcome). Both influence the threshold measured in the classical way, but signal detection theory provides a way of determining detectability independently of the observer's criterion.

Psychophysical scaling. The classical psychophysical methods were described by Fechner not only to provide systematic techniques for measuring thresholds but also to establish a quantitative index of sensory magnitude. That is, he wanted to use the results to scale the intensity of sensations with the precision that scientists apply to scaling physical dimensions, like light intensity, weight, or sound energy. In other words, he wanted to devise units in which sensory intensity could be measured. The unit he selected was the difference threshold or jnd. Therefore any sensation could, in principle, be measured as so many jnds. But what was the starting point? Here he chose the absolute (or what we would now call the detection) threshold as the zero point on the scale. A contemporary of Fechner's, Ernst Weber, had earlier found that the value of the jnd increases with the intensity of the stimulus with which it is being compared. This is now called Weber's law and it can be described very simply: $dI/I = k$, where dI is the jnd, I is the stimulus intensity against which a variable is compared, and k is a constant called the Weber fraction.

We can use as an example a task that was studied intensively by Weber and Fechner—comparing lifted weights. Let us assume that the standard weight is 100 g (I = 100) and a range of lighter and heavier ones are compared with it, and that the jnd is 2 g (dI = 2). This is equivalent to saying: 98 g is judged as lighter than 100 g on 50% of the time and 102 g is judged as heavier 50% of the time. Then: dI/I = 2/100 = 0.02. That is, the Weber fraction (k) is 1/50 (0.02). Now suppose that the standard weight is 1000 g; what weight will be discriminated as different from this? If we know the Weber fraction and the standard we can calculate the jnd: dI/1000 = 0.02, therefore dI = 20. This is equivalent to saying: 980 g is judged as lighter than 1000 g on 50% of the trials and 1020 g is judged as heavier 50% of the time. The value of the Weber fraction is about 0.02 for heaviness, but it will vary for different types of judgement. For example, the Weber fraction for brightness is about 0.08, for loudness about 0.05, and for line length about 0.03.

Fechner also made a critical assumption—that equal differences in jnd give rise to equal sensation differences. Applying these assumptions to any stimulus continuum results in a curve that rises rapidly and then levels off (called negatively accelerating). It can be represented as a straight line if the magnitude of sensation (S) is plotted against the logarithm of stimulus intensity (I). More generally, the relationship can be expressed as: $S \propto \log I$, which we now call Fechner's law. In words, the magnitude of sensation is proportional to the logarithm of the stimulus intensity.

How can this relationship be tested empirically? It would be very tedious to measure an ascending range of jnds, and Fechner did not believe that sensation could be scaled directly. That is, he did not consider that observers could report the magnitude of sensation. Instead, he used an indirect technique called category scaling. In brief, this involved presenting observers with a wide range of stimuli, and asking them to order some of them into, say, seven categories, so that the differences between categories were subjectively equal. Results using this method generally supported Fechner's law. However, with more research, doubts were cast both on the method of category scaling and on the assumptions Fechner made. First, the validity of Weber's law has been questioned by results from experiments on signal detection. Detection and difference thresholds can be modified by the motivation of observers and by the likelihood of stimuli occurring. Second, all jnds do not appear subjectively equal: jnds at the extreme ends of a stimulus dimension do not seem the same as those in the middle region.

S.S. Stevens (1906–1973) spent many years developing direct methods of sensory scaling. The most basic of these is called magnitude estimation. As its name suggests, it involves an observer assigning a magnitude—usually a number—to each stimulus as it is presented. Different individuals will give widely different numbers for any given stimulus, but a given individual is generally consistent in the relative values given. There is a simple way of obtaining greater comparability between the magnitude estimates of different observers, and that is by assigning a number to a standard stimulus. This is called a modulus, and it is presented before each judgement. For example, in scaling line length the modulus could be a line of a particular length assigned the number 100; other lines could then be presented so that the observer estimates their numerical magnitude in comparison to the modulus.

From magnitude estimation experiments using many other stimulus dimensions (like loudness, brightness, heaviness, duration, etc.) Stevens obtained curves that could not be described by Fechner's logarithmic relationship. However, he did find an alternative equation that did describe all the data from magnitude estimates, and other direct scaling methods. This was of the form: $S \propto I^n$ (which is now called Stevens' Power Law). That is, the magnitude of sensation (S) is proportional to the stimulus intensity (I) raised to the power or exponent n. Stevens' law follows from making a slightly different assumption to that of Fechner, namely, equal ratios of jnd give rise to equal sensation ratios. The value of n varies according to the stimulus dimension examined. For loudness n = 0.6, for brightness n = 0.5, for heaviness n = 1.45 and for duration n = 1.1. In the case of apparent length the exponent is 1.0 (i.e., n = 1.0) and so a graph of length estimate against the line length should be a straight line with a slope of 1.0. For other dimensions, like brightness, the exponent can be determined by plotting the data on log–log coordinates; the slope of the straight line is the value of the power.

Stevens' law is generally considered to be preferable to Fechner's law because it is supported by data from methods that are less prone to bias than indirect category scaling. Many different methods of direct sensory scaling (like cross-modality matches and ratio methods) yield similar exponents. There is also growing evidence that the neural responses underlying stimulation might follow a power rather than a logarithmic function.

Modern developments in psychophysics, including psychophysical scaling, are clearly assessed by Coren, Ward, & Enns (1999), Gescheider (1997), and Gordon (1997); Stevens (1975) presented his own account of the evidence in favour of his law.

Physiological indices

Sometimes there may be no overt behavioural indication of perception, and more indirect physiological measures may need to be used. For example, a person may be present at a concert, but give no indication from their behaviour as to whether they are engrossed with the music or bored to the point of sleep. For vision, we usually show by our eye movements that we are observing an event, but this is not invariably the case. However, it may be possible to measure a physiological response, such as a change in brain activity or in the electrochemical state of the retina, using noninvasive techniques. The electrical changes recorded from the surface of the scalp, reflecting the activity of many brain cells, are known as evoked potentials or event-related potentials (ERPs). For example, the event might be a checkerboard pattern that is changing phase (black squares replacing white and vice versa) at a given rate (temporal frequency), and the small potentials evoked by each change could be measured. Because the ERPs are so small (often only several millionths of a volt) the events need to be repeated many times and the potentials averaged by computer, so that the background neural noise can be reduced. Studies of ERPs are of most interest when they can be correlated with verbal or behavioural indices of perception, but they may be of value even when the latter are not available. Similarly, in experimental animals measures of the activity of single cells may be obtained, at various points in the visual system; much of our knowledge about visual processing has derived from such studies, which are summarised in Chapter 3. Electrical changes in the brain are measured by ERPs, whereas the minute magnetic events associated with neural activity can be detected by magnetoencephalography (MEG). The magnetic signals are so small that they can best be detected (using an array of magnetometer coils) from activity close to the surface of the brain.

More indirectly, physiological measures may be taken of functions which are partly determined by perception, such as heart rate or blood pressure. While the occurrence of a physiological response to a stimulus indicates that a corresponding perception may also take place, it is not a guarantee of this. On the other hand, we may have to be careful not to infer the existence of a perception without careful examination of the evidence. A well-known example is that of the "red rag to a bull"; bulls in fact cannot discriminate red rags from green or blue rags of the same brightness, and the effect, if any, is probably due to movement.

In recent years novel methods of neural imaging have been developed, like positron emission tomography (PET scans) and magnetic resonance imaging (MRI). Both rely on computerised tomography which converts small signals from a range of positions into a model of the brain; the images can subsequently be sliced and rotated. They measure activity in the brain and they have proved helpful clinically because the location of lesions or tumours in the brain can be made with greater accuracy. They can also be employed to correlate activity in a variety of brain sites with perception and cognition (see Frackowiak, Friston, Frith, Dolan, & Mazziotta, 1997; Posner & Raichle, 1997). When some radioactive substance has been administered and absorbed into the blood the brain areas that are subsequently most active have the highest radioactivity, and this can be detected by PET scans. Thus, the sites of heightened neural activity associated with a particular perceptual task can be determined following suitable computer image manipulation; these areas receive a greater blood flow and therefore provide a stronger signal for the detector. The computer-manipulated images can be coloured to signify the regions in which activity has been strongest. Because short-lived, radioactively labelled substances are needed for PET scans there are limits to the measures that can be taken from one person. These constraints do not apply to MRI measures; the subject is placed in a strong magnetic field which aligns atomic particles in the brain cells. Bombarding them with radio waves results in them producing signals, which differ according to tissue type, and can be detected. Functional MRI (fMRI) measures are much more useful for perceptual research, as they are concerned with differences in MRI measured in control and experimental conditions. Cells that are active under the experimental conditions utilise more oxygen and can be detected and imaged. The spatial resolution of fMRI is superior to that of PET scans. Both these procedures correlate changes in oxygen or nutrient use with brain activity, whereas MEG measures magnetic consequences of neural activity itself. The temporal resolution of MEG is very high (around 1 ms) and the spatial resolution is best for neural activity close to the surface of the cortex, and so it is well suited to sensory studies.

The techniques mentioned so far record the activity in the brain associated with some pattern of stimulation. An alternative strategy is to disrupt neural activity in some way. This is achieved with transcranial magnetic stimulation (TMS). A magnetic coil is positioned over a particular area of a subject's head (usually defined by prior MRI measures) and a current is briefly passed through the coil. The magnetic field so produced induces an electrical current in a specific part of the subject's brain (see Walsh & Cowey, 1998). The timing of such TMS is very precise and so it can be applied at known intervals after some visual stimulation has taken place. It is as if the technique produced virtual patients because the disruption is temporary.

All the techniques mentioned have virtues and drawbacks, typically depending on their ability to resolve neural activity in space and time. MEG and ERPs measure events in time very well, but it is difficult to determine precisely where in the brain the signals originated. PET scans and fMRI have the opposite problems; their spatial resolution is good (they can localise areas of activity within the brain) but their temporal resolution is poor (they require long periods, seconds or minutes, to obtain their measures). TMS has good temporal resolution for its application but it can be difficult to determine the spatial localisation; brain currents induced in one area might extend beyond the desired brain location.

VISUAL PERCEPTION AND THE PHYSICAL ENVIRONMENT

The investigation of perception must include the definition of those characteristics of the physical environment that can be detected by a perceiver. We need to know at the least what sorts of physical event can act as an effective stimulus for perception. As the example of the "red rag to a bull" demonstrates, we must know that a given event is capable of being perceived before engaging in discussion of its behavioural significance.

Debate has continued for many centuries as whether, and to what extent, we should trust the evidence of our senses, or more precisely, whether we can believe what we perceive. Attitudes towards this issue have ranged from a denial that there is any physical reality at all, to a straightforward acceptance that all perceptions constitute objective truth about the world. Such arguments about truth, knowledge, and reality belong to the branch of philosophy called epistemology, and they remain as intractable as when they were first posed in Classical Greece. For humans and other animals, perception exists as one means of ensuring survival. If our actions are not guided by accurate information about the world, then we make errors and put ourselves and others at risk. The important questions for a psychologist concern how we come to gain information about the environment, the way in which such information is represented in perception, and the limits to our ability to perceive correctly.

Visual stimuli for experiments

The traditional approach in perception has been to define the qualities and quantities of physical energy that can be perceived, as for example in the measurement of the least intensity of light that can be reliably detected, or the difference in wavelength between patches of light needed to make them appear discriminably different in colour. These types of measurement define the limits of perception, so they can be used to find out if any perception is possible. They are therefore useful for identifying perceptual defects, as for instance when an individual's discrimination of certain wavelengths is systematically worse than other people's. Ultimately, the purpose of perception is to enable humans and other animals to guide their behaviour in a way that is appropriate to the real environment, whose most pertinent features are the location and nature of objects in three-dimensional space.

Most perceptual research is now conducted with a computer display, because computers provide more accurate and precise control of both the stimuli that can be presented and the responses that can be measured. Increasingly efficient computers and graphics cards have enabled the monitor screen to replace many of the classical instruments, like the stereoscope, stroboscope, and tachistoscope, for studying perceptual processes (see Chapter 2). The stroboscope varied space and time together, whereas the other two instruments provided a means for the analysis of space and time separately. Devices like these have been used for well over a century to address fundamental questions in perception, and to define the types of answers at the psychological and physiological levels. Present-day research has replaced these instruments with a single scope, the oscilloscope, or its variant, the computer monitor. With the help of computer-controlled monitors stimulus variations are possible, for a modest expenditure, which would have required a whole laboratory a few years ago. Psychology emerged gradually as an independent discipline because a central branch of it, perception, had developed its own methods, which involved both stimulus control and response measurement.

Visual stimuli in the environment

Evolution has ensured that perceptual systems are adapted to the needs of organisms, whether for locomotion, foraging for food or finding a mate. In the most general terms, the environment can be thought of as a source of many varieties of potential stimulation; ranging from vibrations in the atmosphere to electromagnetic radiation of various wavelengths and molecules diffused from an evaporating source. Those aspects of the world that we can perceive depend in the first instance on the senses we possess. The world as it appears to us is therefore based on a selective sample of the many forms of energy that are available. One of the developments of modern technology has been the extension of our natural senses to a wider range of environmental events; we can convert X-rays, ultrasound, and infra-red to forms that can be directly perceived. Whatever the sources of information, however, the outcome is perception of a physical environment that has spatial extent and in which objects can be located in space and time, with a particular size and shape. All perceptual systems must provide some such representation, even it is based on a limited selection of available information, because they would otherwise be of little value for guiding behaviour.

Not surprisingly, it has been argued that we should be cautious about supposing that perception in the real world can be explained by the processes revealed under laboratory conditions. Gibson (1950, 1966, 1979) in particular has argued that natural perception depends on complex patterns of stimulation, involving active exploration of the environment by the perceiver. He reacted strongly against the idea, drawn from the physical sciences, that any complex process can be understood by combining a number of simpler component processes. Under restricted laboratory conditions, perceptual processes are not reduced to their elementary components, but rather to an unrepresentative and impoverished form. Thus, Gibson claimed that visual illusions were simply the consequence of looking at scenes with very little information; under natural conditions in the environment we generally do not see illusions because there is plenty of information to tell us about the true sizes, shapes, and colours of objects. In particular, if the observer is prevented from moving then his or her perceptions will be both unnatural and uninformative. In our view, an adequate account of perception should be able to explain what is seen under any circumstances, whether in a natural environment or in the laboratory.

DEVELOPMENT OF PERCEPTION

Experiments on perception involve communicating the experimenter's requirements to an observer, and the discussion so far has been in terms of studying perception in someone who can communicate with language; but what about cases where this cannot be done? We may wish to investigate perception in infants, in animals, or perhaps in people whose linguistic abilities are impaired. For these, the requirements of the experimenter must be communicated by some other means, and the response cannot be verbal. Clearly, it must be some action that is within the behavioural repertoire of the observer. Thus, for example, it may be possible to use the methods of conditioned learning to study discrimination between stimuli. If one response, like turning the head or raising a paw, can be conditioned to a red stimulus, and another to a green one, then we may be justified in concluding something about the ability to perceive colour; provided of course that the discrimination is not based on some other characteristic like the brightness of the stimulus. If an infant spends more time looking at a picture of a face than at a random collection of lines, then this preference may demonstrate an ability to recognise faces as a special class of object. Clearly it would also be necessary to establish that these measurements did not simply reflect a preference for symmetrical patterns, or even for looking left rather than right. Such behavioural measures are not intrinsically different from verbal ones, and similar sorts of inference may be made from them. However they are less subject to biases, and the inferences are therefore likely to be more secure.

It is possible to be seriously misled by measurements of perception, due to their simplified and inferential character. We may suppose from observable behaviour that perception is limited or even nonexistent, when in fact this is not the case. The traditional view of perception in early infancy was that human babies could see very little, and recognise essentially nothing. Only with the development of better methods of measurement, more closely related to the behavioural repertoire of infants, has it been shown that their perceptual abilities are in fact quite considerable. This finding has been important for the early diagnosis of sensory defects, and has given new significance to the potential effects of neonatal perceptual experience.

Perceptual development is not restricted to infants. There are changes in vision over the whole life span, and particularly systematic ones in the later decades of life. One obvious and well-known change is that associated with the ageing eye; the lens loses much of its elasticity, so that it cannot focus or accommodate over the same range. Other changes are more subtle, and often go unnoticed. For instance, the lens thickens and yellows with age, both reducing the amount of light striking the retina and changing its spectral composition: More short wavelength (bluish) light is absorbed by the lens. However, much more research has been conducted on early than late perceptual development.

Infant vision

William James (1842–1910) remarked, from his armchair, that "The baby, assailed by eyes, ears, nose, skin, and entrails at once feels it all as one great blooming, buzzing confusion" (1890, p. 488). The conclusion concerning infantile confusion was based on the observation of their seemingly random and chaotic movements. More detailed scrutiny indicated that some aspects of behaviour were systematic and could be used to determine what interests infants. Many novel methods were devised to study infant vision in the 1960s. For example, it was noted that infants spent different amounts of time fixating on visual patterns and so infant perceptual discrimination was inferred from the patterns of preferential fixation. Recordings of eye movements in infants only a few days old showed that they were concentrated on contours or corners of simple patterns. When a stimulus is presented many times the response to it typically declines or habituates. Habituation to repeated presentations of patterns provided another source of inference regarding discrimination, particularly when novel patterns were presented; if the infants dishabituated then it was assumed that the novel pattern was discriminated from the habituated pattern. Operant conditioning techniques were applied to demonstrate the emergence of perceptual constancies. These methods were refined and the course of perceptual development began to be charted.

In order to extract the spatial detail from an object it needs to be focused on the retina, and the state of focus will need to change for objects at different distances. This process of accommodation is poorly developed at birth and newborns can only focus on objects within their reach. Indeed, the receptors in the retina are not fully developed at birth nor are the nerve cells in the visual cortex, and so their development is likely to have a profound effect on what can be seen. It is not surprising, then, that the visual acuity of the newborn is more than 10 times poorer than that of adults, but it improves rapidly in the first months of life until it reaches almost adult level at age 6 months. Similarly, infants in the first few months of life are not able to detect low contrast patterns (where the differences between the lightest and darkest parts are small) that are readily detectable by adults. The contributors to the books edited by Slater (1998) and Vital-Durand, Atkinson, & Braddick (1996) describe the capabilities of infants on a wide range of visual tasks, which are being assessed by ever more sophisticated methods like ERPs and MRI.

Perceptual learning

Perceptual development is not restricted to babies. We are constantly learning to discriminate between stimuli that initially appear similar. Our ability to recognise so many individual faces is an example of this. All faces have many features in common, but we are able to determine the identities of particular faces because of the slight differences in the configuration of the parts and the ways in which they move to express emotions. However, our ability to recognise pictures of individual faces is dependent upon their orientation with respect to gravity: If they are upside down we have great difficulty in recognition. Of course, we rarely see actual faces upside down, but we often see photographs of faces that are inverted (for instance when we look at a newspaper that is pointing away from us), and we have great difficulty in determining who is represented. Children engage in perceptual learning when they grapple with the oddities of the patterns we use in written language.

The example of the guide dog described on pages 3–6 indicates that perceptual learning is not restricted to humans; in fact, in the early twentieth century more experimental investigations have been conducted with animals other than humans! One of the features that distinguishes humans from other species is that we have learned to respond to pictorial images of objects as if they had the characteristics of the objects themselves. We derive information about the world from both spatialised and stylised pictorial images (like photographs and written script), and we devote a lot of perceptual processing to these (see Wade, 1990). Clearly there are many important aspects of our lives that are dependent upon accurate interpretation of two-dimensional images, and some of these will be explored in Chapter 7.

WHEN VISION GOES WRONG

We have most difficulty in perceiving, and therefore in acting efficiently, when the information available to the senses is either greatly restricted, or provided by an environment with which we have no natural experience. Examples of the former are given by the gross errors of judgement that occur when attempting to drive a car at speed in fog or at night, and of the latter when people try to perceive correctly in outer space or underwater. In these cases we require special training and experience in order to perceive the "where", "when" and "what" of objects, and without it we are liable to experience distortions of reality. There are also instances in which the mechanisms that underpin perception are not functioning appropriately, either as a consequence of peripheral problems (as in the case of most colour deficits) or central ones (as for visual agnosias). Even when the apparatus for vision is malfunctioning it can be very difficult to discover this. Colour deficiency is a case in point: The use of colour names for particular objects in our environment (like green grass) has delayed the appreciation that not all people have the same colour experiences.

Visual illusions

In some situations what we perceive consistently differs from what we suppose to be correct, and this may be referred to as a visual illusion. There are many examples of these, and a long history of experimentation and theory designed to account for them. It is important to note that the idea of a visual illusion presupposes that the object or pattern concerned would be perceived differently under other conditions. For example, the apparent length of a line is altered by adding oblique lines, known as fins, to either end or the orientation of parallel lines appears distorted because of the angles at which they intersect others (Figure 1.4).

The Müller-Lyer and Zöllner illusions are instances of the distortion of the perceived geometry of simple plane figures—the former of size and the latter of orientation. That they are illusions can only be shown by measuring the lines with a ruler (which assumes correct perception of the ruler itself), or by comparing the perceived lengths of the lines without the inducing parts. Essentially, illusions are defined by comparisons between perceptions,

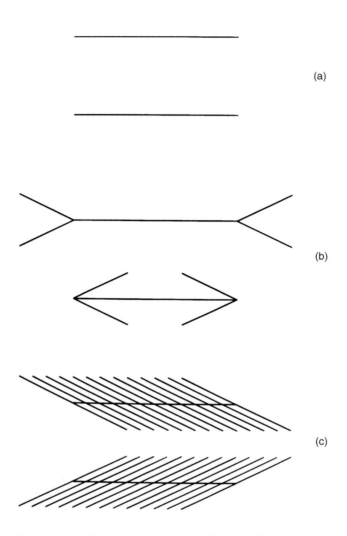

Figure 1.4 (a) Two equal and parallel lines. (b) The same lines with fins (Müller-Lyer illusion). (c) The same lines crossing diagonal lines (Zöllner illusion).

although we naturally assume that at least one of these is physically correct. A more compelling way of demonstrating illusions is by presenting the component parts separately so that they can be combined. In the case of the Müller-Lyer figure the horizontal lines can be shown in isolation and then together with the fins. This technique has been adopted using transparent overlays for a variety of size and orientation illusions in Wade (1982). The same components (like equal, parallel lines) are printed on a transparent surface so that they can be placed over white paper or over the inducing components of an illusion; they can then be shown to undergo perceptual distortion.

One view of illusions is that they can be used as tools to probe the mechanisms of visual perception, because perceptual errors can give us clues about the way in which normal perception takes place. For example, Gregory (1997) has accounted for the Müller-Lyer illusion in terms of depth due to perspective. If we interpret two-dimensional drawings as representing an object in depth, then there may be systematic distortions of apparent size. This would be due to the process which ensures that real objects appear to remain their actually constant size despite being at different distances, and projecting different-sized images on the retina. A normal perceptual process would thus have been revealed by its inappropriate influence on a line drawing, and it could be studied by this means. One problem is that many visual illusions appear to be the result of several different perceptual processes, and it is hard to separate their respective effects.

Analyses of perception typically draw a distinction between the physical description of the external object (called the distal stimulus) and its projection onto the sensory surface (the proximal stimulus). The distinction between distal and proximal stimuli has a bearing on the way illusions are interpreted. In general, measurement of the stimulus is restricted to its distal properties—those that a physicist would employ.

Visual illusions are generally classified as distortions of orientation or size in simple line patterns. Visual neuroscience is generally concerned with neural and/or behavioural responses to contours. For the distal stimulus contours are usually defined as luminance discontinuities, and these can be enhanced by interactions at early stages of visual processing (see Chapter 3 for a discussion of such lateral inhibition). However, one set of stimuli involves seeing discontinuities of brightness where no luminance differences exist. These illusory contours can be produced by gaps in shapes, as in Figure 1.5a. The white triangular shapes that radiate from the centre appear brighter than the white background. The shapes are produced by the white sectors of the dark discs and by the terminations of the concentric circles. The illusory contours even appear to curve between the discs rather than follow the shortest straight line. Illusory contours can also be induced by line terminations as in the case of the central vase shape of Figure 1.5b. Illusory contours behave much like physical ones—they interact with one another and can modify the appearance of subsequently presented patterns, producing spatial aftereffects.

Other pictures are far more paradoxical. For example, the joint in Figure 1.6a appears very strange—almost impossible. However, it is based upon a simple perspective principle: A rectangular rod can be represented by three parallel lines. The central quadrilateral can represent the end of either an upper or lower rectangular rod. Each would be perceptually plausible in isolation, but their connection creates a paradox. A junction between two rectangular rods can be depicted by six lines, with the depth suggested by the

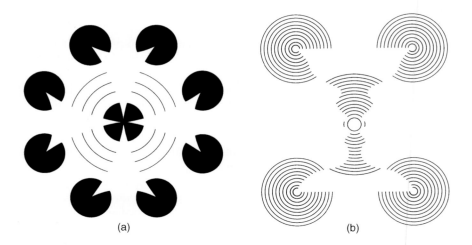

Figure 1.5 (a) Illusory Maltese cross. (b) Illusory vase/faces figure.

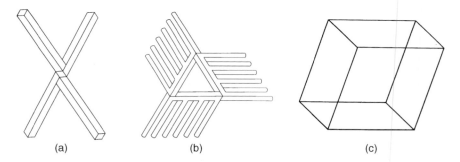

Figure 1.6 (a) Impossible junction. (b) Double impossibility. (c) Reversing figure.

occluded edge. A cylinder, on the other hand, can be described by only two lines and an ellipse, so the lines showing several rectangular junctions would make more cylinders. The central "impossible" triangle in Figure 1.6b has four rectangular rods extending from each side which are transformed into six cylinders at the extremities of the lines. These are called impossible figures because the solid objects to which they allude could not be constructed. Impossible worlds can be drawn by manipulating the rules of perspective, and artists like M.C. Escher have been exceedingly skilful at producing perceptual paradoxes of this type (see Ernst, 1976).

These are not, of course, impossible objects (as they have been called at times) but perfectly possible pictures. Pictures provide us with allusions to objects, and tricks can be played with the transition from three to two dimensions. Indeed, this is grist to the artistic mill: Pictures incorporate ambiguities that are rarely present in objects. One such ambiguity is the depth that is represented in simple line drawings like Figure 1.6c: The apparent orientation of the rhomboid changes so that the front face appears to be pointing either down and to the right or up and left. The picture is interpreted as representing a three-dimensional structure, but there is insufficient detail (for occluding contours, perspective convergence, or texture) to define which parts would be near and which far. However, we do not entertain both depth interpretations simultaneously: Our perception flips from one possibility to the other, so that the apparent depth undergoes reversals. Perhaps the most familiar form of ambiguity relates to drawings which can be interpreted in more than one way, because the same contours delineate two different figures, like the vase/faces motif in Figure 1.5b.

Colour deficits

Colour blindness is a very rare condition, and yet the term is both widely known and widely applied. Very few instances of blindness to all colours have been encountered, unlike the numerous cases of colour defects and anomalies, in which one colour is either not discriminated from others or is not seen as intensely as for the majority of people. It is remarkable that colour blindness came so late on the scientific scene. It must have been present in human societies for thousands of years, and yet the first descriptions of it go back barely four centuries. The likely reason for this is that colour names can mask differences in colour vision (see pages 12–13). The incidence of colour defective vision is markedly less in females than males: Only about 0.5% of females have colour anomalies, whereas they occur in 8% of males. The basis for these sex differences is addressed on pages 126–127.

Colour deficits have had an important bearing on theories of colour vision. There has been much debate on the nature and number of primary colours (see pages 40–43). Normal colour vision is trichromatic. That is, the range of colours that we experience can be matched by appropriate mixtures of just three primaries—corresponding to red, green, and blue parts of the spectrum. Many people with colour defects only require mixtures of two primaries to match any other wavelength presented to them. They are called dichromats, and they are subdivided further into protanopes, deuteranopes, and tritanopes because they are missing the first (red), second (green), or third (blue) detectors, respectively. Tritanopes are much rarer than the other dichromats, but monochromats, who can match any wavelength of light with any other, are rarer still. The largest group of colour defective individuals are anomalous trichromats: They can match any wavelength with three others, but the proportions are different from the normal trichromats.

Visual agnosias

Brain damage can have devastating effects on behaviour. Most of us have seen the consequences of a stroke on people, when one side of the body is partially paralysed due to injury of the brain on the opposite (contralateral) side. The restriction of oxygen to part of the brain results in death of some brain cells, and because of the separate blood supplies to the left and right hemispheres the brain damage tends to be restricted to one side. When the damage is to the left hemisphere there is generally some language disorder, whereas damage to the right hemisphere disturbs spatial orientation and recognition (see Springer & Deutsch, 1997). Such observations of gross differences in the effects of damage to the left and right hemispheres led to the concept of cerebral localisation, with the left hemisphere generally referred to as dominant because of its link to language.

Brain injury frequently has wide-ranging effects on behaviour because the damage is itself often widespread. However, some injuries to specific areas of the brain can manifest themselves in particular perceptual disorders, and important insights into the neural bases of behaviour can be derived from them (see Farah, 2000). The cases are usually very rare but their implications are so profound that they demand detailed attention. One such condition has the enigmatic label of blindsight, because the patients do not seem to be consciously aware of the objects they respond to. When parts of the primary visual cortex have been damaged or surgically removed patients do not detect stimuli presented to areas of the visual field that would project to the damaged cortex; the area of blindness is called a scotoma. They can see normally in the other parts of the visual field, but are unaware of light in the blind region. If asked to orientate themselves towards a stimulus in the scotoma they say they are guessing, but their responses are much better than chance. Thus, despite their blindness they can point to "unseen" objects, indicate the direction in which they have moved, determine their intensity and even aspects of colour (see Weiskrantz, 1990). The ability to orient towards objects that cannot be consciously reported suggests that information about objects in space is processed in more than one pathway from the eyes to the brain. The evidence indicating that there are (at least) two visual systems will be presented in Chapter 3.

Occasionally, the perceptual disorders can be most unusual, even bizarre, as in the tragic case of Dr P, graphically described by Oliver Sacks (1985) in his book *The Man who Mistook his Wife for a Hat*. This was an instance of prosopagnosia (the inability to recognise faces) and the title indicates that it applies to familiar faces; it can even be difficult for individuals so afflicted to recognise mirror images of themselves. Prosopagnosia is a special case of visual agnosia, which refers to the inability to recognise objects. For these conditions to operate, the failure of object recognition should not be due to damage to the sense organs or to any intellectual impairment. There are other specific visual agnosias that can affect recognition in different ways; one person was able to recognise the parts of objects but not the whole object itself, another was said to recognise living as opposed to nonliving things, yet another could not see moving objects. However, the deficits are rarely as specific as these descriptions suggest, and the ways of classifying visual agnosias themselves are still contentious (see Parkin, 1996).

One of the distinctions made earlier in this chapter—between action and recognition—is relevant to visual agnosias. When the injury is in the upper central part of the brain (the posterior parietal cortex) there are difficulties with reaching for and grasping objects, even though they can be recognised. With injury to the central and lateral region of the brain (the inferotemporal cortex) grasping is normal but recognising objects is disrupted (Milner & Goodale, 1995). It is as though action is affected in one case and recognition in the other. One obvious issue raised by these patients is: What do we mean by recognition? Can a patient reach to an object that is not recognised at some level? These and other aspects of recognition will be examined in more detail in Chapter 6. The deficits in action and recognition associated with brain damage in humans have been supported by experimental studies with monkeys. These studies are more precise because the location of specific lesions (or nerve sections) can be ascertained with greater accuracy.

Before the various theories can be appreciated it is necessary to have some understanding of the way in which light is detected by the eyes and processed by the many visual structures in the brain; these topics will be covered in Chapter 3. A concern common to all the issues raised in this chapter is that of levels of representation (or frames of reference) that are operating when we consider tasks like action and recognition. We will argue that our behaviour is guided by perceptual processes that utilise an internal three-dimensional representation of space, and that a rigid distinction between action and recognition might be misguided. These arguments will be developed in Chapters 4–6, and their applications to practical visual tasks will be outlined in Chapter 7.

2 The heritage

Modern accounts of vision draw on the past in innumerable and often unstated ways. The divisions we draw between the physics of light, physiological responses to it, and the psychology of perception represent hard-won battles. The theories applied to these remain matters of debate. We are in a better position to appreciate the massive advances that have been made in understanding the nature of light, image formation, visual anatomy and physiology, and visual phenomena themselves when we can place them in the context of the past. The historical perspective is often overlooked or neglected in books on perception, which is a pity because it implies that we now have a privileged viewpoint, superior to those of the past. In fact, the same theoretical issues often recur, disguised by the new jargon to appear different. Seeing through the shroud of the present can facilitate our understanding of such issues, and remaining ignorant of past attempts to grapple with them can inhibit progress.

All sciences are based on observation. Naturally occurring or experimentally manipulated events are observed and if the observations prove to be consistent they become phenomena. That is, if different observers describe the events in much the same way then they are considered to be aspects of the world rather than aspects of the observer. The phenomena are accumulated and classified in order to interpret them and determine lawful relations between them. The history of vision is somewhat unusual because it is the history of observation itself. For most of its history, the phenomena of vision were those based on observation of natural events like rainbows and reflections, together with the consequences of diseases like cataract and failing sight in old age. Thus, investigations of both the physics of light and the physiology of sight added to the range of visual phenomena, although these two areas were not initially distinguished. The psychological dimension was gradually integrated with these. Vision became an experimental discipline rather late. For most of its long history it has drawn upon observations of naturally occurring events, with relatively little in the way of manipulating the conditions under which they occurred. Colour led the way into the laboratory; when sunlight could be separated into its spectral components and recombined in a variety of ways the nature of light itself could be investigated, as well as its close interrelationship with sight. The experimental study of spatial vision awaited the invention of instruments, like the strobo-scope and stereoscope, in the early nineteenth century. As soon as the nature of the stimulus could be manipulated by devices like these the range of visual phenomena increased dramatically, as did the techniques for investigating them. There are several books on the history of perception and Boring (1942) presents a comprehensive account of the nature of light, of anatomical stud-ies of the eye and nervous system, and of investigations of visual phenomena from the seventeenth to the early twentieth centuries. The developing body of visual phenomena from antiquity until the nineteenth century together with the chronological refinement in their descriptions can be followed in Wade (1998).

The study of perception is essential in trying to understand how we derive knowledge about the world—an endeavour referred to as epistemology. All cultures have struggled to address this question, and their answers have often been radically different. In the following sections we will introduce some of the dominant influences that have shaped the ways in which we presently think about vision. Vision is at the interface of many disciplines, such as art, medicine, physics, and philosophy. Each has influenced the present state of our understanding. Hence, it is instructive to look back at these diverse his-torical strands so that we are in a better position to appreciate the con-temporary approaches to visual perception. This belief in the importance of an historical perspective was voiced clearly by Goethe: "We cannot clearly be aware of what we possess till we have the means of knowing what others possessed before us. We cannot really and honestly rejoice in the advantages of our own time if we know not how to appreciate the advantages of former periods" (1840, pp. xliv–xlv).

This chapter examines the heritage of perceptual research in terms of the disciplines that have influenced it. The first is the study of light itself (optics), followed by that of art and representation. These two were far more intim-ately entwined in the past than they are now, and in the context of vision both made close contact with the life sciences—particularly regarding the way images are formed in the eye. Underlying all these endeavours were distinct philosophical theories, which remain of relevance to the psychology of vision. For those readers who wish to move more quickly to contemporary concerns in the study of vision then the section entitled "Psychology" starting on page 70 will provide the clearest bridge to subsequent chapters.

OPTICS

Optics is now considered to be the branch of physics dealing with the proper-ties of light—how it is propagated through different media, how it reflects from surfaces, and how it is refracted at the boundaries between media. These properties have been studied for well over two thousand years, and the terms to describe them—optics, catoptrics (reflections), and dioptrics (refractions), that were introduced by Hero of Alexandria in the first century AD—are still in use. A distinction is now drawn between physical optics and vision—between light and sight—but this is relatively recent. It is only since the seventeenth century, when the optical functions of the eye were correctly described by Kepler and when its gross anatomy was accurately depicted by Scheiner, that the two have been distinguished.

Among the many philosophers and mathematicians in ancient Greek culture, the most penetrating analysis of optics that has survived was written by Euclid (Figure 2.1a) around 300 BC. Euclid's optics were both physical and psychological; the rays in his diagrams represented not only light but also sight. For example, Euclid's book entitled *Optics* is concerned with describing visual space in terms of visual angles, so that the perception of space was analysed geometrically (see Burton, 1945). For example, the visual cones shown in Figure 2.1b represented both the optical projection and the perception of two equal extents; the visual angle of the nearer object (AB) is greater than that of the distant one (GD) and Euclid contended that AB was seen as larger than GD. The two most important treatments of optics between Euclid and Kepler were by Ptolemy (c. 100–170) and Ibn al-Haytham (c. 965–1039), who is more widely known by his latinized name of Alhazen. The *Optics* of Ptolemy is both experimental and psychological, dealing with colour as well as space (see Smith, 1996).

Euclid's *Optics* was concerned with the geometry of space and did not mention colour. Colour compounds the physical and psychological dimensions of optics, although an appreciation of this was only possible when the physical properties of light had been elucidated by Newton (Figure 2.1c). In his *Opticks* (1704) he illustrated (Figure 2.1d) and interpreted the spectrum produced by sunlight passing through a prism: Differences in colour were related to differences in the amount they were refracted by the prism. He also noted that colour was a subjective experience rather than a property of light: "For the Rays to speak properly are not coloured. In them there is nothing else than a certain power and disposition to stir up a sensation of this or that Colour" (1704, p. 90). That power was dependent in part on the degree to which sunlight was refracted when passing through a prism. A wide range of colour phenomena was available to Newton before he conducted his prismatic experiments, including the prismatic colours themselves. The phenomena concerned colour mixing, afterimages, colour contrasts, and colour shadows; they had accumulated over centuries and spawned competing theories. Most theories were based on the Aristotelian view that colour was a property of bodies, and that it was carried by light through the transparent medium to the eye.

Newton was to provide a unified theory of light and colours: White light was not unitary but compounded, in precise proportions, of many components that differed in their refraction. He was able to analyse the prismatic colours with an armoury of subtle experimental procedures. For example,

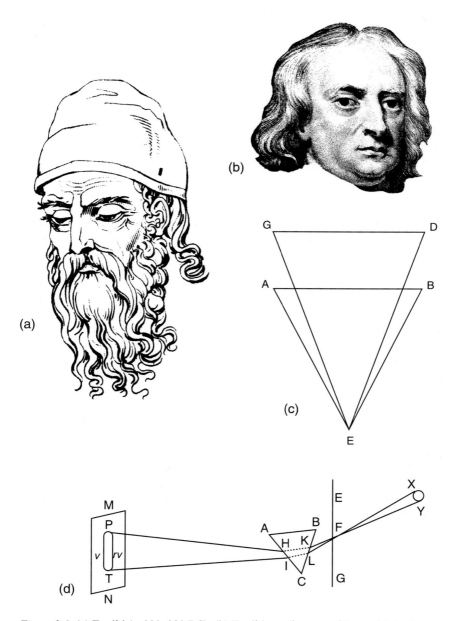

Figure 2.1 (a) Euclid (c. 323–283 BC). (b) Euclidean diagram of lines of light from the eye to objects at different distances. Euclid equated perceived dimensions to the angle subtended at the eye. (c) Isaac Newton (1642–1727). (d) The spectrum produced by sunlight passing through a prism as illustrated in Newton's *Opticks*.

small sections of the prismatic spectrum could be isolated and mixed with other parts, so that the rules of their mixture could be determined. He wished to avoid the speculations entered into by his rival, Robert Hooke, and to base his theory on experiment rather than hypothesis. Indeed, Newton opened his *Opticks* (1704) thus: "My Design in this Book is not to explain the Properties of Light by Hypotheses, but to propose and prove them by Reason and Experiments" (p. 1).

Many books have been written on the history of optics and colour, and those by Lindberg (1976), Park (1997), Ronchi (1970), and Wasserman (1978), are particularly recommended.

Light and sight

We now accept that light is emitted by incandescent sources like the sun, and reflected from objects to enter the eye, so initiating the process of seeing. However, for many years it was thought that light was emitted from the eye to make contact with objects and returned to the eye carrying their images; vision itself was thought to occur in the lens. After all, is it not the case that we cease to see when we close our eyes, thus preventing the emission of light from the eye? Moreover, what we are aware of depends upon where we direct our eyes. Most Greek speculations about sight and the senses generally incorporated elemental philosophy so that fire, earth, water, and air permeated perception. Touch was often taken as the most important sense, and the one relative to which others could be related; qualities associated with it, like hot, cold, moist, and dry were thought to be common to all the senses, and were in turn linked to the four elements. Thus, vision was generally considered to involve some process of contact between the eye and objects and several means of achieving this contact were advanced. These included various versions of emission or extramission theories, in which light originated in the eye and was projected from it. Reception or intromission theories, in which light travelled from objects to the eye, were also advanced, as were speculations incorporating aspects of both emission and reception. Emission theories could have been founded on the experience of light when pressure is applied to the eye and they are consistent with the cessation of sight when the eyes are closed.

A theory based on light passing from objects to the eye was advanced by Democritus (c. 460–370 BC). It could account readily for the absence of sight with eye closure but not for the experience of light when external pressure was applied to the eye. What was received by the eye was often more than light, but some image of the object itself. According to Democritus all nature was composed of atoms in motion, and images were continually emitted from objects to compress the air and carry impressions to the eye. The impression was like a copy of the object that could be received by the eye. The images carried with them the constant features of the objects, and for Democritus these included their three-dimensionality.

A combination of emission and reception was proposed by Plato (427–347 BC), although his theory of vision was always subservient to his philosophy of ideal forms. Plato suggested that light was emitted from both the eye and objects, and vision took place externally where these two streams united. He suggested that we cannot see at night because light is extinguished in darkness, just as heat and dryness are extinguished by cold and dampness. Aristotle (c. 384–322 BC) was scornful of this speculation stating that neither heat nor dryness were attributes of light. For Plato, as for Aristotle, it was not light but colour that was the principal source of interest in vision. Plato distinguished between light and colour, considering that light had its ultimate source in the sun, but colour was a property of objects themselves.

Aristotle's theory is more in line with modern conceptions of light. His interests were in observation, and the phenomena he experienced directed the interpretations he proposed. Thus, he queried the emission theories by the simple expedient of testing a prediction that would follow from them: If light was emitted from the eye then vision should be possible at any time the eyes were open, including night time. The fact that the prediction was not supported led him to suggest an alternative theory of the nature of light. Similarly, he distinguished between vision and touch by noting that an object in physical contact with the eye could not be seen. His alternative interpretation was that vision is the result of some movement in the medium separating the eye from the objects perceived. Aristotle's reception theory was not widely accepted, in part because it could not account for the experience of light in darkness when pressure was applied to the eye.

Euclid adopted an emission theory of light and vision. Vision was restricted to the cone of rays emanating from the eye and meeting the objects within it (see Figure 2.1b). The geometrical projections to these objects were lawful, and this lawfulness was applied to vision, too. Thus, Euclid provided not only an account of optical transmission through space, but also a geometrical theory of space perception itself. The perceived dimensions of objects corresponded precisely to the angles they subtended at the eye, and illumination of those objects had its source in the eye. The emissions from Euclid's eyes were referred to as visual rays, and their properties were conflated with a number of phenomenal features. The visual rays were thought to be discrete, and so small objects could fall between them, and remain unseen; that is, there is a limit to the dimensions of objects that can be detected, namely, a threshold for visual acuity (see pages 96–102). Moreover, those objects illuminated by rays in the centre of the visual cone will be seen more clearly than those towards the edge; that is, direct (foveal) vision has better acuity than indirect (peripheral) vision. It followed, as Euclid stated, that nothing could be seen at once in its entirety, implying that the visual rays would move over an object (by moving the eyes) in order to see all its features.

Ptolemy (Figure 2.2a) appreciated that light rays should be thought of as continuous rather than discrete. His analysis of visual size was radically different from that of Euclid, as it was based on psychology rather than physics.

(a)   (b)   (c)

Figure 2.2 (a) Claudius Ptolemy (c. 100–170). (b) Johannes Kepler (1571–1630).
(c) Christiaan Huygens (1629–1695).

Ptolemy argued that visual size cannot be equated with visual angle, and
introduced the concept that perceived size was derived from visual angle
and distance; that is, he addressed the issue of perceptual constancy (see
page 217). He was in agreement with Euclid about the variations in visual
acuity throughout the visual pyramid (rather than cone). The two pyramids
of vision (one for each eye) needed to be integrated and he conducted
experiments with a board in order to study this binocular combination.
Ptolemy also realised that errors do sometimes occur in vision, and he was
one of the first writers to provide a detailed account of illusions. Indeed,
he devoted over one-third of Book II of his *Optics* to errors of sight; they
were classified, and then considered under the headings of colour, position,
size, shape, and movement. Ptolemy initiated a reconciliation between
physical and psychological analyses of vision which was further amplified by
Ibn al-Haytham.

    Ibn al-Haytham was a mathematician who hailed from Basra and later
worked in Cairo (see Sabra, 1989). He was familiar with the writings of
Euclid and Ptolemy and Ptolemy's influence was particularly marked. Ibn
al-Haytham adopted a reception theory of light, conducted experiments on
image formation in a pinhole camera, extended Ptolemy's experiments on
binocular vision, and classified a wide range of visual phenomena. In short,
he integrated the three theoretical strands in optics that had until then been
dominant but distinct—Aristotle's observations and philosophical stance,
Euclid's mathematical treatment in terms of ray diagrams, and the physiological approach of Galen (c. 130–200), the great anatomist of antiquity. Ibn
al-Haytham's book on optics was translated from Arabic into Latin in the
thirteenth and again in the sixteenth century. This fascinating period in the
history of optics has been chronicled by Lindberg (1976), Park (1997), and
Smith (1998); Lindberg (1992) has also written a general history of science
that gives due prominence to optics.

The belief that light was emitted from the eye rather than transmitted to it was held for over 2000 years until, in 1604, the astronomer Kepler (Figure 2.2b) described how light passed through the eye to form an image on the retina. The similarities between image formation in a simple camera obscura (literally a dark chamber, like a pinhole camera) and the eye were remarked upon in that period, and the emission theory of vision was replaced by a reception theory. Indeed, at that time it was considered by some that the problem of vision had been solved by the appreciation of the image-forming properties of the eye: The picture in the eye was like the scene imaged, and so it corresponded to perception. Kepler was more circumspect in treating the relationship between the inverted and reversed retinal image and perception: "I leave it to the natural philosophers to discuss the way in which this image or picture is put together by the spiritual principles of vision" (Crombie, 1964, p. 147). Natural philosophers have not subsequently spoken with a single voice on this problem, but they have appreciated that physical optics is not the solution to vision.

In addition to the description of image formation in the eye, Kepler made many other contributions to optics, both experimentally and theoretically. Amongst them was the formulation of the basic principle of photometry that the intensity of light diminishes with the square of the distance from the source. Kepler (1611) devoted considerable attention to refraction in his book *Dioptrice* (Dioptrics), but he did not determine the general sine law. Willebrord Snell, in an unpublished manuscript written around 1621, described the relationship between angles of incidence and refraction, upon which the subsequent technical advances in optical instrument manufacture were based.

Snell's law, as it became known, was elaborated by Descartes in his *Dioptrique* published in 1637 (see Descartes, 1637/1902). Light, according to Descartes, acted like a mechanical force which is transmitted through transparent media. His theory of light attracted much criticism in his day because of the inconsistencies it embraced. On the one hand he argued that light was propagated instantly, and on the other that it varied its velocity according to the density of the medium through which it travelled.

Diffraction of light was described and demonstrated by Grimaldi in a book published in 1665; on the basis of this phenomenon he suggested that light might act like a liquid, flowing in waves. Wave theory was supported and extended by Huygens (Figure 2.2c): He proposed and illustrated the wavefronts that could be produced by points on luminous sources, and he made an analogy between light and sound; diffraction was analysed in terms of the wavefronts originating at the aperture. In contrast Newton proposed that light consisted of small corpuscles which collided with one another. Thereafter, the theoretical contrast was between Huygen's wave theory and Newton's corpuscular theory of light. The latter was dominant throughout the eighteenth century, so much so that it became dogma, and those who challenged it were roundly condemned for doubting the genius of Newton. By the beginning of the nineteenth century, corpuscular theory was accepted as a conceptual convenience, but one that found increasing difficulty in accounting for phenomena of diffraction and interference; it was the latter that proved so convincing to Thomas Young in his advocacy of wave theory. The conflicts between supporters of wave and corpuscular theories of light have been detailed by Park (1997) in his excellent history of optics.

With the appreciation that light could be considered as a physical property, and that its reflections and refractions followed physical principles, its study became the province of physicists, whereas the examination of sight was pursued by physiologists and philosophers. The separation of the physics of light from the philosophy of sight was to reflect the ancient schism between materialists and idealists: Light was an external, material phenomenon, whereas sight was internal and subjective.

Colour

Within Greek science colour was considered in terms of an analogy with the four elements, and of these fire and water were dominant. The numeration of four basic colours was clearly stated in the fourth century BC by Democritus, and these were white, black, red, and green; other colours were derived from mixtures of these. Moreover, he adapted the concept of pores in the eye to account for colour vision: Only when the geometrical shapes associated with particular colours corresponded to those of the pores would colour be experienced. Both Plato and Aristotle considered that colour was of paramount importance in perception, and that it could be dissociated from light. They appreciated that pigments could be extracted from certain substances, and they were well aware of the ways in which they could be mixed by artists. However, they stressed the importance of black and white: Plato treated them as opposites, and Aristotle considered that all colours could be made up from these two. It might have been the observation that no colours appeared as light as white or as dark as black that led to this speculation. Consequently, despite the equation of colours with the four elements, black and white tended to dominate the analyses of colour until the time of Leonardo da Vinci (see Kemp, 1990).

The situation changed with investigations of prismatic colours. Although the occurrence of colours due to light passing through or reflected from glass or crystals had been known of since antiquity, their experimental examination had not been undertaken. A preliminary study of the prismatic spectrum was conducted by Thomas Harriot (c. 1560–1627) at the beginning of the seventeenth century, and it was subjected to more detailed analysis later in the century. Descartes (1637/1902) treated the analysis of colours visible in the rainbow in his discourses on *Meteorology*. His mechanistic interpretation of visible colours was in harmony with his concept of light generally: Colours corresponded to different rates of rotation of bodies in the medium.

Newton demonstrated experimentally that sunlight (white light) is made up of rays that can be bent or refracted by different amounts when passing through a prism, so forming the visible spectrum (see Figure 2.1d). He conducted experiments with a prism from 1666, reporting the results in a paper to a meeting of the Royal Society on 6 February 1672; it was published in the *Philosophical Transactions* later that year. The paper stimulated widespread interest as well as opposition, particularly from Hooke and Huygens, who argued that there were only two basic colours. The controversy stirred up by the theory so perturbed Newton that he did not publish his full account of it until his *Opticks* appeared in 1704. By this time, he was President of the Royal Society, and Hooke was no longer a threat. Newton was aware that the range of refractions from a prism was continuous and yet the colours seen were restricted in number. He reported seven colours—red, orange, yellow, green, blue, indigo, and violet—and he arranged them in a particular circular sequence, after the manner of the musical scale. Coloured lights could be combined in such a way that their compound could be defined with respect to the colour circle. Combinations of primary colours that were opposite one another on the circle produced a whitish compound that was positioned near the centre.

Much of the subsequent debate focused on the nature and number of primary colours. For Newton, who introduced the term in 1672, they were the discrete colours that could be seen in the prismatic spectrum, despite his appreciation of continuity across the spectrum. With the formulation of the colour circle they also became the colours from which compounds could be derived. Young (Figure 2.3a) proposed that red, green, and blue were primaries, and that the vast range of colours that could be produced by appropriate

(a)   (b)

Figure 2.3 (a) Thomas Young (1773–1829). (b) James Clerk Maxwell (1831–1879).

combinations of a small number of primaries led to speculations regarding the physiological basis of colour vision. Young (1802) also speculated that colour vision could be mediated by retinal mechanisms that responded selectively to each of the three primaries.

Newton had shifted the analysis of colour towards the physical dimension, while not excluding the subjectivity of colour perception. He also used the analysis of white light into its spectral components to synthesise new colours. For Greek scholars colour seemed to be a property of objects: It could be extracted from some plants and ores, in order to produce pigments that could be mixed with one another. Rough and ready rules for such mixtures were described by Plato, who recognised that the same pigments mixed in different proportions yielded different appearances. Some colours, however, could not be produced by mixing, and Aristotle noted that these corresponded to those seen in the rainbow. Experimental investigations of colour mixing started very early. Ptolemy devised a wheel on which different colours could be painted either as dots or in sectors; when the wheel was rotated the dots appeared as coloured circles or the sectors combined to produce a single colour. Ptolemy appreciated that the disc was required to rotate rapidly, so that the persisting influence of one sector could combine with those of others. Colour wheels continue to be used to demonstrate colour mixture, and indeed were employed by Maxwell (Figure 2.3b) to provide a quantitative analysis of colour combination and he applied it to the analysis of anomalies in colour perception.

Maxwell revived Young's three-colour theory, and also contended that there were three different colour receptors. Support for this derived from his studies of colour defective individuals, who could be classified according to the colour receptors that were absent or anomalous. Most colour defectives could match any colour with only two of the three primaries when using "Maxwell's disc" for colour mixing. The resulting equations led to the proposal of a three-dimensional colour solid, with variables that would now be called hue, saturation, and intensity. In 1861 Maxwell demonstrated the first colour photograph to a meeting at the Royal Institution in London. Separate photographs of a tartan ribbon were taken through red, green, and blue filters and projected through similar filters. The colour triangle had its origins in Young's work, but it was subsequently modified initially by Maxwell and then by Helmholtz.

Painting is much older than science, and so it is natural that the practical skills that the painters had learned by trial and error should have had an influence on ideas about the nature of colour vision. The debate about primary colours was frequently based upon the practice of painting. Newton did distinguish between the mixture of pigments and that of light, noting that pigments reflected the incident light selectively. This could have proved useful to artists and scientists alike, but it was not pursued, perhaps because subsequent artists did not adopt the Newtonian primaries. The stimulus to differentiating light from pigment mixtures was Young's specification of a different set of primaries for light (red, green, and blue) to those for pigments (red, yellow, and blue). The resolution was to await Helmholtz's clarification of the rules governing additive and subtractive colour mixing. When the three primaries for light are mixed white is produced, whereas the three pigment primaries combine to produce black; it is as if lights were added to one another, unlike pigments which subtract wavelengths. A pigment is so coloured because of the components of white light it absorbs and those it reflects; red, yellow, and blue pigments when mixed would absorb all the wavelengths in white light and so the mixture would appear black.

ART AND REPRESENTATION

Colour is not the only dimension that has mixed the art and science of vision. Both are also intimately involved with the representation of space. Pictures are such an integral part of our lives that we tend to overlook their remarkable peculiarities. We readily accept their relation to the objects that they represent even though they have few of the properties of those objects. Indeed, we rarely doubt the equivalence between the pictorial image and the object represented, and when this equation is questioned pictorially we are puzzled. The artist René Magritte painted a picture in the late 1920s that epitomised the problem of pictorial representation: It was called "The perfidy of images" and a variant of it is shown in Figure 2.4. The caption beneath the

Ceci n'est pas une pipe.

Figure 2.4 This is not a pipe. (After Magritte)

pictured pipe reads "This is not a pipe!" If not a pipe, what is it? The simple answer is that it is a picture of a pipe; the pictured pipe cannot be held or smoked, and it is not even supported by anything, as the object would need to be. The title chosen by Magritte for the work indicates that he was acutely aware of the problems associated with equating the pictures of objects with the objects themselves. Magritte was able to make this point forcefully because we can recognise the pictured pipe as representing a curved briar pipe. The orientation he chose for its representation was not arbitrary; had he painted it from other orientations its recognition would not have been as rapid.

Magritte was working within the style of representing objects in space (linear perspective) that has been adopted since the fifteenth century. Almost all Western artistic styles prior to the twentieth century were concerned with representing objects. As such they required a set of rules for generating the pictorial image—a set of relations that linked the object with the picture—which could be followed by the artist and understood by the spectator. Indeed, this was the very function of artistic representation. The fundamental problem that all pictorial artists must address is the difference between objects and pictures of them, namely depth. Over the last 30,000 years different solutions to this problem have been adopted, but all contain some common features that can be linked to optics. Linear perspective is now commonplace because photographic images follow the same optical principles on which perspective is based. However, there have been quite different styles of representing objects in space, and the objects represented can be readily recognised by us. The link between pictorial art and representation has been examined from the viewpoint of psychology by many writers. One of the most popular books is by Gombrich (1960), who combines an extensive knowledge of art history with an interest in perceptual psychology. More specifically psychological treatments can be found in Gregory, Harris, Heard, and Rose (1995), Hagen (1986), Parker and Deregowski (1990), Wade (1990), and Willats (1997).

Styles of representing space

Gombrich referred to the different modes of representing space as "the riddle of style". He posed the question: "Why is it that different ages and different nations have represented the visible world in such different ways?" (1960, p. 3). This was so despite the acceptance that there can have been little genetic change in humankind over the last few thousand years: the cave dwellers would have seen their world in much the same way as we do ours, although the contents of those worlds differed greatly. Objects would have been seen as having specific sizes and locations; they could be approached and grasped or avoided; some, such other animals, moved and their motion through space could be predicted. Survival would not be possible if we did not see the objects in the environment as constant despite changes in our positions with respect to them. One of the aspects that has not remained constant over time is how the objects are represented pictorially. Radical changes of style took place in the ways objects were depicted over the last 30,000 years of recorded art.

Gombrich has referred to the revolution in painting that took place in an early period of Greek art, during the sixth and fifth centuries BC, when the desire to imitate nature was paramount. The artists strived to make the pictorial representations as lifelike as possible, so that, ideally, they would be confused with the real objects. In the first century AD Pliny, in his *Natural History*, related a story about a competition between two Greek artists in which one painted grapes so skilfully that birds tried to eat them, and the other painted a curtain that the first artist tried to draw open! Thus, artists attempted to make the pictorial image match the object so that it would deceive the eye. In this endeavour Greek painters would have had access to the developing science of optics, and basic aspects of projection, like foreshortening, could have been incorporated in their pictures. Most of the surviving examples are on pottery, although some mosaic compositions still exist.

The ancient texts on optics, when they were reintroduced to the West from the thirteenth century, were called *Perspectiva* and they treated direct vision. The term perspective was derived from such texts, which often described aspects of pictorial representation and theatrical scene painting. However, perspective (or more correctly linear perspective) had a particular significance in the Renaissance because it reflected a return to the Greek pictorial ideal of attempting to imitate nature. The rules of perspective were devised in the intellectual cauldron of early fifteenth-century Florence. Linear perspective was demonstrated by architect and painter Fillipo Brunelleschi (1377–1446) and formalised by a contemporary mathematician, Leon Battista Alberti (1404–1472). Basically it was the application of Euclid's visual cone to a glass plane intersecting it, and this device is now known as Alberti's window. Thus, the principles of reducing a three-dimensional scene to a two-dimensional picture were formulated before the image-forming properties of the eye had been described. None the less, the differences between looking at a picture and looking at a scene were clearly appreciated by Leonardo da Vinci (1472–1519). At the end of the fifteenth century he wrote "A Painting, though conducted with the greatest Art and finished to the last Perfection, both with regard to its Contours, its Lights, its Shadows and its Colours, can never show a *Relievo* equal to that of the Natural Objects" (from a 1721 translation into English, p. 178). That is, the allusion to relief or depth in a painting of a scene, no matter how well it is painted, will be different to the perceived depth separating the actual objects in the scene.

Science and art meet in perspective. Perhaps it should more accurately be said that the optics of antiquity met the art of the Renaissance in the context of linear perspective. The technique of perspective painting was rapidly adopted by artists from the fifteenth century onwards, and many textbooks described its rules (Figure 2.5). There are many excellent treatments of the

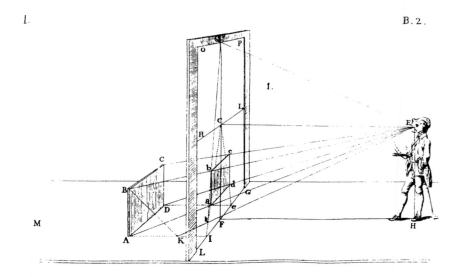

Figure 2.5 An illustration from Brook Taylor's classic treatise on perspective. "1. The *Point of Sight*, is that Point where the Spectator's Eye is placed to look at the Picture. Thus E is the Point of Sight. 2. If from the Point of Sight E, a Line EC is drawn from the Eye perpendicular to the Picture, the Point C, where the Line cuts the Picture, is called the *Center of the Picture*. 3. *The Distance of the Picture*, is the Length of the Line EC, which is drawn from the Eye perpendicular to the Picture. 4. If from the Point of Sight E, a Line EC be drawn perpendicular to any vanishing Line HL, or JF, then the Point C, where the Line cuts the vanishing Line, is called *the Center of that vanishing Line*. 5. *The Distance of a vanishing Line*, is the Length of the Line EC, which is drawn from the Eye perpendicular to the said Line: and if PO was a vanishing Line, then EJ will be the Distance of that Line. 6. *The Distance of the vanishing Point*, is the Length of a Line drawn from the Eye to that Point: Thus, EC is the Distance of the vanishing Point C, and EJ is the Distance of the vanishing Point J. 7. By *Original Object*, is meant the real Object whose representation is sought: and by *Original Plane*, is meant that Plane upon which the real Object is situated: Thus, the Ground HM is the Original Plane of ABCD." (Kirby, 1755)

history of perspective, but that by Kemp (1990) is especially instructive because it deals with the emergence of linear perspective in the fifteenth century, and its subsequent development. The historical connections between optics, painting, and vision are traced by Pirenne (1970), and his book includes many pinhole camera photographs taken to illustrate the principles of optical projection in an eye or camera. He also deals extensively with the art of linear perspective. Greek artists also applied some form of perspective, as Edgerton (1975) argued elegantly.

Image formation

The influence of art was to prove significant because it framed a recurrent concern for theorists of vision: How can we perceive the world as three-dimensional when the image cast in the eye is two-dimensional? Isn't this precisely the problem that confronts the painter? Artists in the new perspective style seemed to answer this in practice if not in theory. An allusion to three-dimensionality could be induced if the rules of linear perspective were followed; this required a single, fixed viewing point and the depiction of objects in the scene in accordance with the angle they subtended at that viewing point. An object, say a person, will subtend decreasing angles at the eye as they walk away from us, even though they remain the same physical size (Figure 2.6). This change in projected size does not correspond to our perception; people appear to remain the same size as they walk away from us. Artists, in common with the rest of us, have a problem in depicting this state of affairs accurately because perception does not correspond to the dimensions projected onto the retina; hence they must use all manner of artificial devices, like matching the angles with an outstretched thumb, in order to discount their perception and record visual angles.

The idea of a particular view of a scene and a surface onto which the principles of optics could be projected is an integral part of linear perspective. Specifying a station point, picture plane, ground plane, and vanishing point permitted depiction of a single image of a scene. Alberti described the rules for capturing the image, and a number of techniques for representing it. Some of these were mathematical, others involved a grid through which the scene is observed and a similar grid onto which the lines can be drawn. A famous woodcut by Albrecht Dürer (1471–1528) shows an artist painting a

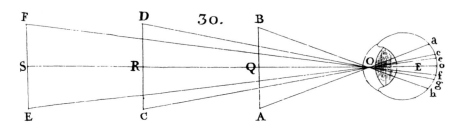

Figure 2.6 Objects of the same size, but at different distances from the eye, projecting differently sized images onto the retina, as was clearly described in Brook Taylor's treatise. "The farther distant the Eye is from an Object, so much less will the Picture of the Object be upon the Retina: for let E be the Eye viewing the several Objects AB, CD, EF at the Distance OQ, OR, OS. Having drawn the several Rays Aa, Bb, Cc, Dd, Ee, Ff, through the Pupil O, it will be manifest, that the Picture of the nearest Object AB, will be painted at the Bottom of the Eye in the Space ab, the Object CD in the Space cd, and the farthest Object, EF, in the Space ef." (Kirby, 1755)

model using such a system. A gnomon or sighting vane was used in order to define a station point, and the figure was viewed with the eye as close to it as possible. Perhaps the simplest means of drawing in perspective was "Alberti's window". If a single eye is maintained at a fixed position with respect to a window then the objects in the scene beyond the window can be represented in accurate perspective simply by tracing their outlines on the surface of the window. Another device, which combined the science and art of optics, was marshalled by some artists to form images in accurate central perspective—the camera obscura.

Camera obscura

The general principles of image formation have a long history. Shadow casting was known to scientists in China as early as the fifth century BC, and the practical optics of the camera obscura, or dark chamber, were described by Chinese scientists in the ninth century (see Hammond, 1981). Little in the way of a theory of image formation is considered to have derived from these experimental enquiries. Ibn al-Haytham described an inverted image in a dark chamber, and pinhole experiments were conducted by late mediaeval students of optics. However, the equation of such optical image-forming devices with the eye appeared much later.

Leonardo da Vinci conducted experiments with a camera obscura, and drew an analogy between its operation and that of the eye. In this regard, as in many others, his ideas were neither published nor widely known until long after his death. A later sixteenth-century artist, Daniele Barbaro (1513–1570), appreciated the assistance that the camera obscura could offer to the painter, particularly when a convex lens was placed in an enlarged aperture. A powerful convex lens was recommended, and the sharpest image could be located by moving a sheet of paper towards or away from the aperture. He also realised that the sharpness of the image could be further enhanced by reducing the size of the aperture through which the light entered the dark room.

The camera obscura was used by both artists and scientists to generate images. The artists realised that the tedium of perspective projection could be circumvented by its application, and scientists considered that it offered a solution to the problem of vision. For example, Giovanni Battista della Porta (1535–1615) argued that the projection of images in a camera obscura provided conclusive evidence against an extramission theory of vision, and that it explained "how vision is made!" Porta still held to the belief that vision took place in the lens. The link between anatomy and optics was still to be forged.

LIFE SCIENCES

Galen, in the second century AD, provided an account of sight which was firmly anchored in a speculative physiology, and it was, in turn, integrated with his description of the anatomy of the eye. He also ventured, with some misgivings, into the arena of optics. In his book *On the Usefulness of the Parts of the Body* (translated into English by May, 1968) he expressed regret for introducing optical concepts in a medical text, since they were at that time deeply unfashionable. His theory of vision was physiological, and it was based on pneumatic concepts: Pneuma, or visual spirit, passed along the hollow tubes of the optic nerves to interact with returning images of external objects in the crystalline lens. The lens was considered to be the primary organ of vision. Galen did not rely on speculation alone; he supported the proposal that the lens was the "seat of vision" by virtue of the blindness that results from cataracts and the sight that is restored when they are surgically removed.

Galen based his anatomy on dissections of animals, particularly monkeys, but most of his ocular anatomy was derived from dissecting the eyes of freshly slaughtered oxen. The restrictions that were subsequently placed on dissections resulted in a reliance on Greek (and particularly Galen's) works on anatomy, and they were recounted dogmatically until the time of Andreas Vesalius (1514–1564) over one thousand years later. From the sixteenth century anatomy became increasingly rigorous, being based on observations from dissection, even when these were at variance with the Galenic dogma. The eye, however, was not subjected to the same detailed scrutiny as the skeleton and musculature until the seventeenth century.

There are many histories of medicine describing the development of ocular anatomy and ophthalmology. Polyak (1957) contains a detailed history of advances in gross and microscopic anatomy of the eye, as does Wade (1998). Finger (1994) places the growth of understanding of the visual process in the broader context of cognitive development and its relation to the brain. A more selective, but very readable, account of the growth of ideas about vision and the brain can be found in the essays by Gross (1998).

Image formation in the eye

Kepler described the manner in which images are formed in the eye before its detailed anatomy had been accurately described and illustrated. The retinal image was inverted and reversed, which was seen as posing a problem for vision, and one that Kepler was not prepared to speculate upon. This problem puzzled many students of vision, even after its solution had been proposed by Molyneux (1692). He argued that the terms erect and inverted are only relative to the direction of gravity; moreover, the process of perception involves the mind as well as the eyes. It took most of the seventeenth century for the distinction between the retinal image and perception to be appreciated.

Following Kepler's insight, students of vision tended to reduce the analysis of vision to an analysis of the image formed in the eye. That is, vision became a problem for geometrical optics, and there was a concrete model for vision (the camera obscura with a lens) that could be used in an experimental way. Scheiner (1619), who provided the first accurate description of the anatomy of the eye, carried out experiments with an excised eye of a bull: when the rear coats were cut away (leaving the dark retina intact) and the eye was placed in a small hole of a dark room an inverted image of the scene outside could be observed. The most famous depiction of this was in Descartes's *Dioptrique* (Figure 2.7).

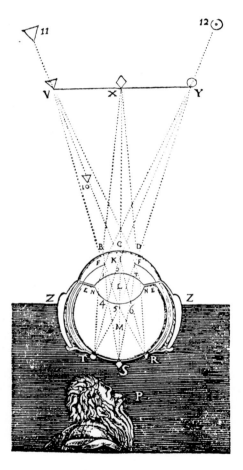

Figure 2.7 A figure from Descartes' *Dioptrique* (1637/1902) illustrating the optical image forming properties of the eye. Rays of light from the object VXY are refracted at the cornea (BCD) and lens (L) to focus an image RST on the retina. (Adam & Tannery, 1902)

Accommodation

The analogy between eye and camera introduced a new set of problems in the study of vision. If the camera can only focus on objects at a particular distance, how is the eye able to focus upon objects over a wide range of distances? This is the problem of accommodation. From the time of Kepler to the middle of the nineteenth century accommodation was one of the most intensively studied and controversial topics in vision. Not surprisingly, since the equation of the eye with a camera had proved so popular, the solutions were often derived from characteristics of cameras. A camera with a small aperture has a much greater depth of focus than one with a larger aperture; moving the camera lens towards or away from the screen onto which images are projected will vary the distance at which objects are sharply focused; conversely, moving the screen itself will have the same effect. Each of these physical speculations was advanced, together with others that were physiological.

Despite the analogies of accommodation with focusing in a camera, Descartes's physiological speculations were to prove particularly astute. The lens itself was considered to change its curvature, becoming more convex for focusing on near objects, and less convex for more distant ones. He even suggested that accommodation provides a source of distance information for objects that are close to the eye. The strongest support for the involvement of the lens in accommodation came from a Scottish physician, William Porterfield (c. 1696-1771); he examined a patient who had had the lens removed from one eye (because of cataract) and was unable to accommodate at all without the aid of a convex lens; moreover, the power of the lens required to be modified for objects at different distances.

Thus, writers on the eye and vision selected one or more of these hypotheses as their candidates for accommodation until the end of the eighteenth century, when Young (1793, 1801) reported his experimental enquiries supporting changes in lens curvature. Such support was not derived from direct evidence, but rather from the rejection of all alternative hypotheses. Changes in corneal curvature were excluded in two ways: The images of candle flames reflected from the cornea did not change with variations in accommodation, and immersion of the eye in water did not abolish accommodation. Elongation of the eye was rendered untenable because accommodation was still possible when considerable external pressure was applied to the eye. The mechanism by which changes in lens curvature could be achieved was proposed by Helmholtz. In order to measure the curvatures of the optical surfaces in the living eye Helmholtz invented the ophthalmometer; he confirmed the speculations of Descartes and the experiments of Young that the lens changes curvature during accommodation, and he proposed the mechanism by which this is achieved: "On contraction, the ciliary muscle could pull the posterior end of the zonule forwards nearer the lens and reduce the tension of the zonule. If the pull of the zonule is relaxed in accommodating for near vision, the equatorial diameter of the lens will diminish, and the lens will get thicker in the middle, both surfaces becoming more curved" (Helmholtz, 2000, p. 151).

Ocular anatomy

Some knowledge of the anatomy of the eye must have been available several thousand years ago because there were not only medical practitioners in Mesopotamia and Egypt but also eye specialists; they must have had a working knowledge of ocular anatomy in order to carry out the operations they are known to have performed (see Finger, 1994). Their skills and understanding would have been passed on to Greek physicians, who both recorded and developed them. Many Greek texts, through their translations, have been transmitted to us, but any illustrations that they might have included have not survived.

Printed figures of the eye were published from the beginning of the sixteenth century, but they were derived from dogma rather than dissection. Following the relaxation of sanctions prohibiting dissection of human bodies in the fourteenth century, knowledge concerning anatomy in general slowly began to be based on more secure ground. The dissecting skills of the anatomist were critical, and the major advances came with practitioners like Leonardo and Vesalius. Leonardo's detailed drawings of dissections did not make any immediate impact because they remained both in manuscript form and in private hands. Unlike his anatomical drawings of the musculature, those of the eye reflected a conflation of dissection and dogma: His rather crude drawings reflected a reliance on Galen, even though he did prepare the excised eye (by boiling it in the white of an egg) for dissection. His drawings of the eye showed the lens as spherical and central in the eye, and the optic nerves passed to the cerebral ventricles.

The renaissance of anatomy is associated with Vesalius, who published his book *De Humani Corporis Fabrica* (*On the Structure of the Human Body*) in 1543. It is taken to be a synthesis of science and art because of the high quality of the anatomical illustrations. His diagram of the eye (Figure 2.8a) did not match the detail or accuracy of those for the skeletal musculature and internal organs: a symmetrical lens was still located in the centre of the eye and the optic nerve was situated on the optic axis. He listed the various structures, but did not pursue their function in any detail. Throughout the sixteenth century diagrams of the eye showed increasing refinement, with more precise locations of the various structures within it. In 1583, the anatomist Felix Platter (1536–1614) stated that the retina rather than the lens was the receptive organ for vision, which received light through the lens, and which could discriminate colour and form. The first accurate diagram of the eye (Figure 2.8b) was that by Scheiner (Figure 2.8c); the lens and its curvatures are appropriately represented and the optic nerve leaves the eye nasally. Scheiner's analysis was rapidly absorbed by both anatomists and philosophers.

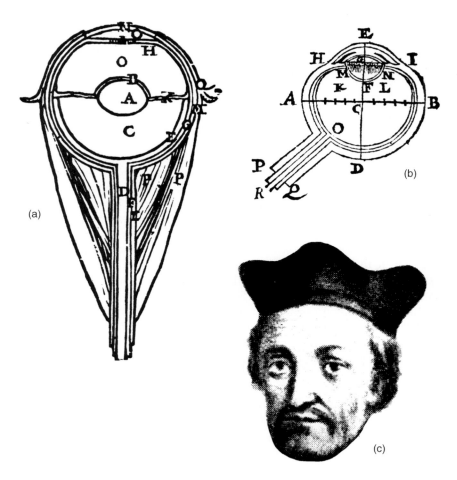

Figure 2.8 Eye after: (a) Vesalius (1543) and (b) Scheiner (1619). (c) Christoph
Scheiner (1571–1650).

Anatomical knowledge increased in the eighteenth and particularly in the
nineteenth centuries—the power of the microscope was brought to bear on
unravelling the detailed structure of the retina and the nerve pathways, and
structure was in turn related to function. For example, in the 1860s the two
different types of light-sensitive cells were found in the eye; they were called
rods and cones because of their shapes when observed under the microscope.
It was noted that the proportion of rods and cones varied over species.
Indeed, some species only had one type or the other, and in all cases this
could be related to the light conditions in which they were active. The retinas
of nocturnal animals had rods but few or no cones, whereas those active only
in daylight had cones but few or no rods: Humans, who are active and can see

under both natural light conditions, have a mixture of rods and cones. Accordingly, it was proposed that rods and cones had differing sensitivities and served different functions. Rods are able to detect light at lower intensities than cones, but cones are involved in colour vision and rods are not. Both rods and cones require appropriate pathways to the brain in order for us to experience light; however, in the nineteenth century relatively little was known about pathways in the brain, and so physiological analyses of vision tended to be restricted to the structures in the eye.

The spirit of these exciting times was reflected in what is perhaps the greatest book written on vision, the *Treatise on Physiological Optics* by Helmholtz. It was originally published in three separate volumes during the 1850s and 1860s, and the complete treatise was translated from German into English in the early twentieth century to mark the centenary of Helmholtz's birth. As an indication of its continuing significance to visual scientists the translation has been reprinted recently (see Helmholtz, 2000). Helmholtz was both a physicist and a physiologist, and he amalgamated the strengths of these two disciplines in the analysis of vision. Amongst his many contributions to visual science were the elucidation of the mechanism of accommodation, the championing of a theory of colour vision based on three colour channels, and the invention of the ophthalmoscope for examining the inside of the eye. The ophthalmoscope is an instrument that directs light into the eye and light reflected from the retina and related structures is magnified (see Millodot, 2000).

Visual pathways

Alcmaeon, in the fifth century BC, proposed that the optic nerves were hollow tubes and this tradition was continued by Aristotle. Galen believed that the origin of the visual pathways was located in the anterior ventricle of the brain, where the animal spirit could interact with the visual spirit (the pneuma), borne by the optic nerves. The optic nerves themselves came together at the optic chiasm, but each of the nerves was considered to remain on the same side (ipsilateral). That is, the visual spirit was unified in the chiasm and then sent to each eye.

For centuries, diagrams of the visual pathways represented the optic chiasm but the passage of the optic nerves through it remained a matter of speculation. Vesalius repeated the separate and ipsilateral projection of the optic nerves, and it became integrated into Descartes's analysis of vision (Figure 2.9). Descartes did stress the correspondence between points on the object, those on the retina, and their projection to the brain, but it is unlikely that he was addressing the issue of corresponding points in the two retinas. His analysis of binocular vision was by the ancient analogy with a blind man holding two sticks, and it was not physiological. The union that was depicted in the pineal body reflected an attempt to match singleness of vision with a single anatomical structure. Thus Descartes's speculative physiology defined

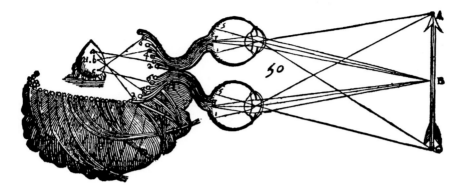

Figure 2.9 Binocular visual pathways according to Descartes (1664/1909): "the filaments 1–2, 3–4, 5–6, and the like compose the optic nerve and extend from
the back of the eye (1, 3, 5) to the internal surface of the brain (2, 4, 6).
Now assume that these threads are so arranged that if the rays that come,
for example, from point A of the object happen to exert pressure on the
back of the eye at point 1, they in this way would pull the whole thread 1–2
and enlarge the opening of the tubule marked 2. And similarly, the rays
that come from point B enlarge the opening of tubule 4, and so on with the
others. Whence, just as the different ways in which these rays exert pressure
on points 1, 3, and 5 trace a figure at the back of the eye corresponding to
that of object ABC, so, evidently, the different ways in which the tubules 2,
4, 6, and the like are opened by filaments 1–2, 3–4, and 5–6 must trace [a
corresponding figure] on the internal surface of the brain." (Descartes,
1972).

his visual anatomy. His achievement was in presenting an account of the
visual pathways in terms of their topographical organisation.

Descartes's analysis of vision was based on his conception of light: When
light strikes the eye it applies force to points on the retina, which is transmitted along the optic nerve to the brain. The significance of Descartes's theories
does not lie so much in whether they were valid or not as in the emphasis they
placed on physiological interpretations of vision. Increasingly, from that time
onwards texts that dealt with vision would have some diagram representing
the pathways from the eyes to the brain, and some speculations regarding the
site at which vision occurs. In the context of the visual pathways to the brain,
it was believed that messages carried by the two optic nerves remained separate
until they were united in the brain, as is indicated in Descartes's figure.

Newton advanced our knowledge of the binocular pathways by describing
the partial crossover of nerve fibres from one optic nerve to the other side of
the brain. This discovery was used to support a mechanistic interpretation of
vision, that is, one that did not make any appeal to nonmaterial sources like
the soul. The messages from each eye were thought to became one, because
the nerve fibres themselves were (wrongly) considered to unite in the optic

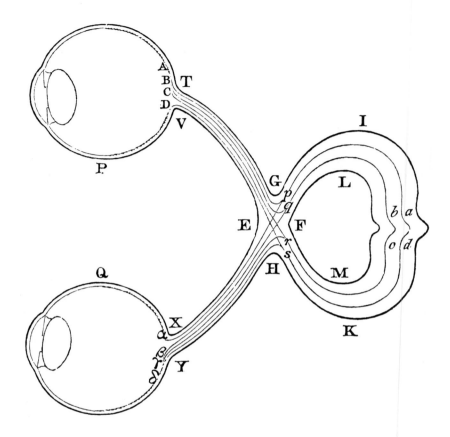

Figure 2.10 Binocular vision according to Newton. "Now I conceive that every point in the retina of one eye, hath its corresponding point in the other; from which two very slender pipes filled with the most limpid liquor, do without either interruption, or any unevenness or irregularities in their process, go along the optic nerves to the juncture EFGH, where they meet either betwixt G, F, or F, H, and there unite into one pipe as big as both of them; and so continue in one, passing either betwixt I, L or M, K, into the brain, where they are terminated perhaps at the next meeting of the nerves betwixt the cerebrum and cerebellum, in the same order that their extremities were situated in the retina's." (As described in Harris, 1775)

chiasm (see Figure 2.10). He also observed that there was almost complete crossing of the fibres for animals with lateral, as opposed to frontal, eyes. Newton was almost correct in his analysis: Partial decussation was appropriate, but he represented the nerves themselves as uniting at the chiasm. That is, optic nerve fibres from corresponding points on each eye formed single fibres in the optic tract. This detail was soon to be rectified in an accurate representation of the partial crossing over and independence of the nerve fibres: Fibres in the optic nerve diverged after the optic chiasm, with those from the left halves of each retina projecting to the left part of the brain, and vice versa. The detailed anatomy of the crossings was described later in the nineteenth century, but few speculated on the more central pathways of vision.

Impact of evolution

At least since the time of Aristotle and Galen anatomical knowledge derived from studying a wide range of species, and similarities of structures between species were often remarked upon. In the early nineteenth century much of this material was systematically classified by Johannes Peter Müller (1801–1858) in his two-volume *Elements of Physiology*. It contained a wealth of information on comparative anatomy and reflected the widely held belief that all species were related, although the mechanism for such an evolutionary process was to await the publication of *The Origin of Species by Means of Natural Selection* by Charles Darwin (1809–1882) in 1859. In the latter part of the nineteenth century the relationship between structure and function was examined over a wide biological spectrum, due to the gradual acceptance of Darwin's theory of evolution. The relationships that were shown to exist between species also supported the extension of physiological discoveries derived from animal experiments to humans. For example, if the processes involved in nerve transmission in the frog could be elucidated then similar processes are probably operating in other species, too, including humans. Comparative anatomists were also able to chart the evolutionary paths of particular sensory organs, like eyes, and it was evident that quite different aspects of information from light were useful to different animals—some can only discriminate differences in light intensity but not differences in wavelength, some can analyse plane polarised light, some can see into the infrared region of the spectrum. Indeed, at an early stage two quite different designs for eyes evolved—one was a multifaceted compound eye (as in insects) and the other a single-lensed image-forming eye (as in vertebrates).

Müller tackled a related problem: Since nerve impulses in all sensory nerves are similar, how can the brain distinguish between impulses originating from the eyes and those from the ears? Müller's solution was to suggest that all sensory nerves have some specific energy or code that signals their particular origin. In this way, he argued, it would be possible for the brain to determine the sense from which the signals originated. According to this doctrine of specific nerve energies all the nerves from the eyes carry a specific signal that defines the quality of the sensation that will ensue; these visual qualities of brightness and colour occur no matter how the nerves are stimulated. For example, a blow to the head or pressure applied to the eye results in an experience of light rather than of pressure. The comic device of "seeing stars" following a knockout punch fairly reflects Müller's doctrine. Later in

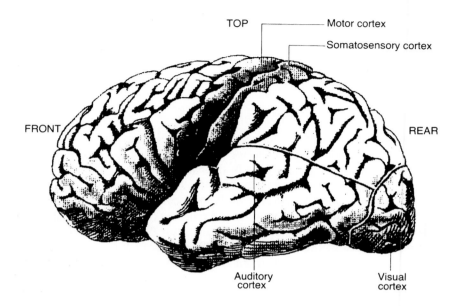

Figure 2.11 Sensory projection areas of the brain.

the nineteenth century physiological recordings indicated that different regions of the brain act as receiving areas for specific senses (Figure 2.11).

Observations of animal behaviour were recorded with increasing skill in the eighteenth and nineteenth centuries. Darwin believed that behavioural patterns could evolve in a similar way to anatomical structures, and he wrote a book on *The Expression of the Emotions in Man and Animals* (1872) charting the relationships between gestures and expressions in different species. Variations occur not only between species but also within them. Most particularly, changes in structure and function take place in the course of development to the mature state of the species. That is, within a given species there will be a developmental sequence for both structure and function. One of the features that seemed particularly perplexing was the ability of newborn animals to seek and find the source of sustenance (e.g., the mother's nipple for mammals) without any prior experience. This led some students, like Müller, to argue that this aspect of their behaviour was instinctive (i.e., innate or inborn) so that it occurred without any learning.

Similar questions can be asked about whether human newborns also possess innate perceptual mechanisms. Paradoxically, the biologists' skills in analysing animal behaviours in the natural environment were not applied to newborn humans. Well into the twentieth century it was thought that the behaviour of very young babies was random and uncoordinated, and this presented problems for determining experimentally what they are able to see.

Rather than refining the techniques for measuring behaviour in infants, it was usually considered that their visual world was as chaotic as their behaviour seemed to be. In the past this might have contributed to the view that the mind of the newborn is like a blank sheet upon which experience writes. In other words, humans were considered to learn the three-dimensional nature of their world, and this learning was dependent upon information delivered by the senses. These concepts of innate and learned behaviours have also been of central importance in philosophical approaches to perception.

PHILOSOPHY

Perceptual experience is subjective. Each one of us is able to reflect upon the nature of that experience, and to describe it to others. Although the experience is subjective, and inaccessible to others, the descriptions of what we perceive can be shared with others. Generally speaking, the descriptions given by different people of their perceptual experiences are in remarkably close correspondence; so close, in fact, that many people equate their perception of the world with the way it is described in traditional physics (or what we might loosely call reality). This has been the topic of much philosophical debate and the equation of perception with external reality is often referred to as naive realism. The close correspondence between perception of the world and other descriptions of it (e.g., as in terms of physical measurement) retarded the analysis of perception in general. The aspects that did demand scrutiny were those in which perceptual and physical descriptions did not match, or in which some disease, injury or intervention influenced perception; that is, when perception is no longer veridical or equated with physical measurements.

We can cite two examples of departures from perceptual veridicality described by Aristotle—afterimages and aftereffects. In one set of observations he directed his eyes briefly at the sun and noticed a rapid sequence of colours when he looked away, followed by a dark disc. It was obviously of interest to Aristotle because there was no visibly coloured object that corresponded to the briefly perceived colours. You should not try to repeat this observation, as it could damage the retina. There is an even more remarkable anecdotal account of such folly in the history of afterimages: A friend of the seventeenth-century chemist Robert Boyle looked at the sun through a telescope, and reported that he could see its afterimage 11 years later! It seems more likely that he was not seeing at all with the part of the retina that had been exposed to the concentrated sunlight because the retinal cells would have been destroyed producing a scotoma. Another phenomenon described by Aristotle was the movement aftereffect. He looked for some time at the stones at the bottom of a river through the rapidly flowing water, then he directed his gaze to the stones on the bank of the river; these appeared to be moving, too. That is, here was a situation in which the same objects, the stones on the river bank, appeared to be stationary at one time and moving at another. Have the stones changed their location or has their perception been modified? This clearly poses a problem for naive realists, who believe that reality is equated with our perceptual experience. The movement aftereffect remains a phenomenon of interest to perceptual psychologists, and it can be elicited with a wide range of moving stimuli (see Mather, Verstraten, & Anstis 1998).

Greek approaches to perception

Philosophy has played a central role in the study of perception because the senses and their functions have been of focal importance to philosophy. Most of the basic ideas were initially expounded by Greek thinkers, and they have been elaborated upon by more modern philosophers. As is clear from the previous references to Aristotle, it was essentially the unusual aspects of visual experience that elicited most interest. Of these, three were of particular significance and they influenced the theories of light described earlier in the chapter. The first concerned the experience of light following pressure or a blow to the eye; the second related to the visibility of a reflected image in the eye. The idea of light being emitted from the eye was founded on the first of these, and the notion of an image being carried back to the eye was the source of the second. A third feature of sight, which distinguished it from the other senses, was that the experience could be terminated by closing the eyelids during daytime.

Plato (Figure 2.12a) distrusted the senses because the evidence they furnished about external objects could change; moreover, the objects themselves could change, as in the process of growth. Accordingly, he believed that the world of appearances was one of illusion, as opposed to the world of thought in which ideal forms existed. The forms reflected the universal qualities of objects rather than the particular features that can be sensed. The abstract forms could be investigated by reasoning rather than observation, and this resulted in a preference for rational rather than empirical enquiry. Plato's position demonstrates the influence that language has had on philosophical thought: particular members of a category that are given a single name (e.g., horse) do not reflect their universal characteristics. These ideal forms are permanent and inaccessible to perception because the senses are concerned with particulars rather than universals. Plato distinguished between the body and the soul: The body was part of the material world, whereas the soul was immaterial. He likened the rational soul to a charioteer steering the competing horses of emotion and appetite; the rational soul was considered to be morally superior to the others and should guide their actions. These distinctions were to have considerable significance because they later permeated both philosophy and Christian theology. Mind–body dualism was at the heart of Descartes's philosophy as well as a constant current in Christian

Figure 2.12 (a) Plato (427–347 BC). (b) Aristotle (c. 384–322 BC).

theology. The latter also placed great emphasis on the moral superiority of reason over irrational feelings and passions.

Aristotle (Figure 2.12b), who was one of Plato's students, displayed detachment from his mentor in developing his own philosophy. He has been referred to as the great realist, because he adopted more naturalistic explanations of phenomena that did not denigrate the senses. He criticised Plato's theory of ideal forms, arguing that the features that distinguish a horse, say, do not have an existence independently of horses; these distinctive features could best be studied by examining actual horses rather than their ideal forms. Therefore Aristotle preferred an empirical approach to a rational one. He is often considered to be the first psychologist because of his emphasis on observation and because he tried to order phenomena in a systematic manner. Many of his classifications of natural phenomena are still used, and he studied a broad range, from botany to behaviour. He placed humans at one end of a continuum of living things that extended to plants. The distinguishing feature was the possession of mind—the ability to reason. Aristotle's studies of the senses were extensive and he suggested that sensations were brought together to form a common sense, which he located in the heart.

The contrast between the philosophies of Plato and Aristotle is that between rationalism and empiricism, and both approaches have been applied to the analysis of vision. The differences between them were brought into sharper focus after the scientific Renaissance in the seventeenth century, when a wider range of visual phenomena was scrutinised.

Rationalism

Descartes (Figure 2.13a) applied mechanistic interpretations to bodily processes while maintaining that the mind was immaterial, thus retaining the Platonic distinction between body and soul. In 1619, during military service in Germany, Descartes had a series of dreams that were to structure his subsequent thinking. They inspired him to search for new methods of enquiry rather than adopting those of past philosophers. His method was to reject all ideas about which there could be any doubt. He was left with the irreducible fact of his own existence—I think, therefore I am. That is, Descartes's sceptical enquiries led him to the view that only thought and reason were beyond doubt, and were the bases upon which philosophy should stand, and these were the province of humans alone. The body, on the other hand, worked by mechanical principles, the understanding of which Descartes did much to advance. Of particular importance is his introduction of the reflex concept, which involved the nerves acting like pipes connecting the receptors to the brain which sent messages to the muscles. Communion between mind and body was achieved via structures in the brain, particularly the unpaired pineal body (the pear-shaped structure labelled H in Figure 2.9).

Descartes gave to the mind properties that were not shared by the body, which was treated as a machine. His mechanistic approach to the senses clarified many issues in perception, but he had the thorny problem of accounting for the interaction of the rational mind with the mechanistic body. This was a task attempted later by Kant (Figure 2.13b), a German philosopher in the eighteenth century. He did not deny that all knowledge begins with experience, but he did not believe that it all arises out of experience either. He considered that certain aspects of knowledge are innate, most

(a)   (b)

Figure 2.13 (a) René Descartes (1596–1650). (b) Immanuel Kant (1724–1804).

particularly the ideas of space and time. That is, Kant suggested that the individual is born with the ability to organise experience in both space and time. Perception is then an active organising process for Kant, rather than a passive receptive process of the type Locke proposed. Kant's influence on Continental philosophy was vast, but it also had numerous repercussions in related disciplines like physiology and psychology. The distinction between innate and learned processes in perception became enshrined in nativist and empiricist philosophies, respectively. The nativists believed that we are born with the ability to perceive space, whereas the empiricists argued that we have no such knowledge of the world at birth, but we need to learn to see the spatial attributes like size, shape, and distance.

Kant developed a transcendental theory of mind that drew upon both rationalism and empiricism without being allied to either. Rather than accounting for ideas in terms of experience, Kant adopted the opposite strategy of accounting for experience in terms of concepts. That is, our conscious, phenomenal world is a cognitive construction. He accepted that all knowledge arises from the senses, but it is not treated in a passive way. The case for nativism was championed in a more specific way than Descartes had proposed. Perception was taken to be an active process of organisation rather than a passive accretion of sensations. Kant made a distinction between the world of things and that of appearances, and was pessimistic about whether the latter (and hence psychology) was open to scientific enquiry. That is, he did not consider that the inner world was open to precise measurement, and therefore its study could not be classified as a science. None the less, Kant's ideas have had a long-lasting influence on psychology in general, and most notably on the emergence of Gestalt psychology.

Empiricism

Modern empiricist philosophy was expounded by Locke (Figure 2.14a) at the end of the seventeenth century. In his *Essay Concerning Human Understanding* (1690/1975, p. 41), he wrote: "Let us suppose the Mind to be, as we say, white Paper, void of all Characters, without any *Ideas*; How comes it to be furnished? Whence comes it by that vast store, which the busie and boundless Fancy of Man has painted on it with an almost endless variety? Whence has it all the materials of Reason and Knowledge? To this I answer in one word, from *Experience*: In that all our Knowledge is founded, and from that it ultimately derives it self." For Locke the mental element is the idea, which is based upon sensory experience. Ideas could be simple (like whiteness) or compound (like snow), and compound ideas are made up from associations between simple ones, by a process like "mental chemistry". Similar associative links can account for our ability to generalise across stimuli: for instance, to form a general idea of a triangle from many different specific instances. Thus, Locke was an empiricist and an associationist: Knowledge derives from the senses and we learn to perceive the objects in the world by association.

Figure 2.14 (a) John Locke (1632–1704). (b) George Berkeley (1685–1753). (c) Thomas
Reid (1710–1796).

The empiricist philosophers were not, however, empirical in their approach
to perception. That is, they rarely carried out experiments to support their
theory, even when they were explicitly suggested. Following the publication
of Locke's *Essay*, Molyneux wrote to him posing an hypothetical question:
Suppose someone was born blind and subsequently learned to discriminate
between a sphere and a cube by touch; if their vision was later restored,
would they be able to name them by sight alone? Molyneux concluded that
they would not be able to name the objects appropriately, and Locke agreed
with this conclusion. It was not possible to check this prediction empirically
at that time, but early in the eighteenth century the oculist William Cheselden
(1688–1752) did perform cataract removals on congenitally blind patients
and noted the recovery of their vision. Unfortunately, neither his study nor
the many others conducted over the last two centuries enable a clear answer
to be given to Molyneux's question, largely because of the poor quality of
vision initially available to the patients after the operation. Morgan's (1977)
delightful book on *Molyneux's Question* carefully dissects the philosophical
ideas underlying Locke's empiricism in the context of surgery to remove
cataracts; he has also translated some articles by French philosophers who
were critical of empiricism.

Locke charted the course for empiricism, but many of the details were
provided by later philosophers, two of whom will be mentioned briefly here.
Bishop Berkeley (Figure 2.14b) argued, in *An Essay Toward a New Theory of
Vision*, that we learn to perceive the dimensions of space by associating muscular sensations with those of vision. He commenced by stating "My Design
is to shew the manner, wherein we perceive by Sight the Distance, Magnitude,
and Situation of Objects. Also to consider the Difference there is betwixt the
Ideas of Sight and Touch, and whether there be any Idea common to both
Senses. It is, I think, agreed by all that Distance of itself, and immediately
cannot be seen. For Distance being a Line directed end-wise to the Eye, it

projects only one Point in the Fund of the Eye, Which Point remains invariably the same, whether the Distance be longer or shorter" (1709, pp. 1–2). He proposed that we learn to see distance by associating sight with touch. Moreover, the degree of muscular contraction involved in converging the eyes are also correlated with distance, and provide a source of association with sight for perceiving distance. Thus, in order to perceive distance visually we learn the relationship between the visual stimulation and the states of the muscles controlling the eyes. The muscular and touch systems were considered to provide direct and undistorted spatial information that could be used to teach vision the dimensions of space.

Berkeley refined the empiricist philosophy of Locke by arguing that appearances are all: Existence is perception. That is, the matter from which materialism is constructed is itself open to question. If all we have are our perceptions, how can we prove the existence of an external world? A problem with this position is that if perceptions are transitory so is existence. Does an object cease to exist when the eyes are closed? Berkeley sought to salvage this slide into solipsism (that nothing other than one's own ideas exist) by arguing that God alone perceived an external reality. Despite this idealist stance, Berkeley made important steps towards understanding how we perceive space, and how the different spatial senses are integrated.

Reid (Figure 2.14c) reacted to Berkeley's idealism by arguing that the evidence of external reality is provided by the common activities of the senses and is supported by common sense intuition. Thus, Reid (1764) founded the Scottish common-sense school of philosophy, whose ideas were to be influential in the development of psychology in America in the nineteenth century. The school was opposed to associationism, particularly when it was couched in physiological language. Reid also proposed a faculty psychology; faculties were innate properties of the mind which exerted control over habits, or behaviour. His descriptive psychology could be studied by reflection on mental activity, by an analysis of the use of language, and by observations of behaviour. He provided a bridge between the extreme rationalists and empiricists. His belief in the power of reason was tempered by a desire to accumulate evidence empirically.

Reid is perhaps best remembered because of the clear distinction he made between sensation and perception. Thus, redness and roundness may be sensations produced by an apple, but its perception includes an appreciation of the object itself. Perceptions also involve projective aspects that are not present in sensations: The apple is perceived as being out there, but the sensations can be internal. Reid's distinction has had far-reaching consequences, and it has persisted well into this century; it has pervaded our language and it even defines the categories of our enquiries. We use the term sensory to describe those areas concerned with the early stages of processing (as in sensory physiology) and the term perceptual to those dealing with later stages (as in space perception).

Empiricist philosophy was initially confined to Britain, but its widest influence has probably been through its adoption beyond Britain's shores—particularly by Helmholtz in nineteenth-century Germany and Watson in twentieth-century America. The seventeenth- and eighteenth-century empiricists challenged the rationalist Continental philosophers who argued that we obtain knowledge about the world by thinking, independently of sensory experience.

Phenomenology

Perceptual experience has always been described in words, when possible, but this has not been the only way of assessing it. Language reflects the nuances that can be applied to the richness of perception, and it has been considered by some, like Goethe (Figure 2.15a), to be the most appropriate vehicle for conveying experience. Goethe, in line with many Romantic philosophers, rejected the experimental approach to the study of nature because it was too constrained. In its place he proposed the astute and intuitive observation of natural phenomena, setting in train the method of phenomenology. This is best seen in his *Zur Farbenlehre* (1810, translated as the *Theory of Colours* in 1840), which contrasted his observational approach to colour with what he considered to be the physicalism of Newton. The purity of white light was taken to be fundamental and indivisible, rather than white being a mixture of different coloured lights. Goethe chose to observe and describe instead of experiment on colour vision. He distinguished between what he called physiological colours (the experience of colour) and physical colours produced by optical refraction. He did borrow a prism to repeat Newton's experiment of

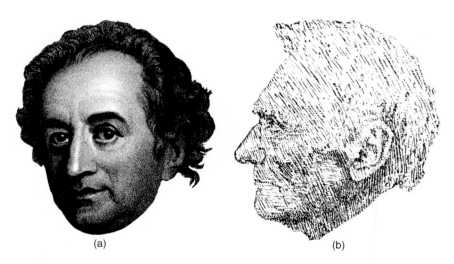

(a)   (b)

Figure 2.15 (a) Johann Wolfgang von Goethe (1749–1832). (b) Jan Evangelista Purkinje (1787–1869)

separating the spectral components of white light, but failed to conduct it appropriately; when asked to return the prism he simply directed it to a light and concluded that it still looked white! Goethe's theory of colour was never taken seriously by the scientific community, but his observations have rarely been challenged. He described many phenomena like positive and negative colour afterimages, irradiation, colour shadows, and colour blindness, in addition to contrast effects—both in the chromatic and achromatic domains. For example, the colour or brightness of a piece of paper can be changed by surrounding it by differently coloured or bright papers, as can its apparent size.

The methods of phenomenology were given a more methodological twist by Purkinje (Figure 2.15b), whose interests in vision were stimulated by reading Goethe's analysis of colour (see Wade & Brožek, 2001). He was encouraged in his researches by Goethe because of his use of the phenomenological method. When Purkinje gained access to one of the new large achromatic microscopes in the early 1830s he put his observational skills to good use. He has left his mark throughout the body. There are Purkinje cells in the brain, Purkinje fibres around the heart, Purkinje images are reflected from the optical surfaces of the eye, a Purkinje tree (the shadows of the retinal blood vessels) can be rendered visible, and at dawn and dusk we can experience the Purkinje shift (the difference in the visibility of coloured objects when seen in daylight and twilight—blue objects appear lighter and red ones darker in twilight). As a medical student he investigated subjective visual phenomena in part because he did not have access to any physiological apparatus, but also because he believed that visual illusions revealed visual truths. Most of his experimental research in both physiology and histology was conducted in Germany, but at the age of 63 he was called to the chair of physiology in Prague, where he became one of the most ardent advocates of Czech nationalism. He was followed in that chair by Hering, who also embraced phenomenology.

Helmholtz and Hering

The contributions made by Helmholtz (Figure 2.16a) to visual science are legion, but his most lasting impact was his theory of perception: he followed the Empiricist philosophers in arguing that perception is like unconscious problem solving—making unconscious inferences about the nature of the external world based upon the inadequate information furnished by the senses. Helmholtz appreciated that the process of perception takes place in the brain, following transmission of the neural signals from the sensory receptors—the brain only had indirect access to the external world, via the senses, and it could only process messages in the language of nerve impulses. This realisation made any equation of the retinal image with perception unnecessary, and it removed a problem that had frequently been raised earlier, and was to return later: If the image on the retina is inverted and left–right

(a)   (b)

Figure 2.16 (a) Hermann Ludwig Ferdinand von Helmholtz (1821–1894) in his diagram of the eye, from Wade (1994). (b) Karl Ewald Konstantin Hering
(1834–1918)

reversed why is our perception not so? Helmholtz argued that this only created a problem if there was a picture in the retina that required further
perception. If all that is available are nerve impulses then the brain can
analyse them and make the appropriate inferences independently of the
orientation of stimulation with respect to the retina.

Helmholtz acknowledged that little he wrote on the theories of vision was
novel, but he marshalled the arguments over a wider range of phenomena
than others had done before. He summarised his position succinctly: "The
sensations of the senses are tokens for our consciousness, it being left to our
intelligence to learn how to comprehend their meaning . . . Evidently, any
other sensations, not only of sight but of other senses also, produced by a
visible object when we move our eyes or our body so as to look at the object
from different sides or to touch it, etc., may be learned by experience. The
content of all these possible sensations united in a total idea forms our idea
of the body; and we call it perception when it is reinforced by actual sensations. The only psychic activity required for this purpose is the regularly
recurrent association between two ideas which have often been connected
before" (2000, pp. 533–534). By adopting a starkly empiricist interpretation
of perception, and by contrasting it so sharply with nativism, he reopened a

debate that has reverberated throughout perception ever since. The debate was personified in the conflict between Helmholtz and Hering, and the main battle-grounds were colour vision and stereoscopic depth perception (see Turner, 1994).

Hering (Figure 2.16b) was a physiologist whose psychology was in the tradition of Goethe and Purkinje. He represented the phenomenological and nativist position in studying perception. His work in vision concerned space perception, colour vision, and contrast phenomena. Like Goethe, Hering stressed the subjective dimension of colour, and he based his opponent process theory on colour appearances rather than on mixing lights of different wavelengths after the manner of Young, Maxwell, and Helmholtz. He adopted the procedure of presenting coloured papers to observers and asking them to name the colours from which they were mixed. Red, green, blue, and yellow were not said to be mixtures of any other colours, nor were black and white. He also examined simultaneous and successive colour contrast phenomena. Together these led him to propose a theory of colour vision based on three oppositional pairs: red–green, blue–yellow, and white–black. He speculated that there are three retinal pigments that are either built up or broken down by light to yield the six elements.

Modern colour theory has shown both Helmholtz and Hering to be correct in principle but wrong in detail (see pages 126–127): The initial stage involves three cone pigments (not three kinds of fibres) the signals from which combine neurally (not in the action of the pigments) to produce opposing pairs of red–green, blue–yellow, and white–black.

In the area of space perception Hering utilised the concept of local sign; each retinal point was considered to have a local sign for height, width, and depth. This conflicted with Helmholtz's emphasis on learning to interpret the retinal signals, largely via information from eye movements. Hering did investigate binocular eye movements and argued that the two eyes move as a single unit: His law of equal innervation states that when one eye moves the other moves with equal amplitude and velocity, either in the same or the opposite direction. Eye movements were also implicated in visual direction: "For any given two corresponding lines of direction, or visual lines, there is in visual space a single visual direction line upon which appears everything which actually lies in the pair of visual lines" (1868/1942, p. 41). The centre of visual direction was called the cyclopean eye. Hering also attracted a large body of able and loyal students who would carry the nativist banner into the twentieth century.

The psychology of the senses led Helmholtz into the metaphysical domain he had assiduously avoided in his physical and physiological endeavours. The philosophical problems remain a matter of constant revision and reanalysis, but many of the issues concerned with the senses that were debated in Helmholtz's day became the topics of experimental enquiry in the then new discipline of psychology.

PSYCHOLOGY

The psychological dimension of vision was exposed as soon as there were phenomena that warranted recording. The experience of light when pressure is applied to the eye is an early example to which reference has already been made. However, its psychological significance was not appreciated because the various stages in the visual process—the physics of light and the physiology of sight—had not been distinguished. Aristotle did describe many visual phenomena, but it was Ptolemy who realised that the spatial vision could not be understood in terms of visual angles. The psychological dimension increased in prominence after the dioptrics of the eye had been adequately analysed. None the less, they were not a part of psychology because there was then no such subject.

Psychology, as an independent discipline, is considered to have been founded in 1879, when Wundt (Figure 2.17), who had been an assistant to Helmholtz, opened his Psychological Institute at Leipzig University. Prior to that psychology was allied principally to philosophy, although perception

Figure 2.17 (a) Wilhelm Maximilian Wundt (1832–1920) from Wade (1995).

was often the province of sensory physiologists. Wundt saw the task of his new institute as that of studying conscious experience. What distinguished his approach from the many earlier ones addressing the same issues were the methods employed. Psychology came of age when it developed its own methodology: The problems of consciousness and perception were examined in novel ways using novel instruments, and psychology became an experimental discipline rather than just an observational one (see Wade & Heller, 1997). Perception has followed the theoretical fashions of psychology generally, ebbing and flowing as the subjective dimension waned and waxed in importance. In Wundt's day it waxed, only to wane under the onslaught of behaviourism; currently it is waxing again in part due to developments in neuroscience and cognitive psychology, and in part because of Gibson's and Marr's analysis.

Many histories of psychology make reference to perception, and Fancher (1996) provides a very readable introduction to the main streams of thought from Descartes to Freud. In addition to the chapters on philosophy and psychophysics, those concerned with the physiology of mind and the theory of evolution are especially apposite. R.I. Watson (1968, 1979) concentrates on the endeavours of many of those mentioned in the present chapter; he has also assembled an extensive list of *Basic Writings in the History of Psychology* in which extracts from the works of Descartes, Newton, Locke, Berkeley, Kant, Fechner, Helmholtz, Wundt, Darwin, and the Gestalt psychologists can be read. These, and many other major players in the field of perception, are portrayed in word and image in Wade (1995). Gardner's (1987) wide-ranging book on the history of the cognitive revolution provides a good link between the distant and recent past. The philosophical precursors of cognition are essentially similar to those for perception, and Gardner provides a clear description of the conflicts between nativist and empiricist approaches to perception and thought.

Wundt and structuralism

Wundt rejected phenomenology and introduced a technique that is now called analytic introspection—the controlled analysis of mental events. He distinguished between the mediated experience available to the physical sciences and the immediate experience investigated by psychology. His use of introspection to study the latter resulted in the proposal that sensations and feelings were the elements of consciousness. Sensations could be combined to yield perceptions, but for these to influence behaviour they required attention: the voluntary control of attention to focus on aspects of perception was termed apperception. It was the active role played by attention that could rearrange perceptions to form a creative synthesis. Wundt was an empiricist and an associationist interested in the universal aspects of conscious experience; the application of psychology to real-world issues held little appeal for him.

Wundt incorporated precise methods for measuring detection and discrimination in his Psychological Institute, and it was in providing alternatives to phenomenology that psychology gained its independence from other disciplines. Wundt used analytic introspection for studying consciousness, but in the area of perception he also applied the psychophysical methods that had been described a few years earlier by his compatriots Ernst Weber (1795–1878) and Fechner (Figure 2.18). As described on pages 13–18, Fechner integrated Weber's fraction to found the discipline of psychophysics. Fechner's insight was that the mental and material worlds could be united mathematically in the domains of sensory and stimulus intensities: "Psychophysics should be understood here as an exact theory of the functionally dependent relations of body and soul or, more generally, of the material and the mental, of the physical and the psychological worlds" (1966, p. 7). Fechner distinguished between an outer and an inner psychophysics; the former was concerned with the sensation and stimulus intensities, and the latter with the relation between brain process and sensations. He realised that experiments in his day would be confined to outer psychophysics, but these were seen as necessary steps towards understanding inner psychophysics.

Figure 2.18 Gustav Theodor Fechner (1801–1887).

Wundt himself did measure thresholds, but his greatest interest was the study of conscious experience. Introspection is looking inward at mental processes and the method differed from phenomenology in that instead of using familiar object names (like book or page) only terms signifying sensory quality (colour or brightness), intensity (extension), and direction were permitted. Thus, the description of the book you are reading could take the form something like "two white surfaces, separated at their centres with one raised with respect to the other; on each surface are black marks, slightly separated from one another horizontally but with larger spaces at irregular intervals . . .". Observers had to undergo extensive training before they were considered to be skilled at analytic introspection. By using this method Wundt believed that he could determine the elements from which perceptions and thoughts were constructed and he was greatly influenced by Locke's ideas about mental chemistry. Wundt was trying to isolate the basic elements and to determine the rules for their combination into more complex perceptions and thought; this approach was later called structuralism. The basic elements were taken to be the sensory attributes (like quality and extension), and these could be combined to make the molecules of perception; the combination was achieved by a process of association. Perception represented a synthesis or building up of the sensory attributes via learning by association, whereas the method analysed or broke down complex perceptions into their component sensory attributes.

Wundt attracted many graduate students from the United States, where psychology was forging a strong foothold. One of his students, Edward Titchener (1867–1927), was from Britain but carried Wundt's method and theory to America. Titchener employed introspection to uncover the structures of human consciousness, thereby giving structuralism its name. The elements of consciousness were said to be sensations, images, and affections. These elements could be isolated by a method of introspection that excluded the use of object names, because describing the meaning of objects introduced "stimulus error". Most of his experimental work was directed at the analysis of sensations, which had the attributes of quality, duration, intensity, extensity, and clearness. Sensations could be combined by association, rather like Locke's mental chemistry, to yield perceptions. Ideas and emotions derived from associations of images and affections, respectively.

Many of Wundt's contemporaries adopted his technique but few were able to obtain the same results as Wundt: Analytic introspection was not a reliable means for plumbing the depths of the processes of perception. By the early twentieth century there was widespread disaffection with the method and its attendant theory, and alternatives were sought. Two major reactions that appeared in the second decade were Gestalt psychology and Behaviourism. Gestalt is a German word that can be translated approximately as configuration, but the German term is retained because of the difficulty of capturing its nuances with a single English word. The Gestalt psychologists were in the main stream of Continental philosophy; they were nativists and phenomenologists. They were nativists because they believed that perception was unitary, and reflected an innate organisation within the brain. Perception was to them an organised process that operated according to rules, and it could not be broken down into its constituent parts. They were phenomenologists because they considered that the subtleties of perception could only be recorded adequately by a system as rich as language. The Gestaltists' main opposition to Wundt's structuralism was theoretical—they did not accept that unitary perceptions could be analysed into smaller parts. Indeed, the cliché associated with Gestalt psychology is that "the whole is different from the sum of its parts"—thus, the perception of a square is different from the separate effects of its four constituent sides.

Behaviourism

John Watson (1878–1936) redefined psychology as the study of behaviour, and he turned his back on its short history as the study of conscious experience. He avoided working with human subjects because he considered that introspection was unreliable and an unsuitable method on which to base any science, and so established the rat and the maze as the subjects for psychology. His views were both radical and initially unpopular, but they were propagated with a religious fervour. Watson launched the Behaviourist attack on structuralism in 1913. His dissatisfaction was with the method rather than the theory; in fact behaviourist theory was also empiricist and associationist. The method of analytic introspection was rejected because it was subjective. Sensations and perceptions were inferences based upon introspections, and were not open to public scrutiny as would be expected of a science. His manifesto was clearly stated: "Psychology as the behaviorist views it is a purely objective experimental branch of natural science. Its theoretical goal is the prediction and control of behavior. Introspection forms no essential part of its methods, nor is the scientific value of its data dependent upon the readiness with which they lend themselves to interpretation in terms of consciousness" (1913, p. 158).

Watson argued that the only aspects of psychology that could be measured reliably were the stimuli (S) presented to subjects and the responses (R) they made. Hence, Behaviourism was often referred to as S–R theory; the organism was likened to a black box about which nothing could be known directly, but only by inference. Watson and the growing band of Behaviourists in America distrusted the study of perception generally, because it could evidently take place without any obvious response. When it was studied, it was in the context of discrimination learning, where the emphasis was more on the process of learning than on perception. Those Behaviourists interested in human perception tended to measure overt aspects of it like eye movements. Thus, the Gestaltists became the heirs to perceptual research, almost by default.

Gestalt psychology

Wertheimer (Figure 2.19a) redefined psychology as the study of configurations or *Gestalten*. Like Watson and at about the same time, he rejected Wundt's psychology, but for different reasons: He opposed Wundt's atomism, considering that complex percepts could not be reduced to simple sensory elements. Gestalt psychology had its origins in perception but its ambit extended throughout the whole of psychology (see Ash, 1995). Its precursors were to be found in Kant's innate categories of space and time, and in Goethe's phenomenology. Wertheimer conducted a series of experiments on apparent movement—motion seen between two stationary and separated stimuli when presented in rapid succession. The inability to distinguish between real and apparent motion was taken as damning any approach that explained perception in terms of its sensations. Perception was considered to be holistic rather than atomistic: "There are wholes, the behaviour of which is not determined by that of their individual elements, but where the part-processes are themselves determined by the intrinsic nature of the whole. It is the hope of Gestalt theory to determine the nature of such wholes" (Wertheimer, 1938, p. 2). Not only was it said that the whole is more than the sum of its parts, but the perception of the whole is prior to that of its parts. Publication of Wertheimer's thesis on the phi phenomenon, in 1912, is taken as the origin of Gestalt psychology; it was principally concerned with perception, and a range of robust demonstrations was devised to support its holistic nature. Much of its attraction lay in the power of the perceptual demonstrations.

Koffka (Figure 2.19b) was the second member of the Gestalt triumvirate. He served as a subject in Wertheimer's experiments on the phi phenomenon, which were conducted in Frankfurt in 1910. After being apprised of their significance Koffka became the leading advocate of the Gestalt approach. He used Gestalt concepts in studies of development and thinking, and he made

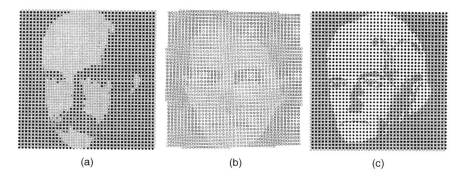

| (a) | (b) | (c) |

Figure 2.19 (a) *Good Gestalt I*: Max Wertheimer (1880–1943); (b) *Good Gestalt II*: Kurt Koffka (1886–1941); and (c) *Good Gestalt III*: Wolfgang Köhler (1887–1967), all as represented in Wade (1995).

American psychologists aware of the new movement in his writings and lectures on Gestalt psychology in the United States. Koffka did pose the fundamental question of "Why do things look as they do?" He also emphasised that visual perception is three-dimensional and that our perception is in terms of the object properties (the distal stimulus) rather than those at the receptor surface (the proximal stimulus).

Köhler (Figure 2.19c) introduced the concept of field forces operating in both perception and in its underlying neurophysiology. Moreover, the brain processes were considered to be isomorphic (having the same form) with the percept, so that principles of brain function could be inferred from perceptual phenomena. He went on to develop a speculative neurophysiology based mainly on the principles of perceptual grouping and on his experiments with figural aftereffects. It could be said that these speculations did more to hasten the demise of Gestalt theory than any other factor: Neurophysiologists failed to find any evidence for such fields of electrical activity in the brain, and so tended to dismiss Gestalt theory in general rather than Köhler's unsuccessful attempt at neuroreductionism in particular. The robust visual phenomena at the heart of Gestalt psychology remained an enigma.

The Gestalt psychologists formulated some descriptive rules for perceptual organisation and produced a wide range of demonstrations that could be used to support them. The principles were described by Wertheimer in two papers published in 1922 and 1923; they appeared in the journal *Psychologische Forschung* (Psychological Research), which the Gestalt psychologists founded to propagate their theory. The figures used by Wertheimer consisted mainly of open and closed circles, hence the use of these motifs to carry their portraits in Figure 2.19. The initial and fundamental perceptual process is the separation of a figure from its background, because all the other grouping principles can only operate with segregated figures. Normally, a figure is defined by contours that surround it completely, whereas the ground is larger or lacking a defined boundary, as in Figure 2.20a. Under certain circumstances neither of these conditions are met (see Figure 2.20b), and perceptual instability ensues—first one part and then the other is seen as figure, and this perceptual alternation continues.

Most of the remaining demonstrations of Gestalt grouping principles have clearly segregated figures; they are usually outline drawings, like those shown in Figure 2.21, and these are shown to observers who are asked to describe what they see. For example, Figure 2.21a is said to look like three columns or three pairs of lines. Although many alternative descriptions are possible (for instance, seven rows of dots) they are rarely given. The elements of the configuration are equally sized dots but these tend to be grouped to form vertical lines; the lines are similar in length and orientation but they differ with regard to their distance or proximity from one another. This was called grouping by proximity.

In Figure 2.21b the dots tend to be described as three columns of black and three columns of white dots. Although all the dots are equally spaced, so that

(a)

(b)

Figure 2.20 (a) A figure, like this black goblet-shape, has closed contours and is smaller than the background against which it is presented. (b) Rubin's crosses. Rubin (1915) examined the reversals of figure and ground that occurs with a pattern like this. Two crosses, comprised of either radiating lines or concentric arcs, have common boundaries, and fluctuate between being figure and ground, but only one can be seen as figure at one time.

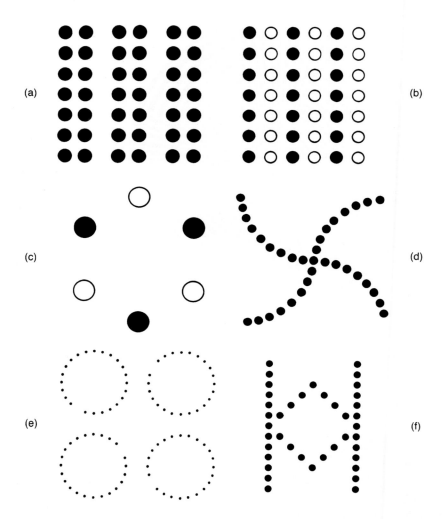

Figure 2.21 Gestalt grouping principles: (a) proximity; (b) similarity; (c) symmetry; (d) good continuation; (e) closure; (f) an example of embedded figures.

proximity cannot be operating, they are grouped according to their similarity; other things being equal, similar elements within a larger configuration will be related perceptually.

The organising principles rarely operate in isolation, more frequently they complement or counteract one another. For example, in Figure 2.21c the dots are typically described as forming two symmetrical triangles, one of white dots and the other of black dots. These are symmetrical figures, and also what the Gestalt psychologists called good figures; simple geometrical shapes, like triangles, squares, and circles, were considered to be good figures because they could not be reduced perceptually to any simpler components. In Figure 2.21c the principle of symmetry is operating, but not in isolation: it is complemented by the similarity of the dots (black or white), but it is acting against the proximity of the dots.

The dots in Figure 2.21d would be most commonly described as following two intersecting curved lines, rather than alternatives like two V-shapes meeting at their points. This organising principle was referred to as good continuation—the lines are seen as maintaining some continuity of direction and not changing direction abruptly. Even the sequences of dots in Figure 2.21e display goodness of figure, in this case circularity. They also illustrate another Gestalt principle, namely that of closure. In each of the four patterns one dot is missing from the regular sequence, but it is not immediately evident. Any irregularities in good figures tend to be smoothed out perceptually.

In Figure 2.21f the various organising principles operate in a way to conceal an aspect of the pattern. This would be described generally as a diamond flanked by two vertical lines, but rarely as a letter W above a letter M. In this instance we are dealing with embedded figures, which are hidden by the grouping rules to yield alternative organisations.

Many more organising principles have been described by Gestalt psychologists, although these are the main ones. Their intention initially was to provide an alternative theory of active, innately organised perception to counter the passive, structuralist views of Wundt and his adherents. The theory was supported by these demonstrations, which drew upon phenomenology. However, it should be noted that the demonstrations themselves were not representative of normal object perception because they were based upon line drawings. That is, the evidence for the principles of organisation is based upon the manner in which two-dimensional pictures are perceived rather than three-dimensional objects. The Gestalt psychologists, and Köhler in particular, extended the theory beyond the realms of phenomenology into the brain. Köhler and Wallach (1944) did conduct more conventional experiments on phenomena like figural aftereffects (see Figure 2.22) and illusions using responses other than verbal descriptions. The results of these experiments were used to suggest a speculative neurophysiology of vision that involved electrical fields in the brain. This strategy was not a wise one because the opponents of Gestalt could attack the physiological speculations far more easily than the robust perceptual demonstrations.

The work of the Gestalt psychologists was originally in German, and many of the source articles are available in a collection of translations edited by Ellis (1938). Here one can find articles by Wertheimer, Köhler, and Koffka on Gestalt psychology generally, as well as on specific issues like the laws of organisation in perception. Gordon (1997) presents a comprehensive account of Gestalt theory, together with an assessment of its impact on modern perceptual research.

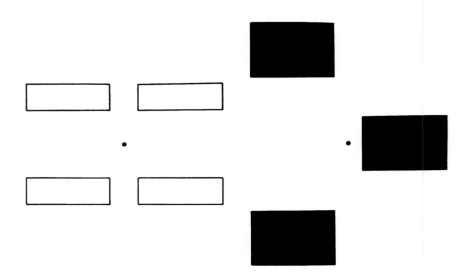

Figure 2.22 A figural aftereffect can be produced by observing these patterns. Initially fixate on the left-hand dot: The left and right pair of outline rectangles will appear to be equally separated from one another. Now fixate on the right-hand dot for about 1 minute, after which shift fixation back to the dot on the left. The outlines will no longer look equally separated—the left pair will seem nearer to one another than will the right pair. Köhler and Wallach (1944) called this a figural aftereffect.

Cognitive approaches

In the second quarter of the twentieth century most research in perception was conducted by Gestalt psychologists, initially in Germany and later in America, where it challenged the prevailing climate of behaviourism. At the same time, an alternative approach was being developed in relative isolation in Britain, and it has had a profound effect on the shape of modern perceptual research (see Wade & Bruce, 2001). Bartlett (Figure 2.23a) examined perception in realistic and dynamic situations and he represents a continuation of the British empiricist tradition with his analysis of perception as a skilled activity. He rejected the application of stimulus–response interpretations of complex tasks like playing cricket or tennis because the actions were highly organised and initiated in advance of any contact with the ball. Indeed, the actions were made with respect to the position the ball would be predicted to occupy at some short time in the future. Complex activities of this type indicated that behavioural sequences had to be programmed in advance and coordinated with predictions based on perception. This led Bartlett to a cognitive theory of perception, one in which the division between perception and thought was difficult to draw. Like Helmholtz,

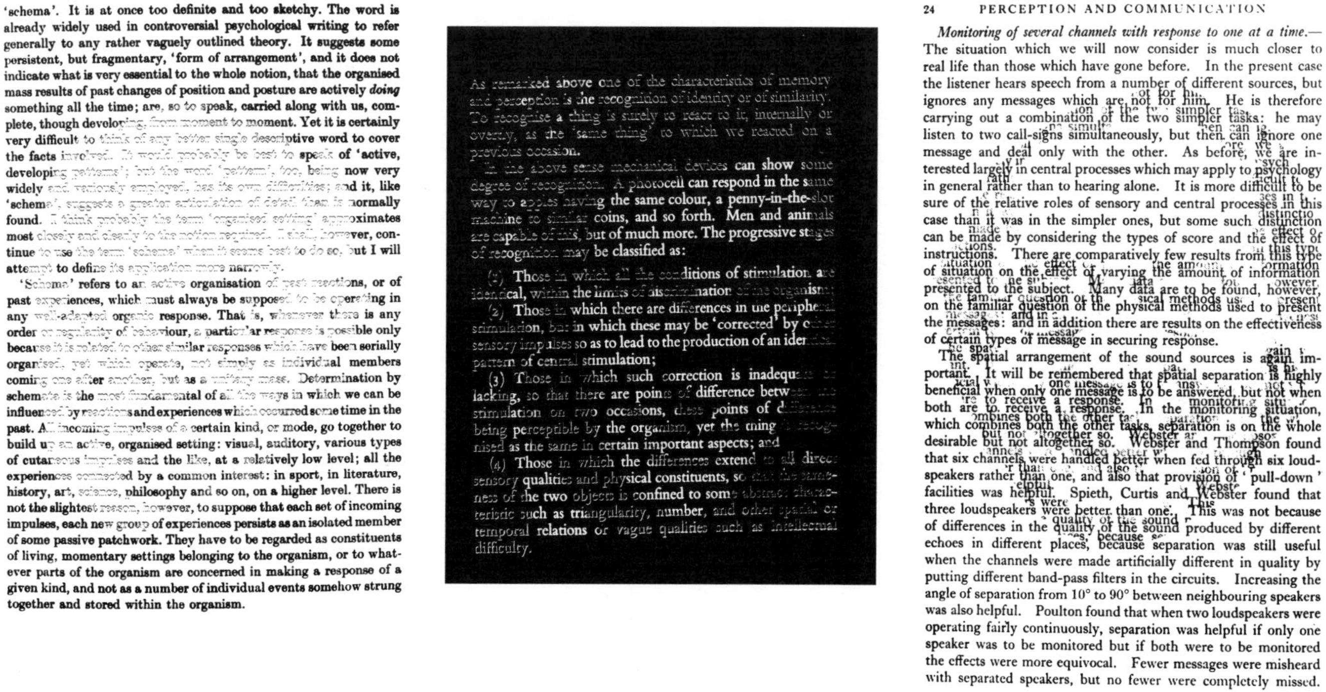
'schema'. It is at once too definite and too sketchy. The word is already widely used in controversial psychological writing to refer generally to any rather vaguely outlined theory. It suggests some persistent, but fragmentary, 'form of arrangement', and it does not indicate what is very essential to the whole notion, that the organised mass results of past changes of position and posture are actively *doing* something all the time; are, so to speak, carried along with us, complete, though developing, from moment to moment. Yet it is certainly very difficult to think of any better single descriptive word to cover the facts involved. It would probably be best to speak of 'active, developing patterns'; but the word 'pattern', too, being now very widely and variously employed, has its own difficulties; and it, like 'schema', suggests a greater articulation of detail than is normally found. I think probably the term 'organised setting' approximates most closely and clearly to the notion required. I shall, however, continue to use the term 'schema' when it seems best to do so, but I will attempt to define its application more narrowly.
'Schema' refers to an active organisation of past reactions, or of past experiences, which must always be supposed to be operating in any well-adapted organic response. That is, whenever there is any order or regularity of behaviour, a particular response is possible only because it is related to other similar responses which have been serially organised, yet which operate, not simply as individual members coming one after another, but as a unitary mass. Determination by schemata is the most fundamental of all the ways in which we can be influenced by reactions and experiences which occurred some time in the past. All incoming impulses of a certain kind, or mode, go together to build up an active, organised setting: visual, auditory, various types of cutaneous impulses and the like, at a relatively low level; all the experiences connected by a common interest: in sport, in literature, history, art, science, philosophy and so on, on a higher level. There is not the slightest reason, however, to suppose that each set of incoming impulses, each new group of experiences persists as an isolated member of some passive patchwork. They have to be regarded as constituents of living, momentary settings belonging to the organism, or to whatever parts of the organism are concerned in making a response of a given kind, and not as a number of individual events somehow strung together and stored within the organism.
As remarked above one of the characteristics of memory and perception is the recognition of identity or of similarity. To recognise a thing is surely to react to it, internally or overtly, as the 'same thing' to which we reacted on a previous occasion.
In the above sense mechanical devices can show some degree of recognition. A photocell can respond in the same way to apples having the same colour, a penny-in-the-slot machine to similar coins, and so forth. Men and animals are capable of this, but of much more. The progressive stages of recognition may be classified as:
(1) Those in which all the conditions of stimulation are identical, within the limits of discrimination of the organism;
(2) Those in which there are differences in the peripheral stimulation, but in which these may be 'corrected' by other sensory impulses so as to lead to the production of an identical pattern of central stimulation;
(3) Those in which such correction is inadequate or lacking, so that there are points of difference between the stimulation on two occasions, these points of difference being perceptible by the organism, yet the thing is recognised as the same in certain important aspects; and
(4) Those in which the differences extend to all direct sensory qualities and physical constituents, so that the sameness of the two objects is confined to some abstract characteristic such as triangularity, number, and other spatial or temporal relations or vague qualities such as intellectual difficulty.
24 PERCEPTION AND COMMUNICATION
Monitoring of several channels with response to one at a time.—The situation which we will now consider is much closer to real life than those which have gone before. In the present case the listener hears speech from a number of different sources, but ignores any messages which are not for him. He is therefore carrying out a combination of the two simpler tasks: he may listen to two call-signs simultaneously, but then can ignore one message and deal only with the other. As before, we are interested largely in central processes which may apply to psychology in general rather than to hearing alone. It is more difficult to be sure of the relative roles of sensory and central processes in this case than it was in the simpler ones, but some such distinction can be made by considering the types of score and the effect of instructions. There are comparatively few results from this type of situation on the effect of varying the amount of information presented to the subject. Many data are to be found, however, on the familiar question of the physical methods used to present the messages: and in addition there are results on the effectiveness of certain types of message in securing response.
The spatial arrangement of the sound sources is again important. It will be remembered that spatial separation is highly beneficial when only one message is to be answered, but not when both are to receive a response. In the monitoring situation, which combines both the other tasks, separation is on the whole desirable but not altogether so. Webster and Thompson found that six channels were handled better when fed through six loudspeakers rather than one, and also that provision of 'pull-down' facilities was helpful. Spieth, Curtis and Webster found that three loudspeakers were better than one. This was not because of differences in the quality of the sound produced by different echoes in different places, because separation was still useful when the channels were made artificially different in quality by putting different band-pass filters in the circuits. Increasing the angle of separation from 10° to 90° between neighbouring speakers was also helpful. Poulton found that when two loudspeakers were operating fairly continuously, separation was helpful if only one speaker was to be monitored but if both were to be monitored the effects were more equivocal. Fewer messages were misheard with separated speakers, but no fewer were completely missed.

(a) (b) (c)

Figure 2.23 (a) *Schema*: Frederic Charles Bartlett (1886–1969); (b) *Recognition of identity*: Kenneth John William Craik (1914–1945); and (c) *Channel capacity*: Donald Eric Broadbent (1926–1993). (a and b as represented in Wade, 1995; c as in Wade, 1990).

Bartlett considered that perception was like problem solving, incorporating processes of inference but also of prediction.

Wundt's "New Psychology" had been virtually ignored within Britain in the late nineteenth and early twentieth centuries, but a "New Physiology" had been actively pursued by Ferrier, Jackson, and others. Indeed, it was the concept of "schema", developed within this new physiology that was applied by Bartlett to memory and perception: " 'Schema' refers to an active organisation of past reactions, or of past experiences, which must always be supposed to be operating in the well-adapted organic response" (Bartlett, 1932, p. 201). The constructive aspects of both memory and perception were emphasised at the expense of their holistic (Gestalt) or sequential (behaviourist) features. Bartlett did not restrict his analysis to laboratory studies, as he examined perception in its social and cultural contexts as well as its application (see Saito, 2000).

Bartlett rejected associationist models of perception and memory and his cognitive theory provided a middle road between those of the molecular behaviourists and molar Gestaltists. He can be seen as ushering in the cognitive revolution that was eventually to replace behaviourism, although his work was neglected in America until the 1950s. Bartlett analysed perception and thought as skilled activities, and he related most cognitive functions to tasks in the real world, seeing little distinction between experimental and applied psychology. "The essential requirement of any performance that can be called skilled becomes much more plain if we look at a few actual instances. The player in a quick ball game; the operator, engaged at his work bench, directing his machine, and using his tools; the surgeon conducting an operation; the physician arriving at a clinical decision—in all these instances and in innumerable others that could just as well be used, there is a continuing flow from signals occurring outside the performer and interpreted by him to actions carried out . . . From beginning to end the signals and their related actions form a series, not simply a succession" (1958, pp. 13–14).

In order to make predictions that involve action we need to have some mental representation of the environment in which the action will take place. This concept of forming a mental model of the world in which we behave was proposed by Craik (Figure 2.23b), a student of Bartlett's, and it is one of the ideas that has proved important in the development of both cognitive and computational theories of vision. The machine metaphor has proved to be particularly attractive to experimental psychologists. Craik was only able to enlist relatively simple machines, but his insight lies at the heart of the cognitive revolution that was to sweep through psychology. He worked with analogue devices as the digital computer was still embryonic. None the less, he appreciated the importance of servo-systems in adapting to the environment: "The main parts of such a system are the sensory device, the law relating its controlling effect on the counteracting cause which it produces, and the nature of that cause . . . The essential feature of the sensory device is its ability to translate the change it is to measure . . . into some form of energy which can be amplified and used to drive the restoring cause . . . The next part is what may be called the computing device and controller, which determines the amount and kind of energy to be released from the effector unit to restore equilibrium. The final part is the power unit or effector (equivalent to the muscles in men and animals) which restores the state of equilibrium" (1966, pp. 23–24). His concern with prediction rather than reaction (shared with Bartlett) reflected his dissatisfaction with behaviourism. Perception is considered to be a process in which information regarding aspects of the world is analysed and utilised to plan behaviour. This information-processing approach has become widely accepted as perception can then be considered as a sequence of representations that are initially crude and become increasingly appropriate to the three-dimensional environment.

Bartlett's emphasis on the constructive nature of perception found an echo in the "New Look" experiments that were conducted in America in the middle of the twentieth century. Many experiments were interpreted as showing interactions between motivation and perception. For example, it was suggested that values influence the perception of size. Another phenomenon was called perceptual defence, because it took longer to recognise taboo words, even when the words were subliminal (presented below threshold). Despite this seeming close association between personality and perception their liaison was not lasting. Vernon (1970) reached the following sober verdict: "It would seem wise to regard with great caution the existence of limitations on speed and accuracy of perception imposed by personality factors, at least in normal observers" (p. 237). Research of this type did hasten the approach of cognition towards perception in an environment that had not been sympathetic to either. Another factor that brought them closer was the impact of information theory, which was developed in the context of telecommunications.

Information in visual patterns could be quantified, and it resided at the boundaries between areas (contours) and where the contours changed direction abruptly (corners). However, it was the qualitative concept of information processing rather than quantitative information measures that was to have lasting appeal. The perceiver was conceived of as a limited capacity information processor, and the information could be filtered, filed, or reformulated on the basis of stored events. Broadbent (Figure 2.23c), a student of Bartlett, presented a model that formalised and represented pictorially the putative processing stages in perception, memory, and learning, and it was addressed to the realistic activity of communication. He examined selective attention to two messages presented separately to each ear, and the effects of noise on behaviour. He stated that the "advantage of information theory terms is . . . that they emphasize the relationship between the stimulus now present and the others that might have been present but are not" (Broadbent, 1958, pp. 306–307). Thus, Broadbent combined Bartlett's approach of examining skilled tasks with Craik's modelling metaphor.

Theoretical attention was shifted towards pattern recognition by both humans and computers because they were both thought of as information processors or manipulators of symbolic information. The patterns were typically outline figures or alphanumeric symbols and there were two major theories, based on template matching and feature analysis. Pattern recognition was the theme that unified physiologists, psychologists, and computer scientists, and it remains a concern of computational theories of vision.

When Bartlett and Craik proposed their theories of perception relatively little was known about the brain mechanisms that mediate perception. This is one of the reasons why the Gestalt psychologists were able to propose their speculative neurophysiology of vision. None the less, Craik characteristically foresaw the principle behind developments that were to take place in visual neurophysiology: "the action of various physical devices which 'recognize' or respond identically to certain simple objects can be treated in terms of such [mathematical] transformations. Thus the essential part of physical 'recognizing' instruments is usually a filter—whether it be a mechanical sieve, and optical filter, or a tuned electrical circuit—which 'passes' only quantities of the kind it is required to identify and rejects all others" (1966, pp. 44–45). In the last four decades of the twentieth century there were major strides in furthering our understanding of neural processes in the visual system. These discoveries have been taken to support the view that vision involves a sequence of stages in which different aspects of the stimulus, like colour and contour, are extracted. These neurophysiological advances will be described in the next chapter, following a description of the stimulus for vision, light, and the organ that responds to it, the eye.

3 Light and the eye

Light is the stimulus for vision and the eye is the organ which responds to
light energy. This chapter will examine two contemporary developments from
the heritage of perception that are actively being pursued. One concerns
advances in our understanding of the nature of the stimulus—visual optics.
The other is about how the visual system responds to light—visual neurophysiology. The image-forming properties of the eye are quite well understood, and most aberrations of the eye can now be corrected optically. The
performance of the human eye is remarkable considering that its optical parts
are so simple. One of the ways of measuring the performance of the visual
system is to treat it as a physicist would a lens, by determining how faithfully
it can transmit patterns of light incident upon it. One outcome of this
approach has been the suggestion that the visual system is most sensitive to
sharply defined contours and also to spatially periodic patterns of parallel
lines (referred to as gratings).

Knowledge about the neuroanatomy and neurophysiology of vision has
advanced because it has proved possible to examine the structures in the
visual system in greater detail. Techniques have been devised to examine
structure and function at and below the cellular level. Thus, there is now
better understanding of how light is absorbed by pigments in the receptors,
how these chemical changes modify the electrical potentials of the receptor
cells, how a nerve impulse is eventually generated, and how the patterning of
light is processed. The methods of recording the electrical activity of individual nerve cells have proved particularly productive, and have demonstrated
that the cells do not respond solely to the presence or absence of light, but
also to its patterning. Single cells in the visual cortex of animals closely
related to humans (like monkeys) respond most strongly to oriented edges.
Accordingly, similar conclusions are being reached from quite different lines
of enquiry: The results from both visual psychophysics and neurophysiology
suggest that the early stages of vision involve the extraction of simple features
from the light stimulating the eye. Indeed, it has been said that the two most
significant ideas in visual science are that the activity of single visual nerve
cells can influence perception and that their characteristics can be inferred
from perception (Lennie, 1998). It is not surprising to find that visual

psychologists have been conducting experiments to relate physiological findings to the phenomena they investigate.

VISUAL OPTICS

In the previous chapter, we saw how the discovery of the eye's ability to form an image of the world was a turning point in the understanding of vision. Once the principles and methods of optics could be applied to the eye, there were immediate advances in visual science, whose consequences have remained important. Image formation is a necessary, but not sufficient condition for vision. Seeing involves a sequence of processes that is initiated by the presence of an image on the retina, so that this is only the first step. Description of retinal image formation, and of the optical characteristics of the eye, requires the use of conventions (such as diagrams showing the path of rays of light) which are very great simplifications of the true state of affairs. In particular, the retinal image is never stationary; that is, it never has the characteristics of a "snapshot" of the world, frozen in time, but this is how it is represented in conventional diagrams. In this section we will be primarily concerned with those aspects of visual optics that have the greatest influence on perception, and thus determine why things look the way they do. Wandell (1995) provides a comprehensive account of visual optics and physiology.

Optical functions of the eye

The environment contains objects which can emit, reflect, or absorb electromagnetic radiation. Such radiation is ubiquitous, but only a small portion can be directly sensed by living organisms, and a smaller part still can be detected by the eye. As was noted on pages 36–40, the nature of light is now thought of as a phenomenon of physics, but those who advanced its science also added to our knowledge of sight. In the late seventeenth century Isaac Newton wrote: "I understand light to be any entity which proceeds directly from a bright body and is able to excite vision". The entities to which he was alluding were corpuscles or particles of light that bounced through the ether. Those present in white light could be decomposed into the spectral components by refraction through a prism, which in turn could be recombined to produce white light. Newton questioned the purity of white but he also appreciated the subjectivity of colour perception: the rays, he said, are not coloured. However, the phenomena of diffraction and interference could be much more readily interpreted using the concept of waves. Furthermore, as a consequence of Maxwell's theoretical work in the nineteenth century, light is now described as electromagnetic radiation—a wave having both magnetic and electrical fields—but so are cosmic rays and radio waves. Light is distinguished from other electromagnetic radiations on the basis of sight: That small part of the spectrum to which the human eye is sensitive is called light.

At the beginning of the twentieth century the principal question was: Is light a particle or is it an oscillation? Evidence could be adduced to support both, and there remained an uneasy ambiguity between Newtonian corpuscles—now called photons—and Maxwell's electromagnetic waves. They have been unified mathematically, in quantum field theory, but this has not transferred readily to experiments on light, or our conceptions of it. Depending on the aspects of light that are measured it can display the properties of electromagnetic waves or photons. The light we experience is typically reflected from objects in the environment—light renders those objects accessible to visual experience, and hence enhances our chances of survival. Classical physics (up to the time of Thomas Young) examined the properties of light using visible phenomena. Particles and waves are conceivable properties of light as they correspond with perceivable aspects of our experience: Larger objects can be divided into smaller and smaller parts and waves are readily seen in patterns of disturbances of water. Modern mathematical analyses of light render its characteristics inconceivable as well as imperceptible.

Electromagnetic radiation can be considered as a wave, and as such can vary in wavelength. Wavelength is defined by the distance between successive peaks in the wave, and for light it is measured in nanometres (nm), where 1 nm equals one billionth of a metre (10^{-9} m). The range of human vision extends from around 380 nm to around 720 nm, and this band of electromagnetic radiation is referred to as light. To someone with normal colour vision, light of different wavelengths appears coloured making up the visible spectrum (Figure 3.1).

Light sources in the natural world are relatively rare, and are limited to celestial bodies such as the sun and stars, lightning, fire, and biochemical processes in living organisms (bioluminescence). Of these the sun is by far the most important, and its location provides a constraint on the appearance of illuminated objects that plays a fundamental role in the perception of depth and shape. The interpretation of three-dimensional structure from shadows seems to be based on an assumption that light comes from the sky above. Our widespread use of artificial sources of illumination may cause misperception of objects, if the light source is located below eye level. Objects that are not light sources can only reflect some part of the light which falls upon them. Generally, objects are neither perfect reflectors nor perfect absorbers of light. Their molecular structure causes certain wavelengths in the incident radiation to be absorbed, and others to be reflected. For example, a blue object appears to be this colour because it absorbs most of the incident light energy with wavelengths above around 550 nm. In practice, the perceived colour of objects is also influenced by factors such as the colour of adjacent objects and of the incident light. The light reflected from one object may in turn fall upon other objects, with their own reflective properties. Our environment is therefore filled with emitted and reflected light, which forms a field of energy carrying information about the environment's characteristics. In order to see,

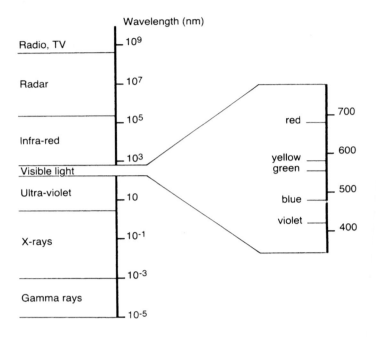

Figure 3.1 Part of the electromagnetic spectrum, showing the small proportion that corresponds to visible light. The expanded section indicates the approximate wavelengths at which certain colours are normally seen.

we must first capture a sample of this radiation, in such a way that the information it carries is not too distorted or degraded.

This sampling of the light field is the function of the image forming components of the eye. The simplest image forming system is an enclosed hollow space, with a small aperture through which light can enter. Any device like this will form an image on the internal surface opposite the aperture (as described in Chapter 2), and is called a camera obscura (Figure 3.2). A sample of the light field enters the camera obscura through the aperture, and if this is small then only a small fraction of the total light energy will be able to enter. However, the rays of light will be limited to those which form an image. The quality of the image (its sharpness and brightness) depends on the size of the aperture. A small aperture will give a sharp image, but it will also be faint. A camera obscura works best when the external illumination is high, and the aperture is small. By the addition of some means of focusing the light from distant objects, the image quality can be maintained with a larger aperture. Focusing consists of bringing together rays of light emitted from a single point in the environment to a single point in the image. Light is emitted in all directions from objects, but if the object is far enough from the imaging

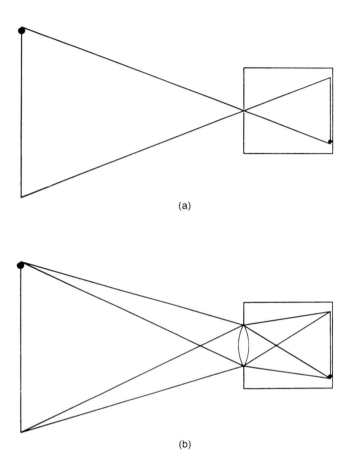

(a)

(b)

Figure 3.2 (a) The formation of an image in a camera obscura. The pinhole aperture allows certain light rays from objects in the environment to enter the camera, where they form an inverted image on the screen. In (b) the addition of a lens increases the proportion of the rays from a point on the object, which are brought to a single point in the camera.

device then the rays which enter it will be approximately parallel, and the object is said to be at optical infinity. This distance is conventionally taken to be 6 metres (20 feet). If the object is close then the rays from a point on it which enter the aperture are divergent, and need greater focusing, or bending, in order to be brought to a single point in the image.

These principles are embodied in the structure of the vertebrate eye (see Figure 3.3). Light first strikes the curved, transparent outer layer of the eye, called the cornea. If the light is not perpendicular to the cornea there is a

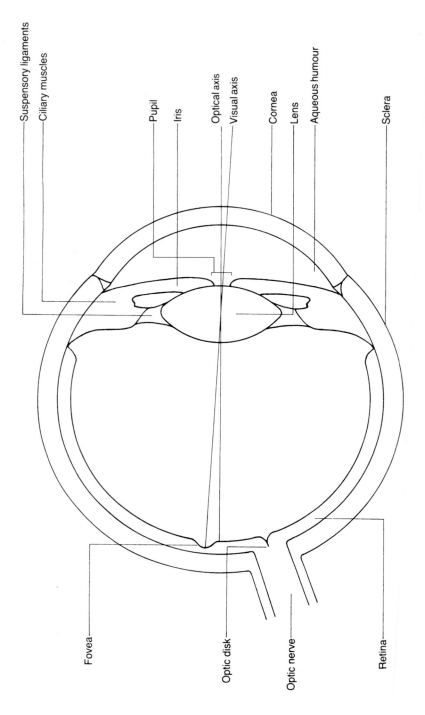

Figure 3.3 Schematic diagram of the vertebrate eye. In reality the eye is not normally a perfect sphere, but is elongated on the horizontal axis. Most of the focusing of light occurs at the curved boundary between air and the cornea. The image formed on the retina is inverted and left–right reversed.

change in the path of light rays (refraction), because the cornea has an optical density higher than that of air, and the velocity of light is reduced. The curvature of the cornea causes the rays of light from an object which strike it at varying points to be refracted by varying amounts, so that they are brought to a focus inside the eye, close to the plane of the retina. The curvature of the cornea also allows it to refract light from directions somewhat behind the observer. The full field of view extends through about 208° horizontally for a forward-pointing eye, although light from this region is imaged on the extreme periphery of the retina, and is blocked by the nose and head on one side. Vertically, the field of view is about 120° (Figure 3.4). Note that these values define the range within which light is imaged on some part of the retina; whether or not anything is seen depends on processes that occur after the absorption of light energy by the retina. It is the difference between the optical density of the cornea and air that causes refraction, which is why vision underwater is usually less distinct; there is very little refraction at the boundary between water and the cornea so that little focusing occurs.

In fact almost all the focusing power of the eye resides in the cornea, rather than in the lens. The lens provides an adjustable fine focusing power, called accommodation, due to the fact that its shape can be changed. Its normal shape is approximately spherical, but this is changed by the application of tension by ligaments attached to the transparent sack in which the lens is

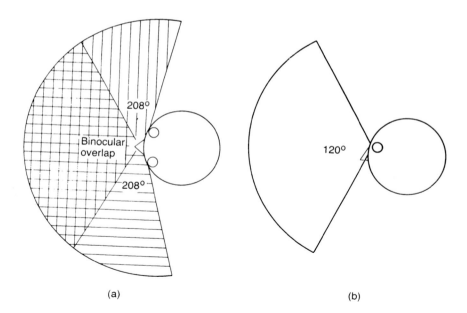

(a)   (b)

Figure 3.4 The horizontal (a) and vertical (b) field of view. The hatched area of the horizontal field represents the area of binocular overlap between the fields of the two eyes.

contained. This tension causes the lens to become more elongated, and to apply less change to the path of light rays. The ligaments themselves are controlled by a circular ring of muscles (the ciliary muscles), which when contracted allow the ligaments to reduce the tension they apply, and the lens to change towards its normal spherical shape. In its most elongated state, the lens in a normal eye will bring rays from an object at optical infinity (defined as a distance greater than 6 m) to a focus on the retina. This is referred to as the far point of accommodation. At its most nearly spherical, it will focus rays from an object at a distance of about 15 cm from the eye (the near point). An emmetropic, or normal, eye is capable of adjusting accommodation within the range between these far and near points. Emmetropia is the result of the focusing power of the lens combined with the length of the eye, either of which may be inappropriate, with results that are described in the next section. When someone's lens is removed, usually due to the presence of a cataract which makes it opaque, then vision is generally little impaired, provided the illumination is high. This is due to focusing by the cornea, and to the presence of a variable aperture in the eye's optical system, called the pupil. The pupil is created by a ring of muscles (the iris), which can expand and contract to adjust the size of the pupil, and thus the amount of light entering the eye. In high light levels, the pupil contracts to a minimum diameter (about 1 mm), and it functions like the aperture in a camera obscura, by assisting in the focusing of light. More precisely, a small pupil diameter increases the depth of focus of the eye, which is the range of object distances for which a clear image can be obtained without adjustment of the lens. By maximising the depth of focus with a small pupil, someone without a lens can see clearly over a reasonable range of distances, but this is reduced in lower light levels. In addition, there is a surprising side-effect: the lens normally absorbs most of the ultraviolet radiation that strikes the eye, and, if it is removed, people report being able to see deeper shades of blue beyond the limit of visibility for normal observers. Pupil diameter can also vary for reasons other than the ambient light level. It is influenced by attention, and dilates when we try to carry out a difficult or important task. Emotions can also have an effect, as the pupil will also dilate with heightened arousal, for example due to fear. The drug atropine, which may be used to cause maximum pupil dilation before clinical examination of the eye, takes its name from the plant *Atropa belladonna* (Deadly Nightshade) from which it can be extracted. The term Belladonna means "beautiful woman" and in the past it was not uncommon for women to use eye drops made from the plant in order to create pupil dilation, perhaps also enhancing attraction. Any beneficial effects may have been due to the implication of attentive interest conveyed by the size of the pupils.

The accommodation of the eye is driven by a reflex response to the retinal image, but the basis of this is not well understood. It does not seem to depend simply on the degree of blur, and is influenced by other factors such as the wavelength of the light. Feedback from the state of accommodation can act as a source of information for the visual system about the distance of objects; the more the accommodation, the closer the object. Clearly, this is limited to the range of distances between the far and near points, and will not convey much information in good illumination, when less accommodative effort is required. In experiments on depth perception it is a common practice to have observers look through an artificial pupil, which is a small aperture about 1 mm in diameter placed immediately in front of the eye. This has the effect of ensuring that the retinal image is in focus regardless of the state of accommodation, which is held constant as a factor in determining the perception of distance.

Limitations of optical function

In practice, the optical functioning of the normal eye falls short of ideal in a number of ways. In addition, individuals may have various sorts of deficiency that further degrade the formation of images. Myopic (short-sighted) eyes are unable to focus rays from optical infinity on the retina, but only to a point in front of it. This is due either to the eyeball being too long, or the power of the lens being too great, or a combination of the two factors (see Figure 3.5). The far point at which myopic vision is distinct is close enough for rays from an object to be divergent, and the near point is also closer than it is for emmetropic eyes. Hypermetropic (long-sighted) eyes are the converse case; rays from optical infinity can be focused, but not those from nearer objects, and the near point is further away. Both these states can be corrected by suitable lenses; myopia with a negative (concave) lens that makes the light rays diverge as if coming from a nearer point, and hypermetropia with a positive (convex) lens that causes a corresponding convergence. In the

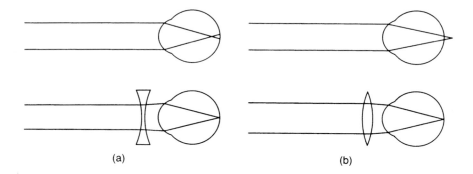

(a) (b)

Figure 3.5 Myopic (a) and hypermetropic (b) eyes, showing the effects of optical correction. In the myopic eye, light rays from optical infinity are brought to a focus in front of the retina, which is corrected with a concave (negative) lens. The focal plane of the hypermetropic eye lies behind the retina, and this can be corrected by a convex (positive) lens.

relatively unusual event that an individual has one myopic eye, and one that is emmetropic or even hypermetropic, each can be corrected with the appropriate lens. However, the resulting images in the two eyes are of different sizes, since a convex lens magnifies the image while a concave one reduces it. This condition, known as aniseikonia, causes problems for binocular vision, since it may not be possible to fuse two such different-sized images, with the result that one is suppressed.

As ageing proceeds, it becomes harder to change the accommodation of the eye, largely due to a loss of elasticity in the lens. This is known as presbyopia, and it affects most people eventually to a greater or lesser extent, even if they were emmetropic as young adults. The effect of presbyopia is most marked on people who were hypermetropic, since it further restricts the range between the near and far points. By contrast, a myopic person will come closer to emmetropia as presbyopia sets in. When visual perception is impaired by presbyopia, it may be some time before the individual is aware of the extent of the impairment, or before he or she is prepared to admit to it, if good eyesight has been a source of pride. This may cause problems particularly in the work place, as errors and accidents may become more probable.

Even if the eye is emmetropic, or has been corrected by spectacles, the image formed on the retina is subject to a number of distortions. The sharpness of the image is reduced away from the centre of vision, which is a point on the retina approximately in line with the centre of the lens; it is therefore traversed by light rays without appreciable refraction. It is not surprising that the highest concentration of light-sensitive cells is found at this point. The best image is still appreciably blurred, and light energy from a point in the environment is spread out across an area, called the blur circle, rather than being concentrated at a point on the retina. This is due to spherical aberration in which light falling on the outer parts of the lens is refracted more than that near the centre. Furthermore, different wavelengths are not focused equally; typically, the focal plane for red light lies somewhat further from the lens than that for blue light, so that if the eye accommodates to bring one wavelength into focus, others are blurred. This difference in focusing power for different wavelengths is called chromatic aberration, and it is quite marked in the human eye. With white light, only the middle (yellow) wavelengths are usually in good focus; the shorter and longer wavelengths are focused in front of and behind the retina, respectively. This means that the image of a white disk consists of a central yellow area surrounded by red and blue coloured fringes. Nevertheless we are not generally aware of chromatic aberration, and there is evidently some process of compensation in the visual system which removes its effects.

Spherical and chromatic aberrations occur even if the transparent surfaces of the eye are parts of perfect spheres. Such symmetry is rare in biological systems, and the eyes usually have optical surfaces that are not spherical. The most common form for the cornea is that the curvature differs in directions at right angles to one another. This has the effect of producing two focal points for the eye, corresponding to each of the curvatures (see Figures 3.6 and 3.7) and is known as astigmatism. Thus if a horizontal line is in focus, a vertical one will not be, and vice versa. When this difference is large enough to interfere with vision, it can be corrected with a cylindrical lens that is shaped so as to focus one orientation more strongly than another, and thus compensate for the deficiency of the eye.

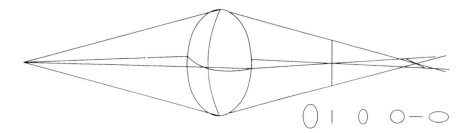

Figure 3.6 Focusing of light by an astigmatic lens. The lens shown is more curved in the horizontal than in the vertical axis. Rays from a point cannot be brought to a single point of focus. Instead there are two focal planes, corresponding to the two axes of curvature. At intermediate positions, as shown, a point source is represented by an elliptical distribution of light. Astigmatism can be corrected with a lens whose curvatures are opposite to those of the lens.

Figure 3.7 The effect of astigmatism on the appearance of lines in different orientations. If you have an uncorrected astigmatism, it will not be possible to bring all orientations into equally sharp focus at the same time. One set of lines in a given orientation will appear darker than the rest. If the page is rotated, the lines concerned will change, corresponding to their orientation with respect to the eye.

In addition to these distortions imposed by the optics of the eye, various effects are produced by the media through which the light passes. The cornea, lens, and fluids inside the eye are not perfectly transparent, and alter the spectral composition of the light. In particular, the lens absorbs long and short wavelengths more than middle ones, giving it a yellowish appearance. This yellowing increases with age, leading to shifts in the appearance of colours. The fluids in the eye may develop small areas of opacity, where light is absorbed more strongly. These appear to an observer as small dark blobs, called muscae volitantes or floaters, which seem to move about as the eyes do. If the basis for the floaters is not understood, their visibility may be attributed to objects in the outside world, which seem to be moving with very high velocities; some of the reported sightings of UFOs have been traced to this source. After the light has passed through the ocular media it must pass through the layer of blood vessels and nerve fibres that lies above them before it strikes the sensitive elements in the retina. This seemingly inefficient arrangement is probably a consequence of biological constraints on the evolution of the retina as an outgrowth of the brain, and it means that light is both absorbed and scattered before it can be detected. You can in fact see the blood vessels in the eye, by shining a small torch into the corner of the eye while in an otherwise dark room. It helps to close the eye partially and to move the torch around. It usually takes some practice to produce the effect for the first time, but it is very striking once seen. The blood vessels appear as a pattern of branches (the Purkinje tree), that appears and disappears as the torch is moved around. In fact you are seeing the shadows of the vessels, since less light reaches the retina behind where they lie. These and other sorts of perceptions produced by the structure of the eye itself are known as entoptic phenomena.

Since such effort is applied to the correction of individual errors in the optics of the eye, it might be thought that the quality of the image was of paramount importance to perception. In fact, most of the distortions of the image pass unnoticed, and it is remarkable how effectively we perceive despite their presence. Why then is it important for the image to be at least approximately in focus? The eye is a means of obtaining information about the outside world, and vision depends on the information available for processing. A blurred edge carries less information, since its location is less precisely specified, and although we can recognise objects when visual information is degraded, the process is slower and more prone to error. The quality of the retinal image imposes constraints on visual performance, and acts as a limiting factor on what we can see.

Measures of optical performance

In the previous sections we have examined the principles of image formation by the eye, and identified some of the common faults that can alter or reduce the information available for perception. An important area of study in vision is concerned with measuring the performance of the eye (see Millodot, 2000). This is useful for various purposes, such as identifying and correcting anomalies, and finding out the limits of normal vision in applied settings. Most people are familiar with the techniques employed in optometry, as the result of having sight tests. Such tests employ a type of psychophysics, modified to take account of the problems of taking measurements from a cross-section of the population. It is important to realise that measurements are usually of perceptual rather than optical performance, in that people are asked to say what they can see when looking at standardised visual patterns. Under these circumstances the response may be influenced by other factors, since even the most skilled observer cannot simply report the events that take place on the retina. Nevertheless, careful use of psychophysical methods can ensure that subjective reports are a useful indication of the quality of the information available to the eye. Although most of our knowledge is obtained in this way, it is also possible to make objective assessments using instruments such as the ophthalmoscope. If the subjective and objective measures differ, then it can be taken that this is due to the processing of information subsequent to the eye. For example, there is a condition known as amblyopia, in which an individual has blurred vision in one eye that cannot be corrected by any optical means. Therefore, the poor acuity is not due to the optics of the eye, but to the ways the neural signals are processed in the visual system. Amblyopia is often a consequence of an uncorrected squint during childhood, leading to failure of normal binocular vision, and the suppression of information from one eye.

The standard of vision is most commonly expressed in terms of acuity, which is, at the simplest, the ability to discriminate detail. Suppose that there are two points of light on a dark background. As described in the previous section, each will be imaged on the retina with a degree of blur, even in an emmetropic eye. More precisely, this means that the light energy will be spread out over some area, and a graph of its distribution would show a central peak with a tailing off at each side. The greater the blur, the more spread out this distribution will be. If the two points are physically separated by a sufficient distance, their two distributions will not overlap; that is, their representations on the retina will also be physically distinct, and are said to be optically resolved. As they are brought closer together, the two distributions of light energy will become increasingly combined, until they merge into one (Figure 3.8). If we ask an observer to indicate the minimum separation at which the points appear separate, then we have a measure of visual acuity. If the observer's eye needs optical correction, then we would expect to find that the minimum separation is larger than that for other people. Clearly, this presupposes some accepted standard of performance against which someone can be assessed, and a standardised test pattern at which to look.

Many such patterns have been proposed, and are useful under different circumstances (Figure 3.9). The familiar opticians' chart (the Snellen chart) uses letters of the alphabet of decreasing size, and tests the ability to

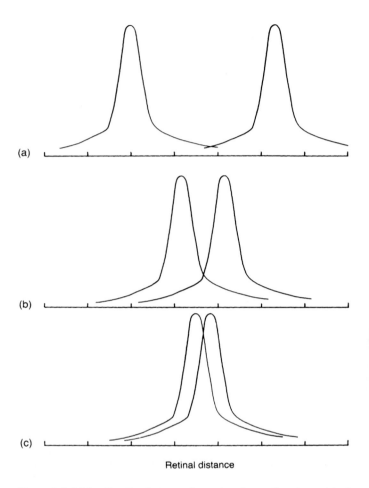

Retinal distance

Figure 3.8 Light distributions on the retina determine the resolution of adjacent
image points. A point source is imaged as a spread-out distribution of
light energy (the blur circle), even in an emmetropic eye. The poorer
the accommodation, the more the blurring of the image. In (a) two
point sources are separated by a distance sufficient to produce distributions that are easily discriminated. In (b) and (c) the two distributions increasingly overlap. At some point the observer will be unable
to see that there are two objects rather than one, and this corresponds
to the limit of visual acuity.

discriminate the separate features of each letter well enough to identify them.
Although this has some relevance to real-life visual tasks, it has the drawback
that we lack detailed knowledge of the processes that underlie the recognition
of letters. A more general measure is the Landolt C chart, which employs a

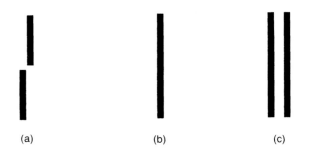

(a)   (b)   (c)

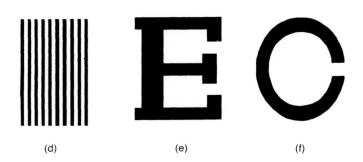

(d)   (e)   (f)

Figure 3.9 Examples of patterns used to test visual acuity. In each case the test is based on establishing the limiting conditions for discriminating a designated feature. (a) Vernier acuity. Detection of misalignment between the two line segments. This is commonly found to be very much better than would be expected from other acuity measures. (b) Detection of the presence of a single line. This depends upon the length of the line, and its orientation. (c) Two-line discrimination. The minimum separation is measured at which two lines are seen, rather than one. (d) Grating acuity. The minimum contrast at which a grating with a given spacing between the lines can be discriminated from a uniform grey field. (e) Snellen letter and (f) Landolt "C", as commonly used for ophthalmic assessments. The Snellen letters are read from a chart on which they appear with decreasing size. The Landolt "C" is shown in different orientations, with gaps of decreasing size, until a point is reached where it cannot be discriminated from a circle with a continuous circumference.

test pattern consisting of a black ring with a section missing, like a letter "C". The ring can be shown in various orientations and the observer's task is to identify the location of the gap, whether up, down, left, or right. As the "C" is made progressively smaller, there comes a point at which performance in detecting the gap is no better than chance, and this is the limit of acuity. In general, visual acuity is expressed in terms of the minimum resolvable visual angle, for which the normal standard is a gap subtending 1 min (1 minute of arc or 1/60th of a degree). Visual angles (the angle subtended at the eye) are measured in degrees, and an approximate indication of 1° is the angle subtended by the index finger nail when the arm is fully extended. Acuity is stated as a fraction, relating a standard testing distance (6 metres, or 20 feet) to the distance at which a gap would subtend 1 min. Thus an acuity of 6/6 (which is the same as 20/20) means that performance is normal, whereas 6/3 means that a gap could be resolved at 6 metres which would subtend 1 min at 3 metres, i.e., a better than normal acuity. Similarly, 6/18 means that the minimum gap that can be seen subtends 3 min at 6 metres, and performance is a third of normal. Although these sorts of test have considerable practical utility, they have a number of drawbacks for scientific research on perception. Even if they are carried out under carefully controlled conditions of illumination, the fact remains that both Snellen letters and Landolt "C"s are complex patterns, from which it is not easy to generalise.

One approach to specifying visual performance in the most general terms derives from measurements of acuity for grating patterns. A grating consists of a number of light and dark lines with a particular width and orientation. Grating acuity is assessed by reducing the width of the light and dark lines until the grating can just be discriminated from an unpatterned grey field of the same average luminance. If the boundary between the light and dark lines is sharp and they are equally wide, then the grating is said to have a square wave profile. This can be seen in Figure 3.10a, which shows a graph of luminance in a square wave grating across the width of the field. A different luminance profile is produced if the change from light to dark is a gradual one. An example of this is the sine wave grating, in which luminance varies across the test field according to a sine function (Figure 3.10b). A cosine grating would have a similar profile, but shifted so that the dark lines coincide with the middle luminance of a sine wave grating (Figure 3.10c). In this case the difference is in the phase of the gratings, that is, in the relative location of the maxima and minima in luminance. Phase is expressed in terms of angles, and a cosine grating is 90° out of phase with a sine wave one. The importance of sine wave gratings lies in their use as general tests of the performance of an optical system. To understand the nature and significance of this work, it is necessary to describe some basic concepts in the specification of signals, whether optical, electronic, or acoustic.

In the early nineteenth century, the French mathematician Jean Fourier (1768–1830) proposed the theorem that any complex change in the state of a system could be described in terms of the combination of simple sine wave

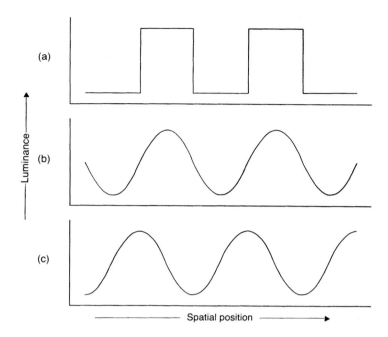

Figure 3.10 Illustration of the way in which luminance varies with spatial position for various spatial waveforms. In (a), a square wave, there are sharp transitions from light to dark, forming a series of bars with sharp edges. In (b) a sine wave and (c) a cosine wave, the transitions are more gradual. Sine waves differ from cosine waves only in the location of the maxima and minima, i.e., in phase. A waveform is fully described by its frequency (the number of oscillations in a given interval), its amplitude (the size of the oscillations), and its phase. Any complex waveform can be created from a combination of sine waves with appropriate amplitudes, phases, and frequencies.

oscillations of different frequency and amplitude. Thus a pure tone is a single frequency of vibration, whose amplitude varies sinusoidally over time. Any complex sound can be described in terms of a combination of pure tones, with suitably chosen frequencies and amplitudes. This provides a very powerful means of specifying sounds, and of testing the response to them by physical systems. By testing the response with a range of pure tones, it is possible to predict performance with any arbitrary sound that might occur. This can be applied, for example, to the specification of performance in loud-speaker systems.

In order to apply these concepts to vision, it is necessary to think in terms of spatial rather than temporal frequencies; that is, rather than measuring the number of cycles of sound pressure in one second the index is the number of cycles of luminance in one degree of visual angle. Visual stimuli have the property of being extended over space, and intensity can vary in this dimension also. Thus a static pattern which changes from light to dark according to a sine wave function constitutes a spatial, rather than temporal, frequency (Figure 3.11).

Any optical system can be tested with a range of such spatial frequencies in order to find out how well they are transmitted. The relevant measure is the contrast of the test pattern emerging from the optical system, compared to that which is fed in. Loss of contrast shows up as a reduction in the difference between the light and dark areas. The overall optical performance is expressed as a modulation transfer function (MTF), which is the relationship between contrast transmission and spatial frequency. Direct measurements of the MTF for the human eye might be made by measuring the contrast of gratings projected onto the retinal surface, for example with an ophthalmoscope and a photodetector. More simply, an observer can be asked to report when the contrast of a sine wave grating with a certain spatial frequency is sufficient for it to be just visible. In this case the measurement is of the MTF of the observer, treated as a single system, and it incorporates the effects of neural as well as optical processes. Such an MTF is called a contrast sensitivity function (CSF), and an example is shown in Figure 3.12.

The human CSF clearly shows a differential response to different spatial frequencies. For example, there is a rapid drop in response above about 12 cycles per degree, and a more gradual decline below about 5 cycles per degree. The high frequency cut-off is probably due to the optical characteristics of the eye, and is related to the diameter of the pupil. It is in fact very close to the ideal performance of an optical system with the dimensions of the eye. The low frequency cutoff is more influenced by signal processing later in the visual system. Note that the scale of spatial frequency is logarithmic, which can give a somewhat misleading impression of the shape of the function. The CSF is an MTF for gratings at threshold contrast, and other techniques can be used to find MTFs for supra-threshold gratings, although this is more difficult. The application of Fourier analysis, and the use of visual stimuli in the form of sinusoidal gratings with a defined spatial frequency, has led to the development of theories regarding the processing of visual information by the brain (see Sekuler & Blake, 1994; Wandell, 1995).

VISUAL NEUROPHYSIOLOGY

Vision, like all other aspects of experience and behaviour, is mediated by activity in the brain. It also depends upon activity in highly specialised cells in the sense organs called receptors. A full understanding of vision will include an appreciation of the neurophysiological processes that are initiated by the activity of light on receptors in the eye. These involve the modification of

Figure 3.11 A square wave (a) and sine wave (b) grating. Note the gradual variation in brightness of the sine wave at the transition from light to dark.

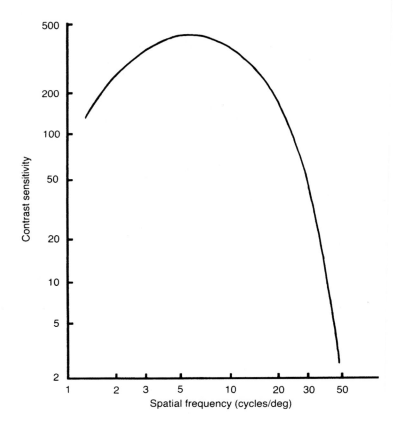

Figure 3.12 A typical human contrast sensitivity function. Contrast is measured by the ratio of the difference between the luminances of lightest and darkest parts of the grating, divided by their sum. Contrast sensitivity is the reciprocal of the contrast at which a grating of a given spatial frequency is just discriminable from a uniform grey field. Peak sensitivity occurs at around 5 cycles/deg. (After Barlow & Mollon, 1982).

light energy into nerve impulses and their transmission to the areas at the back of the brain where they are analysed. Tremendous advances have been made in our knowledge about the neural processes underlying vision, and many of these will be touched upon in the following sections. Many textbooks on perception have good sections on the eye as an optical instrument and on the physiological processes both in the retina and in the brain that follow from light stimulation. For example, Wandell (1995) provides a solid introduction to the anatomy and physiology of the visual system; the use of gratings as stimuli for probing the visual system is explained, and various

perceptual phenomena are interpreted in terms of the underlying physiological processes. The textbooks by Bruce et al. (1996) and by Sekuler and
Blake (1994) are also recommended for their coverage of the visual physiology and of spatial frequency analysis. Similarly, textbooks on neuroscience
usually have a chapter on the visual system. A more detailed and thorough
account of the visual system and neurophysiology generally can be found in
Kandel, Schwartz, and Jessel (2000).

Psychology has constantly tried to link observable function (behaviour)
with underlying structure (anatomy, physiology, genetics, etc.), and these
attempts are often considered to have been most successful in the area of
perception. Some visual phenomena can be reduced to known neurophysiological processes. Reductionism, describing phenomena at one level in terms
of concepts at a simpler level, has been one of the main motivations for
scientific enquiry generally. It is certainly a powerful force in visual science.
Paradoxically, we do not know a great deal about the neurophysiology of
human vision, but we do know a lot about that in some of our nearest
biological neighbours. Much of the material described here is based upon
experiments on other species, particularly monkeys. We assume that equivalent processes occur in the human visual system because of the many biological similarities that exist: the receptors in the eyes, the pathways from the
eyes to the brain, and the anatomy of the visual areas of the brain are all
strikingly similar. Therefore, it does seem justified to relate the wealth of
perceptual data on humans to the neurophysiological evidence from other
species. Modern neural imaging techniques, like fMRI, are strengthening the
evidence to support such inferences (see Posner & Raichle, 1997). In this way
it is possible to interpret visual phenomena in terms of the brain events that
might give rise to them. First, it is necessary to outline the principal features
of the visual system.

Receptors

All sensory systems function by transducing some type of environmental
energy into a form that can be analysed by the cells in the central nervous
system (CNS). The general structure of nerve cells (neurons) is shown schematically in Figure 3.13. Neurons communicate electrochemically: They
transmit signals along the nerve fibres in pulses of fixed amplitude, hence the
term nerve impulse, but it is also called an action potential. Neurons do not
make direct contacts with one another, and the activity of one neuron influences others chemically across the small gaps or synapses separating them via
neurotransmitters. Receptors, like other nerve cells, have a resting potential
difference between the inside and outside of the cell. Processes in the membrane surrounding the nerve cell retain negatively charged molecules (negative ions) within the cell so that the interior is negatively charged (by about 70
millivolts) with respect to the extracellular ions.

The transduction process usually involves a modification of the potential,

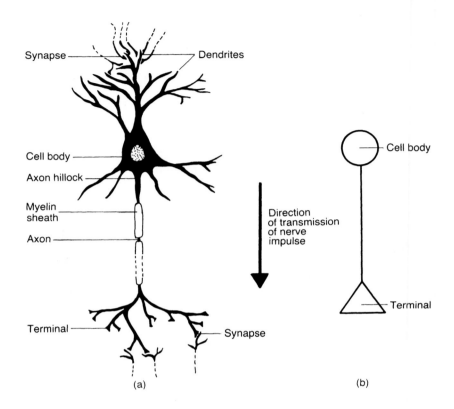

Figure 3.13 The main structures in a typical nerve cell. (a) The dendrites receive inputs, transmitted chemically across the synapses, from many other nerve cells; inputs can be excitatory and inhibitory. If the net activity passes some threshold then an action potential or nerve impulse is initiated in the axon hillock and it is transmitted along the axon to the terminals of the neuron, thereby influencing other neurons. The transmission of the action potential along the axon is facilitated by the myelin sheath, which acts as an insulator. (b) A schematic nerve cell of the type that will be used to indicate the direction of neural transmission in some of the following illustrations. (After Kandel, et al., 2000)

so that the potential difference is reduced; this is called depolarization. These electrical changes are graded, i.e., they will vary with the intensity of the environmental energy stimulating the receptor. The process of vision is initiated by light falling on specialised receptors in the retina (Figure 3.14). The retinal receptors contain light-sensitive pigments that are modified chemically by absorbing light. However, unlike receptors in other senses they hyperpolarize when light falls on them: The potential difference between the inside and outside of the receptor cells increases. Before describing the physiological

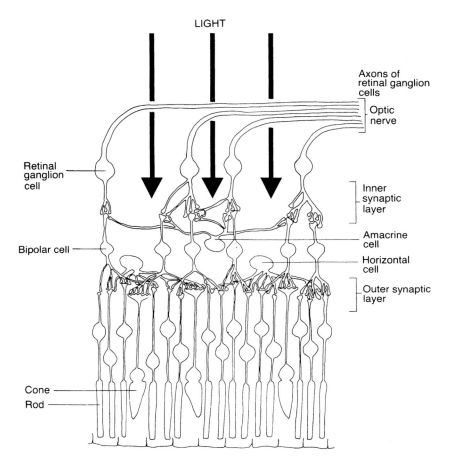

Figure 3.14 The neural structure of the retina. Light passes through the neural layers before striking the receptors (rods and cones), which contain the photo-sensitive pigments. The vertical organisation of the retina is from receptor to bipolar cell to retinal ganglion cell. The horizontal organisation is mediated by horizontal cells at the receptor-bipolar (outer) synaptic layer and by the amacrine cells at the bipolar-retinal ganglion cell (inner) synaptic layer. (After Cornsweet, 1970)

processes at the retinal level, a little more should be said about the structure of the retina itself.

The retina is an outgrowth of the CNS and the receptors are directed towards the back of the eye. Therefore, before the light strikes the receptors it passes through the various neural structures in the retina and also the blood vessels that supply them. There are two types of receptor in the human retina, and they are called rods and cones because of their appearance under the microscope; rods have a cylindrical outer segment (which contains the photo-sensitive pigment molecules) and cones have tapered outer segments. The retina is estimated to consist of about 130 million receptors, the vast majority (over 120 million) of which are rods with about 6 million cones. The distributions of the rods and cones differ in a systematic way. The cones are concentrated in and around a central region of the retina, where there is a shallow depression, called the fovea. There are decreasing numbers of cones as the distance from the fovea increases, and there are none in the peripheral regions of the retina (Figure 3.15).

One part of each eye is devoid of any receptors, and it is called the blind spot (or optic disc). It is located about 17° towards the nasal side of each fovea, and it is the exit pathway of the nerves from the retina (the optic nerve), as well as the region where the arteries enter and veins leave the eye. We are usually unaware of this small area of blindness in each eye, because it corresponds to different parts of the visual field of each eye. Even when we use one eye alone we generally overlook this blind spot, and it is only when we employ some specific procedure, like following the instructions to observe Figure 3.16 that we can locate it.

The light-absorbing pigment molecules in the receptors are distributed in the photosensitive membrane in their outer segments (Figure 3.17). In rods the photosensitive membrane consists of separate discs stacked on top of one another, rather like a pile of coins. The photosensitive membrane in cones has a different structure: It consists of a single surface folded successively over on itself. All rods contain the same visual pigment, which is a complex protein molecule called rhodopsin. There are three different types of cones each with a specific light-sensitive pigment. The cone pigments can absorb light throughout the visible spectrum, but one type is most sensitive to low wave-lengths of light (around 420 nm), another the middle region of the spectrum (around 530 nm), and the third to slightly longer wavelengths (around 565 nm).

Duplicity theory

With all these differences in mind, it is not surprising that the rods and cones operate under different conditions of light stimulation. The rods are more sensitive than the cones and respond in twilight or moonlight; rods become overloaded in daylight and are unable to function. The cones require the more intense illumination of daylight to function. This difference in sensitivity is indicated in Figure 3.18; rods are about 1000 times more sensitive than cones. Indeed, rods are so sensitive that an individual rod can register the absorption of a single photon of light, but the activity of a single rod does not provide an impression of light. Under ideal conditions a human observer can detect a light when less than 10 photons are absorbed. The increased sensitivity of rods is combined with a slow response to light; it is estimated that a rod receptor takes about 0.3 s to signal the absorption of a photon. The

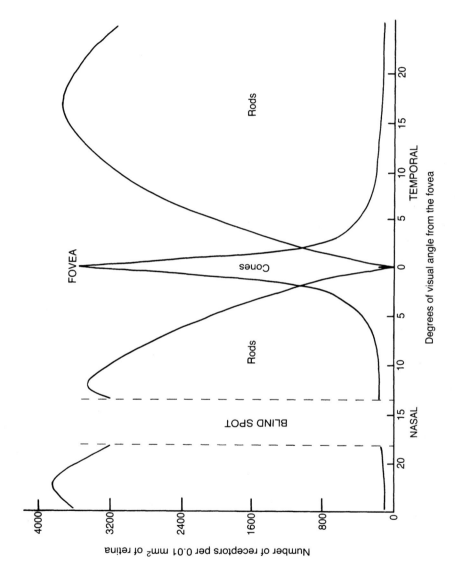

Figure 3.15 Distribution of rods and cones over a horizontal region of the retina passing through the fovea and blind spot.

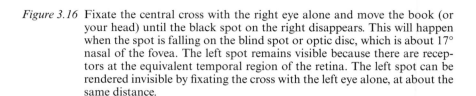

Figure 3.16 Fixate the central cross with the right eye alone and move the book (or your head) until the black spot on the right disappears. This will happen when the spot is falling on the blind spot or optic disc, which is about 17° nasal of the fovea. The left spot remains visible because there are receptors at the equivalent temporal region of the retina. The left spot can be rendered invisible by fixating the cross with the left eye alone, at about the same distance.

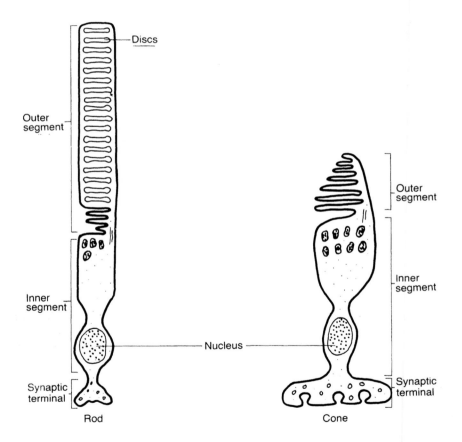

Figure 3.17 Detailed structure of rod and cone receptors. The light-sensitive pigments are located in the outer segments—stacked discs for rods and a single folded surface for cones. The inner segment is concerned with the metabolic functions of the cells. (After Kandel, et al., 2000)

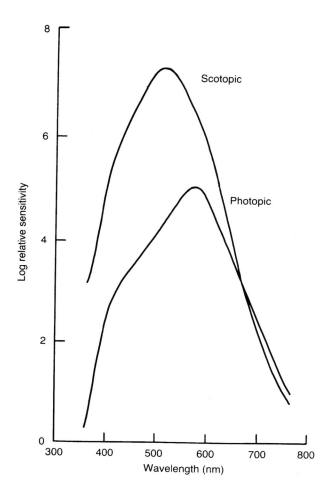

Figure 3.18 Spectral sensitivity of the rods (scotopic curve) and cones (photopic curve). The rods can detect light at lower intensities than the cones, and their peak sensitivity is for lower wavelengths of light. (After Kaufman, 1974)

cones require more light to function, but their response is about four times faster than rods. There is, therefore, a trade-off between sensitivity and response time in rods and cones. Figure 3.18 also illustrates another aspect of rod and cone function: In dim light rods respond to the whole visible spectrum but they are most sensitive to wavelengths around 505 nm; the spectral sensitivity under bright conditions is somewhat different, showing a peak at around 555 nm. This could be the basis for some differences in our sensitivities to colours under dim or bright light conditions. Bluish-green objects appear to be brighter in dim light than they do in daylight, and conversely greenish-yellow objects appear brighter in daylight than under dim conditions. This is called the Purkinje shift, after the physiologist who first described it in 1825. We are most sensitive to light of around 505 nm in low illumination (reflecting the function of rods) and around 555 nm in bright conditions (reflecting cone function).

Another feature of this distinction is the time taken for the receptors to recover from intense light adaptation. When we have been exposed to bright daylight and then enter a dark environment (like a cinema) we are initially unable to distinguish any detail, but gradually our sensitivity improves until after about 30 min we can see quite well. It is referred to as dark adaptation; it can be measured accurately by adapting the observer to bright light for a few minutes, then placing them in darkness and measuring the detection threshold for light at regular intervals. The resulting dark adaptation curve (Figure 3.19) has two components, the initial phase shows the fast recovery of the cones and the final phase the slower recovery of the rods. If the detection

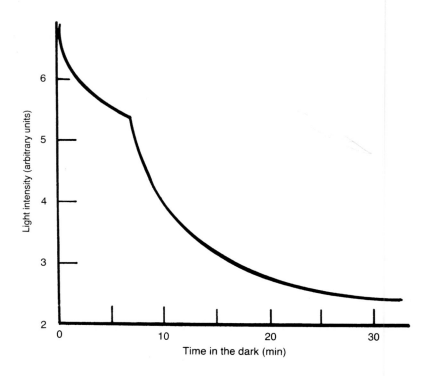

Figure 3.19 Dark adaptation or the recovery from light adaptation. The curve represents the increasing sensitivity (or decreasing thresholds) for light detection with time in the dark. The initial rapid phase reflects the recovery of the cones and the slower phase that of the rods. An asymptote is reached after about 30 min in darkness.

threshold is measured with a small red spot presented to the fovea then only the initial component will be found, because the spot would stimulate cones alone. Some individuals do not have any cones in the retina, and their dark adaptation curves would have the second phase alone.

Any photoreceptor can only signal the absorption of photons of light. The signals delivered will depend upon the wavelength of the light as well as its intensity, because of the differences in spectral sensitivity described earlier. Therefore, the same signal can result from a wide range of combinations between intensity and wavelength, and no photoreceptor can distinguish between these two dimensions. This is referred to as the principle of univariance. This principle is important when discussing differences in wavelength sensitivity between rods and cones because it applies to both of them. All rods contain the same visual pigment and so they could not discriminate on the basis of wavelength. The same is true for any given type of cone: it can only respond in one dimension, by hyperpolarising by some amount. However, there are three different types of cone, and their combined activities can mediate wavelength discrimination or colour vision. It is now considered that colour vision is based upon signals from the three cone types being combined at subsequent neural stages. This is demonstrated with regard to our ability to see colours in different regions of the visual field. Colour vision is best in and around the fovea. However, in the peripheral retina, where there are rods but no cones, we are all colour blind (Figure 3.20).

The differences in function described previously are attributable to the characteristics of rods and cones, and this is referred to as duplicity theory. However, we should be cautious of treating the rods and cones alone as the bases for the effects described; the effects are the consequence of activity occurring throughout the visual system, not just at the initial stages. The activity of the rods and cones defines the limiting light conditions under which vision is possible. Beyond these the manner in which neural information is processed will be of importance, and therefore it is necessary to examine the neural interactions within the retina and the pathways to the brain.

Retinal structure

The retina is a complex neural structure, as was evident from Figure 3.14. An even more simplified and schematic diagram of its structure is shown in Figure 3.21. It can be thought of as having both a vertical and a horizontal organisation: The vertical organisation corresponds to the connections leading to the brain, and these have horizontal (or lateral) connections between them. Receptors make synaptic connections with bipolar cells, which in turn make synaptic contact with retinal ganglion cells. The ganglion cells are much larger than receptors or bipolar cells; their cell bodies are in the retina, but their axons (or nerve fibres) leave the retina to form the optic nerve. There are about 1 million axons in each optic nerve, so an enormous

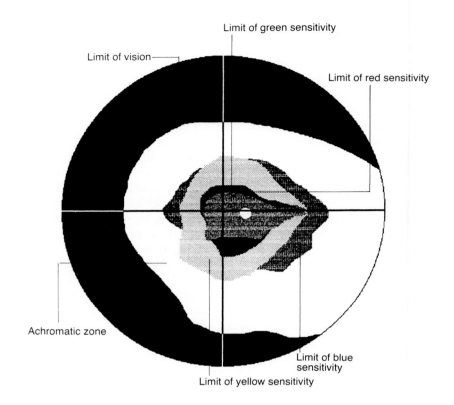

Figure 3.20 Colour regions of the right eye. Colour sensitivity can be determined by means of an instrument called a perimeter, which can present coloured spots of light to peripheral regions of the retina. All colours can be detected in the central area of the retina. The areas for red and green sensitivity are similar but smaller than those for blue and yellow.

neural convergence has taken place in the retina—from about 130 million receptors to 1 million ganglion cells. This convergence is not evenly distributed over the retina, and is least for the foveal region. Conversely, the convergence is much greater than average in the peripheral retina. The horizontal or lateral connections occur at the first and second synaptic layers. At the first synaptic layer, between receptors and bipolar cells, there are horizontal cells, and at the second layer, between bipolar and retinal ganglion cells, there are amacrine cells. Retinal ganglion cells can be classified according to the sizes of their cell bodies. In primate retina the vast majority (about 80%) have small cell bodies and receive their input from foveal cones; the remainder with larger cell bodies receive input from more peripheral regions of the retina in which the rods predominate. The distinction

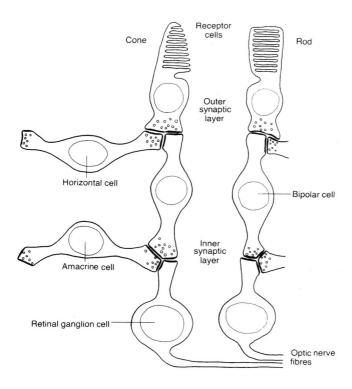

Figure 3.21 Detailed representation of the neural structures in the retina. At the outer synaptic layer the receptors can influence the activity of the bipolar and horizontal cells, and the horizontal cells can affect the receptor and bipolar cells. At the inner synaptic layer the bipolar cells can influence the activity of both the retinal ganglion and amacrine cells, and the amacrine cells can in turn affect the bipolar and retinal ganglion cells. (After Werblin, 1976)

between these two cell types is maintained in subsequent processing at more central sites.

Visual pathways

The axons of the retinal ganglion cells leave the eye forming the optic nerve. This nerve is situated at the base of the brain, and the two optic nerves travel towards one another and appear to meet at the optic chiasm (see Figure 3.22); it was so called by Galen because it resembled the shape of the Greek letter chi. The axons do not in fact meet, but they project to different cerebral hemispheres according to the area of the retina from which they originate: Axons from the outer (temporal) side of each retina (the left half-retina for the

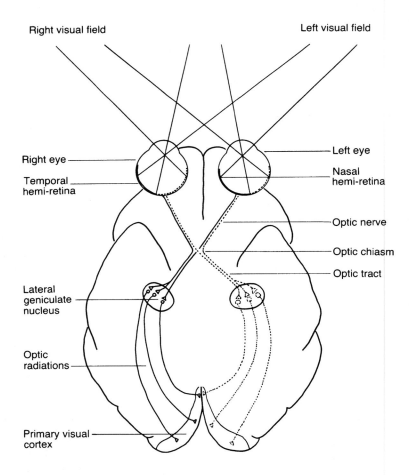

Right visual field

Left visual field

Right eye

Temporal hemi-retina

Left eye

Nasal hemi-retina

Optic nerve

Optic chiasm

Optic tract

Lateral geniculate nucleus

Optic radiations

Primary visual cortex

Figure 3.22 Pathways from the eyes to the visual cortex, viewed from below. The axons of the retinal ganglion cells form the optic nerves which pass under the frontal lobes of the brain. Fibres from the nasal halves of each retina cross over to the opposite hemisphere, while those from the temporal halves project to the hemisphere on the same side. This partial decussation occurs at the optic chiasm, and it results in signals from the same regions of the visual field projecting to the same hemispheres. The optic tracts consist of fibres from both eyes, and the axons terminate in a large subcortical body called the lateral geniculate nucleus (LGN). The cells from the LGN project to the primary visual cortex, also called V1.

left eye and the right half-retina for the right eye) project to the ipsilateral hemisphere (on the same side), and the axons from the nasal halves of the retinas cross over and project to the contralateral hemisphere. There is a narrow vertical strip in the centre of both retinas, subtending about 1°, that projects to both hemispheres. Animals that have lateral rather than frontal eyes, with little or no binocular overlap of their two visual fields, have almost complete crossover at the optic chiasm. The partial crossover of fibres in humans results in the transmission of signals from equivalent parts of the visual field to the same hemispheres. Thus, the right half of the visual field projects to the left halves of the retinas, and they in turn send neural signals to the left hemisphere.

The axons from the retinal ganglion cells continue beyond the optic chiasm as the optic tract, and they form synaptic connections in the thalamus, in a structure called the lateral geniculate nucleus (LGN). The LGN consists of six layers, rather like an onion. The fibres from the contralateral eye project to layers 1, 4, and 6, and those from the ipsilateral eye to layers 2, 3, and 5 (see Figure 3.23). The cell bodies in layers 1 and 2 are larger than those in layers 3 to 6; the former are called magnocellular layers and the latter parvocellular layers. The small retinal ganglion cells project to the parvocellular layers, and the large ones to the magnocellular layers.

Axons from the LGN cells project to the visual cortex, which is situated at the back of the brain. The visual cortex also has a vertical and a horizontal cellular organisation (Figure 3.24). Vertically (perpendicular to the cortical surface) it can be divided into six layers, on the basis of the cell types that can be distinguished microscopically. The horizontal organisation is in terms of the lateral fibre connections between ocular dominance columns.

Neural activity in the retina

Having outlined the structure of the retina and the pathways to the brain, we can examine the activities of these cells. The initial stages of light absorption in the receptors results in hyperpolarisation. The measurement of such small graded electrical changes is possible by the use of minute pipettes (micropipettes) in contact with the surface of the cells or inserted into the cells themselves. The amount of hyperpolarisation that occurs is proportional to the light energy absorbed. The receptors form synaptic connections with bipolar cells and horizontal cells. The electrical activity of the bipolar cells depends on the source of stimulation: Direct influence from the receptor cell results in hyperpolarisation, whereas indirect influence from horizontal cells produces depolarisation. The horizontal cells in synaptic contact with receptors also hyperpolarise. All these electrical events are graded, that is, they vary on a continuous scale according to the intensity of stimulation.

Quite a different electrical response can be recorded from the amacrine and retinal ganglion cells: They produce action potentials (or nerve impulses), which can be measured extracellularly with microelectrodes.

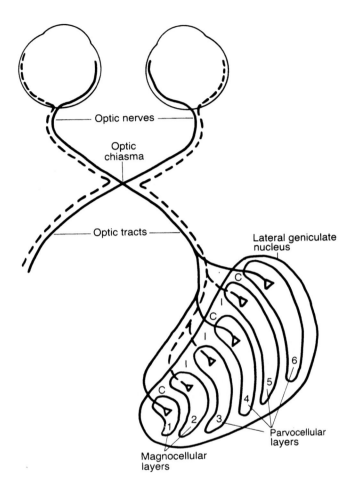

Figure 3.23 The lateral geniculate nucleus (LGN) consists of six layers. The cell bodies in layers 1 and 2 are larger than those in layers 3–6; the former are called magnocellular and the latter parvocellular layers. Projections from the contralateral (C) eye synapse in layers 1, 4, and 6, and those from the ipsilateral (I) eye synapse in layers 2, 3, and 5. (After Kandel, et al., 2000)

Action potentials are all-or-none electrochemical events that have a fixed amplitude; they are the rapid depolarisations that occur along the axons of nerves. Much more is known about the activity of retinal ganglion cells (and subsequent stages in the visual pathway) because extracellular recording has been technically possible for longer than has intracellular recording. Indeed, the activity of retinal ganglion cells can be measured without entering the retina—by recording from single axons in the optic nerve or optic tract. This

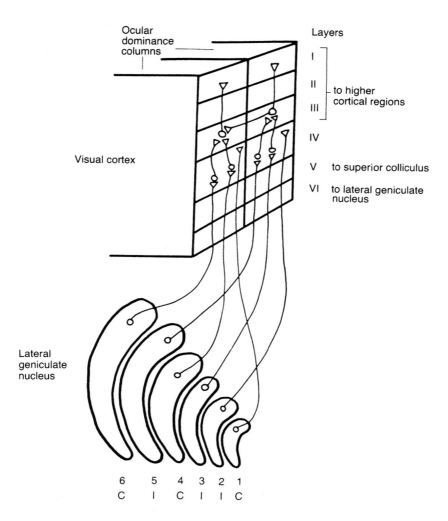

Figure 3.24 Projections from the LGN to the primary visual cortex (V1). All cells project to layer IV of V1; those from the magnocellular layers project to higher locations in layer IV. Fibres from the ipsi- and contra-lateral layers of LGN project initially to adjacent regions of V1, maintaining a distinction based on the eye stimulated. There are also lateral connections between these adjacent regions. V1 has six distinct layers. Incoming fibres to layer IV project upwards to layers III, II, and I, and are concerned with analysing the visual signals. Layers V and VI send signals back to sub-cortical structures, such as to LGN from layer VI. (After Kandel & Schwartz, 1985)

technique has generally been applied to experimental animals like cats and monkeys, and it has furnished us with important information concerning the ways in which patterns of light are coded in the visual system.

Prior to the use of microelectrode recording it was thought that the cells in the visual pathway were excited simply by the presence of light. Now it is known that it is the pattern of light that is of importance, not solely its presence. Experiments on Limulus (the horseshoe crab) first indicated that the neural activity of one cell can be influenced by the state of its neighbours, a process called lateral inhibition. This is evident at the retinal ganglion cell level of vertebrate eyes. When experiments were performed to determine the adequate or appropriate stimulus for these cells it was found that they did not fire (produce nerve impulses) when the whole eye was stimulated by diffuse light. First, light had to be presented to a particular part of the retina, and second it had to have specific dimensions. Some retinal ganglion cells could be excited by small spots of light, but they ceased firing when the spot was increased in size (Figure 3.25). These are called on-centre cells, as they are characterised by excitation when the centre is stimulated by light and by inhibition when the annular surround is also stimulated. Retinal ganglion cells, like other neurons, have a resting discharge rate, i.e., they continue to produce nerve impulses at irregular intervals in the absence of light. Neural inhibition can be demonstrated by stimulating the surround alone with light, as the resting discharge rate then declines. Other retinal ganglion cells display the opposite pattern of activity: They are excited by the presence of light in the annular surround and inhibited by its presence in the centre. These are called off-centre cells.

The activity of each retinal ganglion cell can be influenced by a particular pattern of light falling on the appropriate part of the retina. This region is called the receptive field for that cell. Most retinal ganglion cells have con-centric receptive fields with central and surrounding regions that are antagon-istic in their function. Thus, the processes of neural excitation and inhibition are vital in determining the ways in which cells in the visual system respond to the patterns of light falling on the retina. The retinal ganglion cells respond to changes in the pattern of illumination, rather than to steady states of uniform illumination. These changes can be spatial and temporal. So far we have described the spatial characteristics—the centre-surround receptive fields—but there are differences in the responses of retinal ganglion cells to the duration of stimulation and the speed of conduction along their axons. Prolonged stimulation (for a few seconds) of the small-bodied retinal gan-glion cells results in an initial reduction of the firing rate, levelling off to a steady rate, and they conduct slowly (at around 6 metres/s). These have a sustained response; that is, they continue to discharge at above their resting rate with prolonged stimulation. Because they project to the parvocellular layers of the LGN they are considered to be part of the parvocellular (or P) pathway. The large-bodied retinal ganglion cells respond briefly to the onset or offset of stimulation, and then revert rapidly to the resting discharge rate

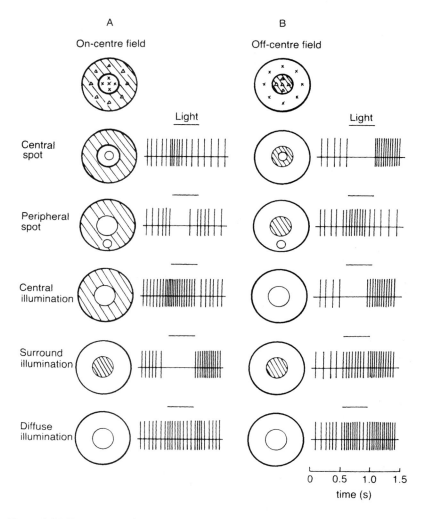

Figure 3.25 Responses of on- and off-centre retinal ganglion cells to a variety of light patterns falling on their receptive fields. The cross symbols in the upper figures refer to excitatory influences and the triangles signify inhibition.

even if stimulation is continued; they also conduct nerve impulses more rapidly (at about 15 metres/s). Thus, they have a transient response and project to the magnocellular layers of the LGN, and are part of the magnocellular (or M) pathway. As noted earlier, the P pathway receives input from predominantly in and around the fovea, where visual acuity is best, and they have smaller receptive fields than cells in the M pathway, which are distributed more evenly throughout the retina. The receptive fields of retinal ganglion cells are antagonistic with the centre stimulated by the opposite character-istics to the surround. Cells in the M pathway code luminance differences between centre and surround whereas those in the P pathway code wave-length as well as luminance differences.

The excitatory and inhibitory interconnections in the retina are the basis for the receptive field properties of the retinal ganglion cells. The antagonistic interaction between centre and surround also determines the type of stimulus that will produce a response in these cells. As we have seen, the maximum response is elicited by a small white or dark spot, but large responses will also be produced by the grating stimuli described in the previous section. That is, the light bar of a grating will produce a large response if its projected width on the retina corresponds to the dimensions of the on-centre receptive field; con-versely, a dark bar of the grating would produce a large response in an off-centre retinal ganglion cell with a receptive field of the appropriate dimensions.

Contrast phenomena

The lateral inhibitory interactions within the retina act to increase the differ-ences between neural signals for edges or boundaries in the stimulus. There-fore, the neural coding of light falling on the retina depends on changes in its spatial distribution over time; these changes are enhanced by the neural machinery within the retina. Indeed, the enhancement is such that it can lead to the visibility of patterns that are not present physically in the stimulus. Mach bands are one phenomenon of this type; they are named after the physicist Ernst Mach (1838–1916) who described them in the nineteenth cen-tury (Figure 3.26). The areas of constant luminance on the left and right are separated by a ramp of increasing luminance: If a light meter was passed horizontally across the whole pattern it would register a constant level then a gradual increase followed by another constant (but higher) level of lumi-nance. This does not correspond with what is seen in the pattern, as there appears to be a dark vertical band on the left side of the ramp and a light band on the right, which are the Mach bands.

Shortly after Mach had described his phenomenon (in 1865), a related effect was reported by Ludimar Hermann (1838–1914) when looking at a grid of black squares on a white background (Figure 3.27a): The background does not appear uniformly white, but dark grey dots are apparent at all the intersections apart from the one fixated. The reverse occurs with white squares on a black background, as was reported by Hering. These are now referred to as the Hermann–Hering grids, and they have been related to the properties of concentric receptive fields in the retina. Consider two equivalent on-centre receptive fields stimulated by different parts of the white back-ground in a Hermann grid (see Figure 3.27b). The one that falls between the intersections would be inhibited by a smaller white area surrounding it than will the one falling at an intersection.

Figure 3.26 Mach bands refer to the light and dark bands that can be seen flanking the boundaries between the luminance ramp. A dark band is
visible on the darker side of the ramp and a light band on the lighter
side, despite the absence of such differences in the pattern when
measured with a light meter.

The dimensions of concentric receptive fields are smallest in the retinal
ganglion cells receiving their input from the central fovea, and they increase
in size with increasing distance from the fovea. This is probably the reason
why the Hermann–Hering dots are not visible at the fixated intersection:
Both the centre and surround would fall between the squares and within the
intersections, so that there would be no differential response from them, and
no illusory dots. If the separations are made sufficiently small then the dots
can be seen at the fixated intersections. In fact, measuring the limiting dimensions of grids that yield the illusory dots has been used to estimate the sizes of
receptive fields at different eccentricities in human vision.

Mach bands and Hermann–Hering grids can be encompassed within a
wider class of phenomena, namely simultaneous contrast effects. These generally refer to the apparent brightness or colour of one region in a pattern
when it is surrounded by another having a different brightness or colour. For
example, in Figure 3.28 the central grey squares all reflect the same amount
of light, i.e., they have the same physical luminance, but there is a difference
in their brightness. This difference in brightness (a perceptual dimension)
where there is no difference in luminance (a physical dimension) is due to the
surrounding regions in each case. When the surround is lighter than the

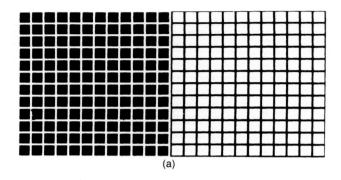

(a)

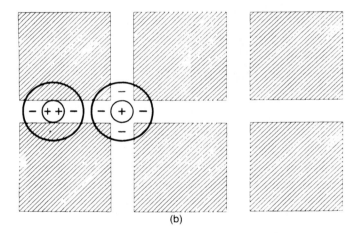

(b)

Figure 3.27 Hermann–Hering grid. (a) Dark grey dots appear at the white intersections on the left and light dots are visible at the black intersections
on the right. Note that these might not be apparent at the intersection
you fixate upon. (b) The interpretation of the Hermann grid effect in
terms of on-centre receptive fields. The surround inhibition is greater
at the intersections of the white lines than between the squares,
because more of the surround is exposed to light. A similar interpretation of the Hering grid can be given in terms of off-centre cells.

central grey square it appears darker than when the surround is darker than
it. If the surrounds were coloured then the central grey areas would also
appear slightly coloured, but in the complementary colour of the surround.
For instance, if the surround was red then the physically grey centre would
appear greenish; if it was blue then the centre would appear yellowish. These
effects have often been manipulated systematically in art, particularly in the
Pointilliste paintings of Georges Seurat (1859–1891).

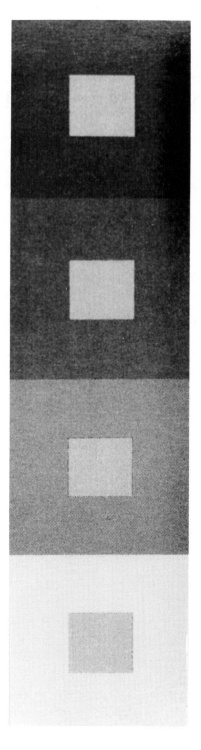

Figure 3.28 Simultaneous brightness contrast. The central squares are all the same luminance, but their brightnesses are influenced by the area surrounding them. If the surround is darker then the grey square looks brighter, and vice versa.

Colour

Seurat also sought to capture colour on canvas as if it was light. Painters traditionally mixed pigments on a palette before applying them to the canvas; Seurat adopted another technique, which is more akin to additive than to subtractive colour mixing. The colours were applied as small dots of (principally) primary colours; they could then mix in the eye like light. His influence was Helmholtz, who had written on the relationship between painting and perception, and who advocated a theory of colour vision based on three primaries. The Young–Helmholtz trichromatic theory of colour vision has received support from studies of the different photopigments in retinal cones. Both psychophysical and physiological studies have provided evidence for the view that there are three different types of cone receptors, with peak sensitivities at around 420, 530, and 565 nm (see Figure 3.29a). These are sometimes referred to as S (short), M (medium), and L (long) wavelength receptors and at other times, more loosely, as blue, green, and red receptors. Neither set of terms is strictly appropriate for the cone pigment that has a peak sensitivity at 565 nm, largely because it is neither a long wavelength in light terms nor does it correspond to the perception of red.

The complement of colour cones varies markedly between species. The retinas of mammals, other than primates, have only two cone pigments, responding to short and medium–long wavelengths. Most Old World primates have three cone pigments, but some New World primates have four. It would seem that in humans the differentiation between the medium and long wavelength cone pigments is of relatively recent origin (see Mollon, 1989). The genes for the medium (green) and long (red) wavelength pigments are almost identical and they both lie on the X chromosome, which defines the sex of individuals. Females have XX chromosomes, whereas males have XY, with the Y chromosome being shorter than the X. This can account for the

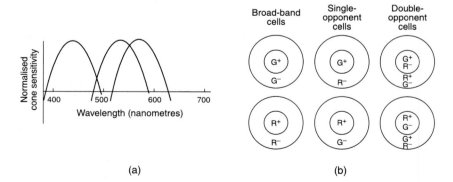

(a)   (b)

Figure 3.29 (a) Cone sensitivity functions for the three cone types, normalised to indicate the peak spectral sensitivities (after Hubel, 1995). (b) Different types of opponent process receptive fields found in the retina (after Kandel & Schwartz, 1985).

wide divergence of colour defects in females and males (see page 29), because a recessive on one X chromosome of a female is likely to be paired with a dominant allele; a recessive on the X chromosome of a male will have no allele with which to combine and so will be expressed. The short wavelength cone pigment is coded on a different chromosome.

The signals from the three cone receptors are combined neurally in many ways, as indicated by the receptive field properties of retinal ganglion cells in the P pathway. For example, some cells are excited when long wavelength (red) light falls on the centre and inhibited when the complementary (green) falls on the surround. All excitatory and inhibitory combinations of these colour opponent cells have been found with pairings between long and medium (red-green) and short and medium-long (blue-yellow) wavelengths (Figure 3.29b). Thus, there is support for the Young–Helmholtz trichromatic theory at the receptor level, and for Hering's opponent process theory at the retinal ganglion cell level.

Neural activity in the lateral geniculate nucleus

This distinction between large- and small-bodied retinal ganglion cells, in the M and P pathways, respectively, is amplified in the projection to the LGN (refer back to Figure 3.23): the small colour-opponent retinal ganglion cells project to the parvocellular region (layers 3–6) and the large cells project to the magnocellular region (layers 1 and 2). Therefore the large and small cells that were intermingled in the optic tract project to separate sites in the LGN. Moreover, these separate M and P pathways display other functional differences in addition to wavelength sensitivity: P cells respond (1) more slowly, (2) to higher spatial frequencies, and (3) with less sensitivity to luminance contrast than M cells.

Neural activity in the visual cortex

The axons from the LGN project to visual area 1 (V1) of the visual cortex, and enter it in layer IV (refer back to Figure 3.24). Again the distinction between the P and M projections is preserved, with the P fibres terminating in the lower and the M in the upper half of layer IV. The cells form synaptic connections with neurons projecting vertically to upper layers of V1. In addition to separate regions in layers I–III receiving input from P and M systems, there is another which receives input from both. The regions are shown up by specific staining procedures as oval blobs separated from one another, and microelectrode recordings show that cells in these regions have quite different receptive field properties. In fact, almost all the cells in the visual cortex have receptive field characteristics that differ from the concentric organisation found at earlier stages in the visual system. The neurons in the blobs receive inputs from both the P and M systems: They can be excited by coloured or white light falling on the retina, but they are not as sensitive to its precise position on the retina. The cells in the interblob regions receive inputs from the P system: They are excited by edges or bars in a particular orientation, but are relatively insensitive to wavelength. That is, a cell will respond to a line at a specific orientation no matter what its wavelength or intensity, but it will not respond to lines that are inclined away from the preferred orientation (Figure 3.30). The cells in layer IV that receive their inputs from the M pathway are excited by lines or edges in a specific orientation, particularly if they are moving; they are not selective for wavelength. For example, a given cell might respond most strongly when a horizontal line moved vertically.

These orientation selective neurons were once considered to make up the majority of cells in the visual cortex. Indeed, such was the interest elicited after their discovery, by David Hubel and Torsten Wiesel in 1959, that they became called feature detectors. This was because the cortical neurons were selectively tuned to extract certain features contained in the pattern of retinal stimulation—in this case orientation. Direction of edge motion is another feature extracted, as are binocular disparity and colour. The orientation selective neurons have a highly ordered organisation over V1, both perpendicular to the cortical surface and parallel to it, as is shown in Figure 3.31. If a microelectrode is inserted at right angles to the surface and all orientation cells encountered are recorded, then they will have the same preferred orientation, say 45°. This has been called a cortical column. An equivalent insertion in the neighbouring column will record a slightly different orientation selectivity, say 30°; the next column would have cells displaying a preferred orientation of around 15°, and so on, each column differing by about 15° from its immediate neighbour. In fact, the orientation selectivity of the cortical cells is not quite as precise as might have been suggested here; there is a particular orientation that will produce the maximum response from each neuron, but it will also respond, though with decreasing intensity, to lines within 10–20° either side of the preferred orientation. Accordingly, a given line falling on the retina will excite a range of orientation selective neurons, but to varying extents. It is clear that area V1 has a vertical organisation in terms of orientation selectivity, and a horizontal organisation in terms of orientation change. This results in all orientations being represented for a given retinal region. The cortical blobs code the wavelength characteristics of the stimulus; the cells are non-orientation selective and they have double opponency. The receptive fields have a centre-surround organisation with the centre, say, being excited by long wavelengths and inhibited by medium ones (denoted by R + G–) with the reverse influence on the surround (R–G +) as indicated in Figure 3.29b. These cell types are more common than those coding for B + Y– centre and B–Y + surround or the converse.

So far, nothing has been said about combining signals from the two eyes. The fibres in the optic tract are from similar halves of both eyes, but they project to different layers in the LGN. The first stage at which binocular integration of the neural signals occurs is in V1. The cortical neurons can be excited by appropriate stimulation of either eye, although one eye will

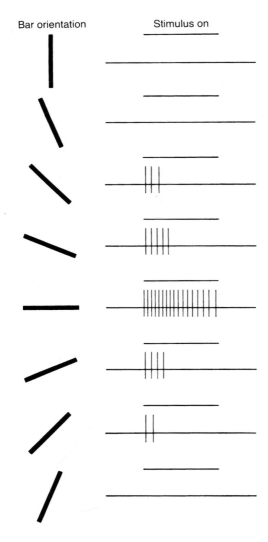

Bar orientation

Stimulus on

Figure 3.30 Receptive field properties of a cortical orientation detector. The orientation at which a bar is presented to a specific part of the retina is shown on the left. On the right the upper horizontal lines indicate when the stimulus (a black bar on a light background) is presented, and the vertical lines denote nerve impulses. For this cortical cell the firing rate is highest for a horizontal bar, and it declines sharply when the orientation differs from horizontal, not responding at all for bars at right angles to the preferred orientation. Neighbouring cells respond most strongly to different orientations, so that all orientations are represented for all retinal regions. (After Kandel & Schwartz, 1985)

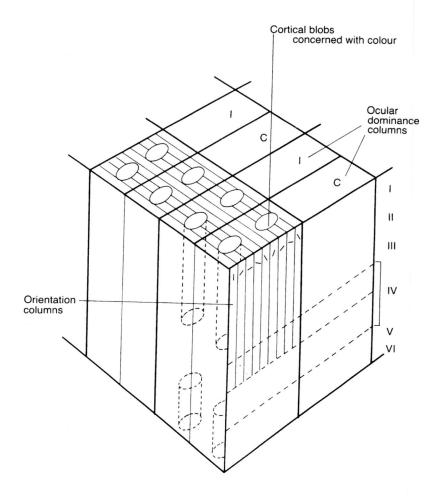

Figure 3.31 The organisation of cells in the primary visual cortex (V1). Cells in layers I, II, III, and the upper part of layer IV respond to contours in specific orientations. A column, perpendicular to the surface of the cortex, contains cells having the same receptive field orientations, and is referred to as an orientation column. Neighbouring columns display a shift of preferred orientation of about 15°. There are also cortical blobs, receiving inputs from both magno and parvo cells in LGN, that respond to the wavelength of the original light stimulus. Projections from the ipsilateral (I) and contralateral (C) eyes remain separate in V1, resulting in a larger horizontal organisation based on ocular dominance. Within cortical areas of about 1 mm² both eyes and all orientations are represented for a small region of the visual field. Hubel and Wiesel referred to these as hypercolumns. (After Kandel & Schwartz, 1985)

generally have a greater influence than the other. This aspect of eye preference represents yet another horizontal organisation over the surface of V1: Neighbouring orientation columns tend to have the same eye preference. However, at intervals of about 0.5 mm the eye preference changes abruptly to the other eye, and the sequence of orientation selective columns is repeated, as is represented schematically in Figure 3.31. Figure 3.32 shows the pattern of eye preference regions that have been established in monkey visual cortex. The eye-preference slabs can be identified by particular staining procedures and they are striped, rather like the stripes on a zebra. All the cells in the regions shown in white have one eye preference and those shown in black have a preference for the other eye. The combination of binocular signals to furnish information about relative depth (stereopsis) takes place at the next visual area.

V1 is, therefore, a highly organised structure. It appears to break down the pattern of light falling on the eye into discrete features, such as retinal location, orientation, movement, and wavelength, as well as maintaining a difference between the signals from the two eyes. These features are further differentiated in the subsequent cortical processing in visual areas shown in Figure 3.33c. Axons from neurons in V1 project to a variety of other visual areas in the cortex (Figure 3.33d). The adjacent visual area (V2) receives inputs from the three receptive field types in V1, but subsequent visual areas appear to specialise in the processing of particular features extracted in V1. The binocular combination in V1 is primarily for inputs from corresponding areas of each eye. That is, most binocular V1 neurons are excited by cells from the two eyes with equivalent receptive field characteristics and equivalent retinal locations. In V2 there are binocular cells that respond most

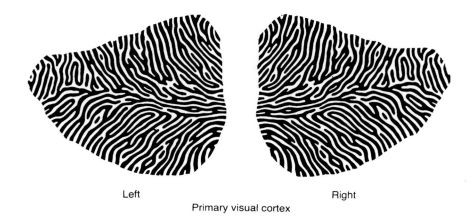

Left   Right
Primary visual cortex

Figure 3.32 The pattern of ocular dominance columns, represented by black and white areas, over the left and right hemispheric regions of V1. (After Hubel, 1995)

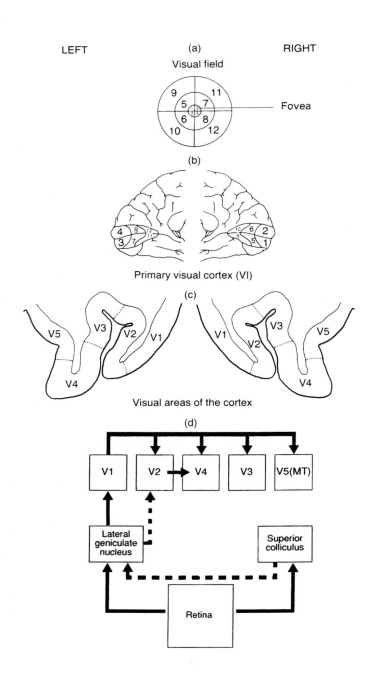

LEFT   (a)   RIGHT

Visual field

Fovea

(b)

Primary visual cortex (VI)

(c)

Visual areas of the cortex

(d)

strongly when the receptive field characteristics are slightly different. The inputs from each eye would have the same orientation selectivity, but the retinal locations associated with the receptive fields would be slightly different. These have been called disparity detectors because they appear to be responding to specific disparities (or horizontal retinal separations) between the stimulating edges in each eye. There are some disparity detectors at the level of V1. In addition to the analysis of retinal disparity further specialisations can be found in other visual cortical areas. For example, area V4 is principally concerned with the analysis of colour, with cells in areas V5 (also referred to as MT) processing movement. There are even cells in a more central area that can process complex stimuli like faces (Perret, Hietanen, Oram, & Benson 1992).

The projections from the retina to the LGN and onwards to the multiple visual areas retain the basic mapping of the retinal surface: Adjacent regions on the retina project to adjacent regions in LGN, V1, V2, etc. This is called retinotopic projection because the distribution of stimulation on the retina is preserved at more central sites. In turn, the pattern of retinal stimulation is geometrically related to the layout of objects in space. Although adjacent regions on the retina project to adjacent regions in the visual cortex, the precise separations are not retained. The fovea is only a small area in the retina, but its projection to the cortex is disproportionately large. Conversely, the large peripheral areas of the retina are represented by small areas in the cortex (see Figure 3.33a and b). If you think of the retinal surface as a balloon with a very weak central area (analogous to the fovea) then inflating it results in a huge expansion of the central region, but relatively little of the surrounding area. Neighbouring regions are still adjacent, as in retinotopic projection, but the relative separations are changed. This is a general scheme found in the cortical projections of sensory systems: Those parts of the sensory surface that have the greatest sensitivity also have the greatest cortical projection. For example, the cortical representation of the sensitive fingers is far more extensive than that of the arms, even though the area of the skin surface is much less. Similarly with vision, the retinal region serving the sharpest acuity (in and around the fovea) also has the largest cortical

Figure 3.33 (a) The visual field considered schematically as 12 regions, centred on the fovea. (b) The cortical representations of these regions. The diagram represents the posterior portions of the occipital cortex spread apart, exposing area V1. Note the inverted and reversed relationship between the visual field and its cortical representation, and also the cortical magnification: the largest areas of V1 process signals from the small foveal area of the retina, corresponding to areas 1–4 in (a). (c) A horizontal section through the occipital cortex showing visual areas 1–5. Signals from LGN are processed in V1; V2 is principally involved in processing retinal disparities, V4 with wavelength, and V5 with movement. (d) A schematic diagram of the connections between visual cortical areas. (a and b after Kandel, et al., 2000; c after Barlow & Mollon, 1982; d after Tovée, 1996)

representation. It has been estimated that the central 10° of the retinal surface is represented by about 80% of the cells in the visual cortex. This concentration of cortical processing to the central visual field would present a problem if the eyes remained stationary, because stimuli of significance could move out of the region where acuity is highest. In fact, the problem does not arise because of our exquisite control over eye movements, so that we can pursue moving objects to keep them projecting to the fovea or we can move our eyes rapidly and accurately to locate novel objects in the visual field. These control processes are mediated by pathways in the midbrain that have not yet been mentioned.

The excitement of research in the area of visual physiology is conveyed in the well-illustrated books by two researchers who have added substantially to our understanding of visual processing (Hubel, 1995; Zeki, 1993). There has been widespread acceptance of the idea that the various cortical areas are concerned with a modular organisation of vision (for orientation, colour, stereoscopic depth, motion, etc.) although this idea is now subject to scrutiny (see Lennie, 1998).

Midbrain structures associated with vision

The discovery of multiple mapping in visual areas of the cortex is relatively recent, and as many as thirty such areas have now been found in monkey cortex. However, the concept of a second visual system was first proposed in the 1960s. Unlike the multiple maps in the cortex, this one is subcortical and older in evolutionary terms. The pathways that have been described so far comprise the classical projection system. Some fibres branch off the optic tract before the LGN to make synaptic connections in a structure in the midbrain called the superior colliculus (Figure 3.34). The paired superior colliculi also receive inputs from layer V of V1. In evolutionary terms the superior colliculus is far older than the visual cortex. In many animals, like reptiles, all visual processing occurs in the optic tectum (which is equivalent to the superior colliculus in mammals), as there is no cortex present. In mammals its function is related to localizing objects in peripheral vision and directing eye movements towards them. Experimental animals that have had the visual cortex removed can still locate objects on the basis of collicular activity, but they do not demonstrate recognition behaviour when tested.

The midbrain also contains a number of oculomotor nuclei that control the movements of the extraocular muscles within the orbit. All eye movements are rotations generated by the coordinated activities of pairs of muscles attached to the eye ball. There are three pairs of muscles, which can rotate the eye in the three dimensions of space (Figure 3.35). We commonly refer to eye movements in terms of the directions the eyes point rather than the axis around which they rotate. The most frequent movements are up and down, and right and left. The former are coordinated in the two eyes, i.e., both move up and down in the same way.

Neurophysiological interpretations of visual phenomena

Very little is known about the neurophysiology of the human visual system. Most of the experimental findings summarised earlier have been derived from experiments on many animals, but principally cats and monkeys. It might be the case that the human visual system behaves in quite a different way. This is, however, very unlikely. The anatomy of the visual system in humans is very similar to that of monkeys, and some species (e.g., macaque monkey) have

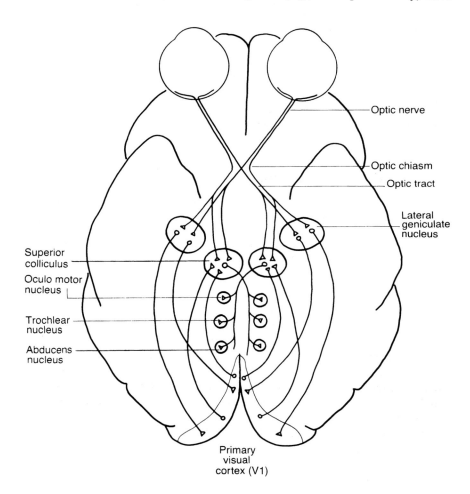

Figure 3.34 The classical projection pathway from the eyes to the brain via LGN, and the older pathway, in evolutionary terms, to the superior colliculus. Fibres from the optic tract synapse in superior colliculus, and the collicular fibres project to three nuclei concerned with the control of eye movements. Note that the superior colliculus also receives feedback from (layer V of) V1.

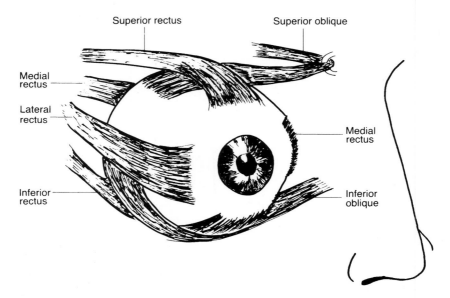

Figure 3.35 Extraocular muscles of the right eye. Rotations of the eye about a vertical axis (left and right) are controlled by the medial and lateral rectus muscles, those about a horizontal axis (up and down) by the superior and inferior rectus muscles, and those about the optical axis (torsion) by the superior and inferior oblique muscles. (After Sekuler & Blake, 1994)

about the same visual acuity and colour discrimination as humans. Therefore, we assume that the physiological processes measured in related species also applies to our visual systems. This extrapolation seems reasonable because the processes in cats and monkeys are closely comparable, even though the differences between their brain structures is greater than those between humans and monkeys.

Some phenomena have already been described in terms of the physiological processes that might give rise to them. For instance, the phases of dark adaptation were attributed to differences in rod and cone recovery times, or Hermann–Hering grid effects were related to differences in surround inhibition operating on the receptive fields of retinal ganglion cells. In attributing the phenomena to these particular processes we should not think that the phenomena are experienced at the levels these processes occur; the phenomena require those retinal processes but it is likely that they can only be experienced if the information is transmitted to more central sites. In order to sustain neurophysiological interpretations we need to assume that changes coded at one level in the visual pathway are retained throughout subsequent processing. The search for neurophysiological interpretations of visual phenomena has proved to be a driving force in vision research over the last few decades, especially since the discovery of feature detectors in the visual cortex. The phenomena interpreted in this way tend to be rather simple, and they reflect the operation of the relevant stimulus dimension (like orientation or motion) in isolation.

Under normal circumstances we can judge orientation very accurately. Even in a darkened room we can adjust a light line to within about 1° of the direction of gravity (vertical). This accuracy in perceiving the vertical can be biased by observation of a nonvertical pattern. For example, the gratings on the left in Figure 3.36 will initially appear to be vertical and aligned. Following inspection of the pattern on the right for about 1 min, the gratings on the left will appear neither vertical nor aligned. This is called the tilt aftereffect, and it has been interpreted in terms of orientation selective cortical neurons. According to this interpretation, a vertical grating will stimulate a range of orientation selective cells in the visual cortex—those with preferred

Figure 3.36 Stimuli for producing a tilt aftereffect. Initially look at the black spot on the left: The gratings above and below it will appear to be vertical and aligned. Then inspect the figure on the right by looking at the black rectangle for about 1 min; move your eyes slowly back and forth along the rectangle to avoid generating an afterimage. Looking back at the spot on the left will result in the lines appearing slightly tilted with respect to one another: The upper grating will look tilted anticlockwise, and the lower one clockwise. This aftereffect will only last for a few seconds after which the gratings will again look vertical and aligned.

orientations inclined slightly away from the vertical as well as those for vertical (see Figure 3.37). Initially the balance for those inclined clockwise of the
vertical will match that for those inclined anticlockwise. During inspection of
the inclined grating an overlapping distribution of orientation selective
cells will be stimulated. However, since the inspection is prolonged these
will undergo adaptation, i.e., their firing rates will be reduced by constant

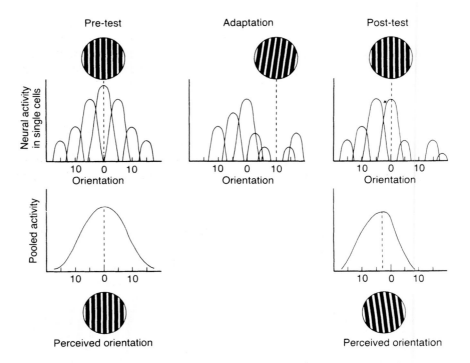

Figure 3.37 An interpretation of the tilt aftereffect based on adaptation of cortical
orientation-selective cells. The vertical pre-test grating has the maximum
neural effect on those cortical cells with vertically oriented receptive
fields, but there will be smaller effects on other cortical cells having receptive fields within about 15° clockwise and anticlockwise of the vertical. The pooled activity of these cells is shown on the lower left. The
effects are symmetrically distributed around the vertical, and it is
assumed that the peak of this distribution represents the perceived orientation of the grating. During adaptation to a grating inclined 10° clockwise of the vertical the cortical responses will adapt as shown in the
central figure. On post-test, the vertical grating will stimulate some cells
(clockwise of the vertical) which have been adapted and others (anticlockwise of the vertical) that have not. The resulting pooled distribution
of activity (shown on the lower right) has its peak biased in an anticlockwise direction, with a consequent shift in perceived orientation. The
adapted cells recover quite rapidly to their normal sensitivity and so the
aftereffect also dissipates. (After Blakemore, 1973)

stimulation, and the cells will require some time to return to their original sensitivity. When the original pattern is observed again, the balance between the clockwise and anticlockwise influences will be disturbed and shifted in the opposite direction to the inspection orientation. This shift in the distribution has been used to account for the shift in orientation that we can see. The effects of adaptation for seconds or minutes are relatively short lived, and so the two gratings return to alignment after a few seconds; longer adaptation results in longer lasting aftereffects.

The tilt aftereffect represents an example of successive biasing: Some orientation selective cells are adapted and the recovery from this adaptation is evident in the misjudgement of orientation. Related orientation biases can be induced simultaneously in patterns like that in Figure 3.38. The grating in the central circular region is vertical, but it does not appear so because of the inclined grating surrounding it: The central grating appears to be tilted in the opposite direction to the surrounding grating. This tilt illusion has been interpreted in terms of inhibition between orientation selective cells in the cortex.

The motion aftereffect is an example of motion biasing: Following observation of a moving pattern (like descending water) a subsequently viewed

Figure 3.38 Tilt illusion. The central lines are parallel to the edges of the page, but they look tilted clockwise because of the surrounding anti-clockwise lines.

stationary pattern appears to move in the opposite direction. It has been interpreted in a similar way to the tilt aftereffect, but incorporating motion detecting cortical cells rather than orientation detecting cells. Studies of tilt and motion aftereffects have also provided evidence for the ways in which signals from the two eyes interact. If a moving pattern is observed by one eye and a stationary pattern is subsequently observed by the other then the movement aftereffect can still be measured, but it only lasts for about 50% as long as adapting and testing the same eye. This is called the interocular transfer of the aftereffect, and it has been used to infer the nature of binocular interaction in the human visual system. For example, the fact that interocular transfer occurs at all suggests that there are binocular cells that share the same information: They can be stimulated equivalently by either eye. The fact that transfer is less than complete suggests that there are also some monocular cells contributing to the perception. In addition to the binocular cells that are excited if either eye is stimulated there are others that are only excited if both eyes are stimulated at the same time. Some of these respond only when contours fall on corresponding locations in each eye, that is, when the receptive fields in each eye are exactly in register. Such binocular cells probably mediate binocular single vision—the perceptual experience of a single world. Other cortical cells respond only when there are small horizontal displacements between the locations of stimulation on each retina. These are called disparity detectors because they may be implicated in stereoscopic depth perception or stereopsis. Binocular single vision and stereopsis will be discussed in the next chapter. Interest in stereopsis has increased in recent years because neurophysiologists have found regions in the brain, like V2, which appear to extract and process retinal disparities in comparative isolation. Other brain regions process features like colour and movement. However, we know relatively little about the ways in which these "feature maps" are subsequently integrated to provide us with unified percepts of objects having a particular shape, size, texture, and location in space.

Neurophysiological investigations are conducted under conditions that are far more controlled than those operating in perceptual experiments. The animals are generally immobilised so that the experimenters can define precisely both the area of the retina stimulated by light and the response that is elicited in the brain. Perceptual experiments, involving active and intact subjects, are open to much greater variability. The eyes move around resulting in the stimulation of a range of retinal regions, and the responses, like pressing a switch, are much more complex. There are several strategies that can be adopted to accommodate these differences. One is to try to simplify the stimulus and response conditions in perceptual experiments to match, as closely as is feasible, those obtaining in neurophysiological experiments. This is the approach that has been adopted in the study of spatial aftereffects described previously. It has the advantage of proposing and testing explicit hypotheses linking neurophysiological and psychophysical data. The disadvantage is that the phenomena investigated are very simple, and the conditions of their occurrence are far removed from perception of objects in the world. Another strategy, and the one adopted in this book, is to examine functional aspects of perception, like location, motion and recognition, and to draw on the neurophysiological evidence when it is pertinent. This will enable the investigation of both simple and complex phenomena, but with respect to the latter it is more difficult to draw on our knowledge of neurophysiological processes underlying perception.

Visual streams

In the past two decades functional distinctions between two pathways of neural processing in the visual cortex have been made. Both start from the visual cortical areas mentioned on pages 127–34, but one passes dorsally to the posterior parietal areas of the cortex and the other ventrally to the infero-temporal cortex (Figure 3.39). These streams have been called the dorsal and ventral streams by Ungeleider and Mishkin (1982), and they are also referred to as the parietal and temporal streams; they could be involved in parallel processing of the visual input. The distinction between the M and P pathways described earlier could be retained in these streams, with the dorsal stream analysing aspects of movement and depth in the pattern of stimulation, and the ventral stream extracting spatial detail and colour. Lesions or sections in the posterior parietal cortex (involving the dorsal stream) result in failure to

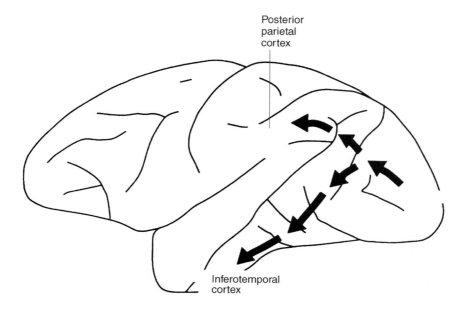

Figure 3.39 A simplified representation of the dorsal and ventral visual streams. (After Milner & Goodale, 1995)

discriminate the spatial location of objects whereas lesions in the inferotemporal cortex (damaging processing in the ventral stream) impairs object recognition. Accordingly, perceiving the location of an object was attributed to the dorsal stream while the ventral stream determined its identity—the *where* and *what* dimensions of vision (see Goldstein, 1999).

A recent revision of the functions served by these streams is in terms of action and perception: The dorsal stream is said to be concerned with motor control and the ventral stream with perceptual representation. Milner and Goodale (1995) have argued that the representation and conscious awareness of external objects is a consequence of processing in the ventral stream. That is, our experience of a perceptual world is a consequence of this neural pathway. The control of our actions, on the other hand, is said to be due to the dorsal stream and it operates without our conscious awareness. One of the differences associated with the distinction relates to visual illusions: The difference between the way size illusions look to us and the way we respond to them is taken to support the distinction between action and recognition. Although our perception is distorted by these patterns, our motor control is not. If two horizontal sticks were placed in the Müller–Lyer configuration (as in Figure 1.4b on page 26) the upper one would look longer than the lower one but observers would adjust their fingers to the appropriate physical length rather than their perceived inequality. Thus, we might be able to fool the eye, but not the fingers!

Neuropsychological studies of individuals who have suffered accidental injury to specific regions of the brain, like those mentioned on pages 30–31, lend support to the latter position. However, as we will argue in the following chapters, both action and recognition systems can only operate effectively if there is a representation of three-dimensional space available to them. We will suggest how such a representation might be achieved.

4   Location

Perception of the location of objects in the environment determines many other perceived characteristics. The example of crossing the road, described in the first chapter, illustrated some of the ways in which the perception of location is necessary before other aspects of a scene, like motion or recognition, can be determined. Our perceptual-motor coordination relies upon localising objects accurately, so that we can step over them, reach for them, avoid them or orient appropriately to them. Perception is a platform for action, and actions take place in a three-dimensional environment. It is necessary, therefore, for spatial perception to share the three-dimensional coordinate system in which behaviour occurs. The aspect of visual perception that will be examined in this chapter is location. Specifying the location of an object requires information for its direction and distance. Direction and distance will be considered separately, although they almost always function in tandem: Information that an object is a given distance away is of little assistance for guiding behaviour if its direction is not also detected, and vice versa.

Any statement about the locations of objects requires the specification of a frame of reference relative to which the objects can be assigned. No better description of such relativities can be given than that by the empiricist philosopher, John Locke (1690/1975, pp. 76–77):

> Thus a Company of Chess-men, standing on the same squares of the Chess-board, where we left them, we say are all in the *same Place*, or unmoved; though, perhaps, the Chess-board hath been in the mean time carried out of one Room into another, because we compared them only to the Parts of the Chess-board, which keep the same distance one with another. The Chess-board, we also say, is in the *same Place* it was, if it remains in the same part of the Cabin, though, perhaps, the Ship it is in, sails all the while: and the Ship is said to be in the *same Place*, supposing it kept the same distance with the Parts of the neighbouring Land; though, perhaps, the Earth hath turned round; and so both Chess-man, and Board, and Ship, have every one *changed Place* in respect of remoter Bodies.

The fundamental point that Locke was making is that statements about position require the definition of a frame of reference, and that there are many such referents which can be nested within one another. First it was the chess piece, then the board, then the cabin, then the ship, then the earth, then the solar system. Any statement about location and motion is meaningless unless the frame or frames of reference are specified.

Accordingly, when discussing any aspect of space or spatial perception it is necessary to define the frame of reference relative to which measures are made. This is commonplace for physicists, who are accustomed to defining the framework within which any measurement is expressed. Surprisingly, it is less common among perceptual psychologists, even though they are dealing with a system that has detectors in a moving eye, two eyes that can move with respect to one another, and eyes that can be displaced when the head or body moves. Information about where the image of an object falls on the retina could alter because the object moves, because the eyes move in the head, because the head moves with respect to the body or because the body moves in space. Any of these changes, alone or in combination, will result in the displacement of a retinal image. Generally we perceive the world while there are complex patterns of eye, head and body motion, but our perception of objects is not disturbed. To understand how this might be achieved, we need to understand how frames of reference can be specified, and how they can apply to visual perception (see Wade & Swanston, 1996).

FRAMES OF REFERENCE

Our language is replete with terms relating to where things are with respect to one another. For example, is this book on the table or beneath the light or beside the window or above the floor? All these questions refer to relations between objects. In these statements there is an implicit assumption of the greater stability of one of the objects (table, light, window, floor) relative to the book. Some objects may be considered to be more stable than others, but those objects could be changing place, too. If the book is being read on a train then all the objects would be moving in the same direction. These statements would still apply if the carriage was taken as a frame of reference, but the carriage (and its contents) could be located with respect to a larger frame of reference, like the surface of the earth.

A physicist would describe the locations of objects in this way, and also draw attention to the fact that the earth is moving relative to the sun, which is not, of course, the final reference. A physicist assumes that these nested frames of reference can be defined in abstract terms; the descriptions do not make any reference to the location of an observer. In our example, the reader of the book can change location both to it and to the other frames of reference like the floor. Physicists relate objects in the world to other objects; they are not (as physicists) a part of that world themselves. If we are to discuss perceived location then we must also take the perceiver into account. Thus the situation is somewhat different, and more complex, for perception than for physics.

The concept of frames of reference is, accordingly, of critical importance in understanding the issues in this and subsequent chapters. By way of analogy, Locke's chessboard could be likened to the retina, and the location of a piece could correspond to a particular point on the retina. If the chessboard (or retina) is adopted as a frame of reference then the location of a piece with respect to it would be called, in our terminology, *retinocentric*. All that is required to specify a particular square is the adoption of a point on the surface as the origin with specified units of separation. On a chessboard (Figure 4.1) the convention is to adopt the black square with the White Queen's Castle as column *a* row *1* (*a1*) and then the rest of the 64 squares can be given specific locations (like *b6*). In the case of the retina it is likely that the origin would correspond to the fovea.

However, the situation is a little more complex for vision because we have two retinas: It is as though we had two similar chessboards, side-by-side; which one should we use? Our perceptual experience is not in duplicate: We see objects singly with two eyes and in a single direction. This direction does not correspond to that from one or other eye but from a point between them. We refer to this as the *egocentric* frame of reference and it provides a single origin from which the direction of objects can be assigned. It is as if we have derived a line of direction in which objects are seen, but it does not enable us to determine how far along the line they are positioned. In order to do this we need to have some indication of distance as well as direction, and this

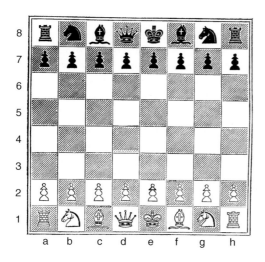

Figure 4.1 The layout of a chessboard with symbols for rows and columns, so that every square can be specified.

involves adopting yet another frame of reference, called *geocentric*. It is three-dimensional, and it can be used to guide our actions. This is not, of course, the final frame of reference that could be adopted, but it is the one that is vital for our behaviour and survival. We know that the earth rotates around the sun, but our experience each day is that the sun rises and appears to rotate around the earth. When we need to use larger frames of reference (as in navigation by air and sea) we tend to use instruments rather than rely on the senses because there have been no evolutionary pressures for us to develop detectors for them.

The use of retinocentric, egocentric, and geocentric frames of reference enables us to discuss the perception of location in terms of natural articulations of the body—the stimulation of the retina, the rotation of the eyes, and the motion of the head. However, Locke's example of spatial relativity was based on a single chess piece. Suppose that there are several pieces on the chessboard. Each could be specified with respect to the origin (equivalent to retinocentric coordinates), but they could also be described with respect to one another. To state that the King's pawn can take the Black Bishop (or that the Black Bishop can take the King's pawn) does not indicate where the two pieces are on the board, but only their relative locations. Similarly, it is possible to determine retinal locations in this way, so that they relate to the particular pattern of stimulation. We will see in Chapter 5 how certain motion phenomena can best be understood by introducing such a frame of reference, which we have called *patterncentric*. One potentially useful feature of patterncentric information is that it does not change as the eyes move; the relative position of two stimuli on the retina remains the same even if the retina moves. Under normal circumstances the patterncentric frame of reference will correspond to the geocentric, but there are circumstances under which they are dissociated, and we can learn a lot about spatial vision by studying these.

In summary, the retinocentric frame of reference relates to location on the retina, the fovea can be considered as the origin from which coordinates are assigned. The patterncentric frame of reference can take any point on the retina as an (arbitrary) origin and assign the coordinates of another point with respect to it. The egocentric reference frame combines signals from the two eyes to define a single origin, which is typically between the eyes; directions are assigned with respect to this egocentric origin. The geocentric frame of reference adds distance to direction so that objects can be located in three-dimensional space; the origin remains within the observer. The dimensions used at the geocentric level are those that apply to three-dimensional space. This enables us to perceive space three-dimensionally and to control our actions in it. Unlike physical descriptions of space, which are viewpoint free, we carry the origin of our geocentric representations around with us.

The discussions of location, motion, and recognition in this and the following chapters will all be couched in terms of these four frames of reference as we believe that they provide a logical basis for understanding vision. Frames of reference are being incorporated explicitly in many theories of perception, but neither the terminology nor the concepts themselves are equivalent. This applies particularly to theories of object recognition, and the issue of terminology will be returned to in Chapter 6.

Coordinate systems

In order to use the information available from a frame of reference we require a defined origin and also units which determine the separation of points from the origin. That is, a coordinate system is required. The one with which we are perhaps most familiar is the Cartesian system for drawing graphs; it uses X and Y axes, which are usually represented as horizontal and vertical, respectively. Such a graph is two dimensional, one for breadth (X) and the other for height (Y). If a third dimension is added at right angles to the other two then depth can be specified along the Z axis. The description made earlier in terms of a chessboard can be amplified with respect to points drawn on a two-dimensional graph. Figure 4.2a shows a graph with the X and Y axes marked. Any point within the graph can be specified; here it is at values X = 2 and Y = 2, and it is marked by a circle. The location and intersection of the coordinate axes define a frame of reference relative to which the point is located. Figure 4.2b represents a similar graph with the point (marked by a square) at the same location (X = 2 and Y = 2) with respect to the origin. If we take the axes as the only frame of reference in each case then the points have the same locations because they have the same coordinates on axes of the same scale.

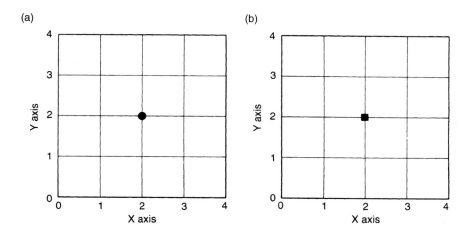

Figure 4.2 Two graphs with circular (a) and square (b) symbols at the same X and Y coordinate values (2,2).

Hierarchies of coordinate systems

The intersection of the X and Y axes defines a point (the origin) relative to which all other points are plotted. It is only when a further frame of reference is adopted that a measure of the enclosed one can be taken. For instance, the graphs represented in Figure 4.2 are positioned differently on the printed page: If the page is taken as a frame of reference then the locations of the two graphs on it can be measured, and differences between them can be described. Therefore, taking the page as the frame of reference the circle and square symbols have different locations, even though their coordinate values (2,2) are the same. The page itself can be in different positions, but this can only be measured if a larger frame of reference still is adopted, like the table, the ceiling, or the surface of the earth. In such a descriptive system no informa-tion about locations with respect to one frame of reference is lost by moving up to another one; rather information that was not available is introduced by adopting a superordinate frame of reference. Again, this is like considering the chessboard, the cabin, and the land as frames of reference in Locke's example.

Statements about the location of objects are restricted to the highest frame of reference in operation. For example, at the level of the graph in Figure 4.2a, the coordinates of the circular symbol can be specified, but no state-ments can be made about the location of the axes, because they define the frame of reference relative to which all other points are specified. It is only when a higher frame of reference is adopted, like the page, that the location of the axes can be described, and the location of the page can only be speci-fied if we consider a frame of reference relative to which it can be located, like the surface of the earth.

The graphical example is conceptually similar to what is happening in spatial perception, because the perceiver has many articulating parts: The eye can move in the orbit, one eye can move with respect to the other, the head can move on the shoulders and the body on the ground. The retina in one eye is somewhat like the drawn X and Y axes on the graph paper; different points on the retinal surface can be stimulated, but they can only be measured with respect to the retina itself. The second sheet of graph paper is like the other eye. The information about locations on each eye could be derived by adopt-ing a similar frame of reference for both, like the coordinate axes of the two graphs. In the example that we have drawn in Figure 4.2, the coordinates on each graph are (2,2) and (2,2), and the units of length are the same in both. If the axes of the two graphs were superimposed on one another, then the points would be in correspondence. The page can be likened to the head; whenever the page moves the two graphs move with it. Similarly, whenever the head moves the two eyes are displaced in space. Therefore, changes in retinal stimulation can be produced by movements of the eye with a fixed head, by movements of the head without eye movements, or by a combin-ation of the two. The changes in position of the page (or head) occur with respect to a larger frame of reference, namely the surface of the earth. For all practical purposes, the surface of the earth will be taken as the final frame of reference and will accordingly be defined as stationary.

VISUAL DIRECTION

Visual direction can be considered as a line extending from a point in the perceiver. We will start our treatment of visual direction by considering simplified situations, like a stationary observer. This has the advantage of building up a scheme of spatial representation in a systematic way. The information available at early stages (like the retina) is generally inadequate for guiding behaviour, and it needs to be amplified successively by other sources of information (like eye and body positions) in order to achieve a representation of three-dimensional space.

Retinocentric direction

Suppose a point of light in an otherwise dark room is observed by a single, stationary eye. How can observers determine its direction? One of the sources of information that must be used is the location on the retina that was stimulated. This is referred to as a local sign (see Rose, 1999). Essentially, a local sign can be considered as a two-dimensional coordinate reference on the retina itself. It is likely that the fovea acts as the origin for the retinal frame of reference, and positions with respect to it can be discussed in terms of the familiar Cartesian coordinate system (see Figure 4.3), although other coordinate systems could equally well apply. Within this retinocentric frame of reference there is no information about the position of the retina itself, only about points on it. If one eye moved slightly, as is illustrated schematically in Figure 4.4, then different retinal coordinates (or local signs) would be stimulated. At the retinocentric level there would be no means of determining whether this was a consequence of motion of the point or displacement of the eye.

Patterncentric interactions

Now consider a situation in which two points of light are present in an otherwise dark room. If the directions of each point are determined independently then their directions with respect to one another could also be computed. This is essentially the comparison of the two retinocentric values (see Figure 4.5). Thus, the coordinates of one point $(x1, y1)$ could be subtracted from those of the second point $(x2, y2)$ to determine their separation. It would also be possible to derive the relational directions of the two points without determining their retinocentric values: One could be so many retinal units away from the other, so that their separation alone was coded. For

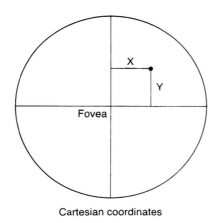

Cartesian coordinates

Figure 4.3 Circular schematic of a retina representing a point at a given location in terms of Cartesian coordinates. The fovea is taken as the origin for the coordinate system.

example, in Figure 4.5 one point (x1,y1) could be taken as the origin of a coordinate system and the separation from (x2,y2) would be given by its coordinates; alternatively, the second point could act as the origin. Such a relational (or patterncentric) system can take either point as the frame of reference for the other. So, for example, point A could be the origin and point B is separated from it, or vice versa. With just two points there are no advantages in taking A or B as the relational frame of reference. It is difficult to present an illustration of such a patterncentric scheme because the page on which it would be printed provides an implicit frame of reference! That is, the directions of one light source with respect to the other could be described independently of their local sign values (their locations on the retina)—they could be anywhere as long as both were imaged in the eye. The relational values would code separation independently of direction or orientation.

Such a relational system operating on its own could not account for our ability to determine the directions of isolated lights, but we will see later that the joint operation of retinocentric and patterncentric values assists in the interpretation of several movement phenomena.

When an isolated target is presented to the peripheral part of the retina it initiates a fixation reflex—the eye moves automatically to locate the target on the fovea. Indeed, the adequate perception of the spatial detail is dependent upon light from the object falling on the central region of the eye, because acuity is best in and around the fovea. Therefore, we need to be able to direct our eyes to objects that require more detailed spatial resolution in order to

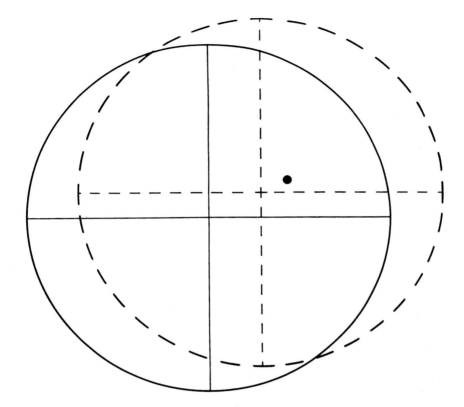

Figure 4.4 A point (the black dot) located at a constant position in space would stimulate different local signs (retinal coordinate values) if the eye moved, as indicated by its position relative to the solid and dashed circles.

determine whether they are of interest to us. For this to occur the retinocentric coordinates must be involved in the control of eye movements. For example, the retinocentric coordinates corresponding to an isolated point of light could be x2,y2, and these values are used to bring the point onto retinocentric coordinates of 0,0.

We can determine the visual direction of a point falling on the fovea (with retinocentric values of 0,0). A different visual direction is perceived if the eyes have to rotate to fixate the point on the fovea, and the retinocentric signals remain (0,0). Thus, different visual directions can arise from stimulation of the same retinocentric coordinates. Clearly, the difference in visual direction could not be registered at the retinocentric level. However, there are signals for the position of the eye in the orbit, and if these eye position signals are combined with the retinocentric signals then differences in the direction of

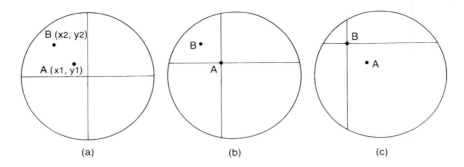

Figure 4.5 (a) Two points (A and B) could be described by their Cartesian coordinates (x1,y1 and x2,y2), and their locations relative to one another could be determined from the difference between the coordinates. Alternatively, (b) point A could act as an origin and define a patterncentric frame of reference, (c) as could point B.

points could be discriminated. Therefore, visual direction is dependent upon both retinocentric and eye movement information.

Egocentric direction

So far, we have considered situations in which a target is observed with one eye, whereas normal vision is binocular. When we rotate an open eye the closed one rotates, too. This can easily be demonstrated. Close one eye and gently place the index finger of one hand on the upper eyelid. Look at the other outstretched index finger with the open eye, and follow its movements. You will feel the closed eye rotating in its orbit, yoked to the movements of the open eye: the two eyes work as one. This principle was stated by Ewald Hering, and it is known as Hering's law of equal innervation: "The two eyes are so related to one another that one cannot be moved independently of the other; rather, the musculature of both eyes reacts simultaneously to one and the same impulse of will" (Hering, 1868/1942).

The integration of eye movements between the two eyes affects visual direction, too, because the direction in which a stationary monocular target is seen depends on the position of the occluded eye. When one eye is occluded, it tends to rotate inwards, towards the nose, and this rotation of the closed eye results in changes in the visual direction of the target seen with the open eye, as is illustrated in Figure 4.6. Moreover, when both eyes fixate on a target its visual direction does not correspond to the retinocentric direction of either eye alone, but it assumes an intermediate direction, midway between the eyes. Not only do the two eyes work as one, but the visual direction of a target appears aligned with a single central eye, rather like the mythological cyclops. Indeed, this position between the eyes is often referred to as the cyclopean

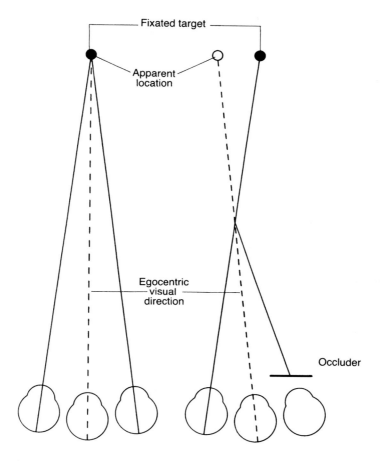

Figure 4.6 The change in visual direction when one eye is occluded. When one eye is occluded it rotates inwards, thereby modifying the egocentric visual direction of the target. (After Ono, 1990)

eye, as well as the egocentre. This can easily be demonstrated with the aid of a sheet of paper and two coloured pens. Make two marks at one end of the sheet separated by about 60 mm (somewhat less than the distance between the eyes) and join one to a central fixation point at the opposite end using a red pen and the other using a green pen (see Figure 4.7a). Now, place the sheet slightly below eye level and fixate the point at which the lines intersect. Although each line is pointing directly at one eye, the impression is of a single line pointing between the eyes (to the cyclopean eye), with two flanking lines pointing wide of the left and right eyes. The central line might also appear to fluctuate between red and green, as a consequence of binocular rivalry.

An even simpler demonstration of the same general point can be made

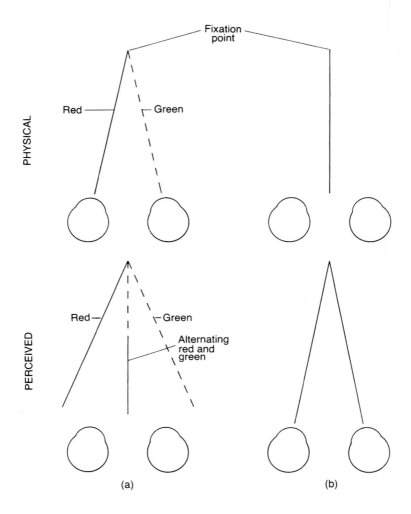

Figure 4.7 (a) The visual direction of red and green lines directed along the optic axes of each eye. (b) The visual direction of a single line in the median plane. (After Ono, 1990)

with a single line drawn on a sheet of paper (see Figure 4.7b). If the line is aligned with a point midway between the eyes and the far point is fixated with both eyes then two lines will be visible, one directed at each eye. In this case, the central line appears to be directed to the opposite eye, as can be ascertained by closing the eyes in turn. The initial registration of direction is dependent upon a retinocentric frame of reference, but any judgements made by an observer are dependent on the integrated activity of both eyes. This egocentric frame of reference yields a single visual direction with respect to the egocentre or cyclopean eye. One of the most fundamental aspects of vision is the integration of information from the two eyes to provide a single percept of the world. We have already described how the two sets of eye muscles operate like a single unit; does the same apply to the two sets of retinocentric signals? The evidence suggests that the signals from both retinas are combined independently of those for eye movements. The egocentric frame of reference is based upon information derived from the combination of a binocular retinocentric signal and a binocular eye movement signal (see Wade & Swanston, 1996).

If the information from each eye is equally weighted the egocentre is located midway between the two eyes. This is not always so, because one eye can have a greater influence than the other. For example, if the influence of the right eye is stronger than that of the left then the egocentre would be shifted towards the right eye. It was noted on page 128 that the neural signals from each eye go to adjacent eye preference slabs in the visual cortex, and so the possibility of the eyes contributing differentially to egocentric direction is present in the processing of information in the visual system. In fact one of the oldest tests of eye dominance is based upon assessing visual direction. It was described by a Neapolitan natural philosopher called Porta in 1593 (see Wade, 1998). If you look with both eyes at an object a few metres away and then point at it with your index finger, the finger will appear somewhat blurred but pointing at the target. While keeping the head and finger still, alternately close one eye and then the other. The finger will remain aligned when one eye is open, but not when the other is used. This is a test of sighting eye dominance. It can be refined somewhat by carrying out the task not by pointing a finger but by locating the target in a hole in the centre of a card held in both hands; this avoids problems associated with changing fixation from the far object to the nearer finger, as well as a possible bias from using the preferred hand. About 65% of the population are right eye sighting dominant, 30% are left eye dominant, and the remainder do not have a preferred sighting eye. Porta believed that right-handed people were also right-eyed, but there is no simple link between hand and eye preference.

Binocular single vision

Porta also proposed an intriguingly simple theory to account for binocular single vision. He suggested that we only use one eye at a time! We know that such permanent suppression of signals from one eye does occur in about 4% of the population, usually arising as a consequence of an uncorrected squint in childhood. These individuals can see with each eye alone, although the acuity is much poorer in the deviating eye. When both eyes are open such individuals are functionally monocular, in that neural signals from the normal eye suppress those from the deviating one, as though they only had one eye open. A similar form of suppression can be demonstrated in people with normal binocular vision. The vertical and horizontal gratings shown in

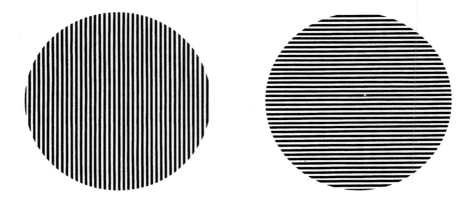

Figure 4.8 Rivalry patterns. Binocular rivalry can be seen with suitable observation of
these gratings. If your eyes converge on a point between you and the gratings then the latter can both appear to have the same visual direction.
Some people can achieve this without any assistance, for others it is necessary to align, say, a finger-tip with the vertical grating when using the right
eye and the horizontal grating when using the left eye. When this is
achieved three gratings will be visible—vertical on the left (as seen by the
left eye alone), horizontal on the right (as seen by the right eye alone) and
the central area where they overlap. Binocular rivalry occurs in this central
region, resulting in the fluctuating appearance of the gratings.

Figure 4.8 have different visual directions upon initial inspection. However, if
you look at the tip of a finger held between the patterns and your eyes its
position can be adjusted so that it will appear to point towards the vertical
grating when the right eye is open and to the horizontal grating with the left
eye. Move the finger until you find a position that is aligned with the base of
the centre of the vertical grating with the right eye and the horizontal grating
with the left. Keeping your finger as steady as possible fixate its tip with both
eyes. Initially the gratings will appear a little blurred, because the state of
accommodation is closely linked to the degree of convergence between the
eyes. If you persevere for a minute or so the vertical and horizontal gratings
will have the same visual directions, but they will not both be visible at the
same time: Occasionally only one grating will be seen, but more often a
complex mosaic made up of local vertical and horizontal regions will be
visible. The mosaic is itself dynamic, undergoing constant changes in its
composition. This phenomenon, which is called binocular rivalry, is of particular interest because we do not see a stable grid, but rather an alternation
between parts of the two differently oriented gratings. Binocular rivalry also
occurs when different colours are presented to each eye—rather than seeing
an additive combination of the colours (as would be produced by projecting
them independently onto a screen) we see an alternation between them (see
Howard & Rogers, 1995).

The mosaic patterns that we see are made up from local regions in one eye that are suppressing the corresponding regions in the other eye. The fact that such percepts occur at all contradicts Porta's theory, but it does indicate that binocular vision involves aspects of competition as well as cooperation. Competition, or rivalry, takes place when corresponding regions of each eye are presented with different patterns. This provides yet another means for determining eye dominance. If rivalling patterns are viewed for some fixed duration, say 1 min, and the duration for which each pattern is completely visible is measured, then the two durations could be compared. The eye receiving the pattern that was seen longer is called rivalry dominant and, surprisingly, it is not necessarily the same as the sighting dominant eye. That is, sighting and rivalry measures reflect different aspects of eye dominance.

The alternative theoretical view concerning binocular single vision to Porta's was proposed at about the same time—at the beginning of the seventeenth century. It was that objects are seen as single when they have the same visual direction, and that visual direction results from stimulation of corresponding points on the two retinas. Corresponding points have the same retinocentric coordinate values with respect to the foveas: If the two retinas were exactly superimposed on top of one another then contacting points would be corresponding. Returning to the example of the graphs mentioned earlier, the origins of the two graphs are like the foveas in the two retinas, and the two points on the graphs would be corresponding because they have the same coordinates (2,2) with respect to the origin. Corresponding points can also be described geometrically: With fixation on a given point, all other points lying on a circle passing through the fixation point and the optical centres of each eye fall on corresponding points. This definition of corresponding points was formulated nearly two centuries ago by two German physiologists, Vieth and Müller, and it is now referred to as the Vieth–Müller circle. The geometrical values of the projections to each eye also apply to the egocentre (see Figure 4.9). The geometrical definition is too restrictive in practice; it would predict that only those objects falling on the Vieth–Müller circle would be seen as single and having the same visual directions for each eye.

As the distance of the fixated object from the eyes increases the Vieth–Müller circle becomes very large, and for all intents and purposes it can be thought of as a plane, and so corresponding points lie on a fronto-parallel plane (at right angles to the straight ahead). In fact, the conditions that have been mentioned above approximate stimulation in a fronto-parallel or frontal plane. When we fixate on an object in the frontal plane we can still see objects singly when they are slightly in front or behind it. However, they do not then share the same visual directions for each eye, and neither of these correspond to the egocentric visual direction. The difference in visual direction from each eye is referred to as retinal disparity. Thus, we see the objects separated in depth with respect to the fixated object, and in directions defined with respect to the egocentre.

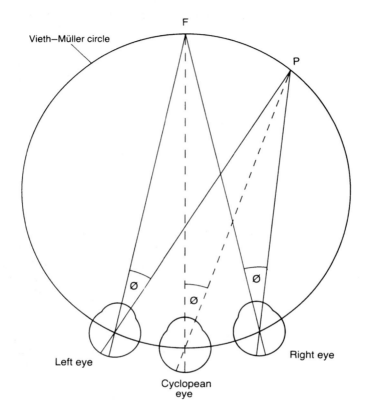

Figure 4.9 Vieth–Müller circle. With binocular fixation on a point (F) a circle
can be described that passes through the point and the optical
centres of each eye. Any other point (like P) on the circumference of
the circle will stimulate corresponding points in each eye. The angle
subtended by the two points will be the same at each eye, and also at
the cyclopean eye. (After Howard, 1982)

There is a limit to the disparity that can be processed to yield depth perception. Only stimuli quite close to the Vieth–Müller circle, in a region referred
to as Panum's fusional area, can be seen in depth on the basis of disparity
alone. Beyond the range where noncorresponding stimulation results in perceived singleness and depth, it would be expected that objects would be seen
as having two visual directions. However, we are rarely aware of seeing double
images, even though the conditions for their visibility occur constantly.
Whenever you fixate on a near object, more distant ones can have radically
different alignments for each eye, but they are not often seen double. This can
easily be demonstrated by fixating a finger, held about 20 cm from the eyes,
and then closing each eye alternately. You will probably be surprised at the

large differences in alignment that are evident between the finger and the background objects, and yet they pose few problems for normal perception. One of the reasons for this is likely to be that the nonfixated objects are slightly out of focus because of the state of accommodation required for viewing the near finger. Another factor is the operation of binocular rivalry: The corresponding regions of each eye will be stimulated by quite different patterns, and so singleness can be served by suppressing one or the other in local regions.

A single target is seen singly when it falls on both foveas, but under circumstances such as observing the rivalling patterns in Figure 4.8, it is possible for a single target to be seen double, i.e., for one object to have two different visual directions. When the vertical and horizontal patterns were projecting to corresponding retinal regions, by converging on a point between them and the eyes, three patterns were visible—a vertical grating on the left, the rivalling patterns in the centre, and a horizontal grating on the right. Another way in which a single object can have two visual directions is by passively moving one of the eyes. Passive movement of an eye means it is displaced by means other than the extraocular muscles themselves. If you look at an object that is in relative isolation (like a clock on the wall) then gently press the corner of one eye, you will probably see two objects; one remains steady and the other appears to move as the eye is passively displaced. As soon as the pressure is removed from one eye the object appears single again. Passive eye movements of this type are distinguished from active or voluntary eye movements because the former do not modify our perception of direction in the way voluntary eye movements do. Voluntary eye movements are recorded internally and can be used to compensate for retinal image motions that occur as a consequence of them. No such compensation occurs for passive eye movements (see Ono, 1981).

The outcome of the computations based upon patterncentric, retinocentric and eye movement information from both eyes provide a representation of egocentric visual direction. This is a representation of the line along which a single target can be located or an angle between two targets. The lines or angles do not locate the targets unambiguously because their distances have not been determined.

VISUAL DISTANCE

Information about the direction of objects with respect to the perceiver is clearly important, but insufficient by itself to control anything but very simple sorts of behaviour, such as guiding oneself towards a target. For example, the tendency (called tropism) of plants and animals to grow or move towards certain sources of stimulation, and away from others, can be based on a sensory estimate of the direction in which the stimulation is strongest. However, an object could lie anywhere along a line of visual direction, and for most behaviour it is necessary to know the distance as well as the direction of objects in the environment. Together, distance and direction specify the location of an object in three-dimensional space. The size of an object cannot be known from direction alone, either. The lines of visual direction, which define the boundaries of an object, could correspond to any of a large number of identically shaped objects, with different sizes and distances. All that would be known is the angular size of the object, and this would not generally be sufficient for recognition or appropriate action. For human behaviour, and probably that of most vertebrates also, perception involves recovering both the direction and the distance of objects in the environment, so that their location is specified unambiguously.

Egocentric distance is the distance separating the observer from some environmental feature. This is sometimes misleadingly called absolute distance, although it is in fact relative to the observer. Relative distance is the term normally given to the separation in space of one object with respect to another. If the objects are stationary, their relative distance remains constant, despite any movement by an observer. As will be seen, one of the critical requirements of the visual system is to recover relative distances and directions in the environment despite movements of the observer's eyes, head and body.

Just as with direction, there is always a frame of reference involved in any specification of distance, and it is important to make this explicit in discussing distance perception. We are familiar with physical measurements of both egocentric and relative distances, using devices like rulers and tape-measures, and scales with units like inches and feet, or centimetres and metres. These scales provide metric distance information, which conveys not only the order of objects in depth, but also the distances between them. One reason such scales are needed is that experience teaches us not to rely on judgements of distance "by eye", if accuracy is required. Nevertheless, we obviously do perceive distances, whether accurately or not. Most people can apply familiar units to express their perception of distances, and are able to report how far away something appears, for example in centimetres. No doubt this is due to our constant use of such scales since childhood. However the guide dog that featured in Chapter 1 would have no such familiarity, but could still perceive distances and act accordingly.

Essentially, a perceptual system should represent distances in a way that is lawfully related to physical distances in the outside world, at least for the range of distances which cover the space where we can carry out actions. In effect, this means that perception should conform to the nature of the three-dimensional space in which we live. Such a requirement is unlikely to be met with complete accuracy, or to hold for longer distances. However, it is hard to imagine behaviour of any complexity without effective distance perception. Many of the activities needed for the survival of humans and guide dogs would be impossible if perceived distances did not correspond to the physical space in which the activities are carried out. Since we have evolved to survive in a three-dimensional environment, it is hardly surprising that we have developed perceptual systems capable of representing that environment with sufficient accuracy to guide our behaviour.

It is striking that many of our units of distance have their origin in human anatomy, like the length of the forearm or foot, or the stride when walking. Possibly, in the absence of verbal scales, distance may be expressed in terms of the muscular effort needed to reach a given point in the environment. Even someone who had difficulty in stating the apparent distance of a target might be quite good at reaching out and touching it. Human distance perception is quite poor at longer ranges, such as more than a few metres, as is well known to drivers, pilots, mountaineers, and golfers. Our ability to represent distances decreases outside the range of action of an unaided individual, and this may have important consequences for our ability to function effectively, or even survive, in a mechanised environment quite unlike that in which our species evolved.

How do we come to perceive distance at all? This question has been at the heart of perceptual investigation for centuries, and it is generally answered by description of the various sources of information about distance which are available to us. These sources of information are known as cues, and their identification and analysis has been an important achievement, although primarily on the part of artists rather than psychologists. There are a number of these cues, which under normal circumstances give rise to a reliable perception of distance. When failures occur it is generally because of the lack of strong cues to distance, which causes inaccurate perceptions. The major cues to distance are described in the following two subsections, in terms of their contribution to the perception of egocentric and relative distance.

Egocentric distance

Suppose that you are seated in a dark room, and a small illuminated disc appears in front of you. The disc will be at a particular physical distance, but at what egocentric distance, if any, will it be perceived? The apparent direction of the disc would vary, and it would appear to move around randomly (the autokinetic effect, see page 186). However, its distance would appear fixed and it would not seem to move towards or away from you. Under such reduced conditions, your perception of distance may be quite inaccurate, but the disc will still appear to be at some distance, even if this is erroneous. In fact, in a situation like this, observers will see an object as being at a particular distance, generally around 1.5–2 m, regardless of its physical distance. This has been called the specific distance tendency by Gogel (1969, 1973). The specific distance tendency ensures that some value of perceived distance will be present in the perception of any object. Generally, we are not strongly influenced by the specific distance tendency, because there are other, stronger, cues available. Gogel's work has demonstrated the strong influence of distance perception on the perception of other visual characteristics such as shape, orientation and motion. Gogel (1990) provides a good introduction to this approach to the analysis of perceived space.

One egocentric distance cue, accommodation, was described in Chapter 3. In principle, the accommodative state of the eye could provide information about distance, although as was discussed earlier this will be confounded with the light level in the environment and with the wavelength of the light. The question of whether, and to what extent, accommodation actually does play a part in determining perceived distance remains controversial. Probably it is at best a weak cue, which comes into play mainly at short egocentric distances, or when other sources of distance information are reduced.

Distance can be determined from ocular convergence provided the distance separating the two eyes is known (see Figure 4.10). This interocular distance (IOD) averages around 65 mm in adults, but varies quite considerably between individuals. It also changes within individuals as the result of growth, but presumably any changes are slow enough for us to adapt to them as they occur. Provided an object is straight ahead, its distance can be found from the ratio of the convergence angle to the IOD. More precisely, for this case, the distance is equal to half the IOD divided by the tangent of the angle by which each eye deviates from the straight ahead position. For objects away from the straight-ahead position, the relationship is more complex, but still solvable. It is not likely that the nervous system actually performs the operation of taking the tangent of an angle, but rather that there is in practice a consistent relationship between the state of the muscles that move the eyes, and the distance of centrally fixated objects. Such a relationship would be established as the result of visual and manipulative experience with objects, and the nervous system is good at detecting and recording the way in which one sensory event is correlated with another.

There is some disagreement as to exactly how information about ocular convergence might be obtained; the alternatives are either feedback from detectors in the ocular muscles themselves, or more likely, a copy of the commands sent to the muscles from the brain. In either case, for convergence to be an effective cue to distance, such information must be available, from whatever source. In order to show that convergence affects perceived distance, it is necessary to devise experimental conditions in which convergence can be controlled and altered, and other cues are eliminated or held constant.

Changes in convergence can lead to paradoxical effects on the perception of distance and size, which have caused some controversy as to whether convergence is a reliable cue to egocentric distance at all. Typically, if convergence is reduced so as to correspond to a greater distance, while the physical distance to the target remains constant, the perceived size of an object also increases. Similarly, perceived size decreases if convergence is increased. The paradoxical effect is that an observer may not also report that the perceived distance has changed, when the convergence does. Possibly we modify our judgement of distance on the basis of perceived size. A larger appearing object may be judged to be nearer, even though the information

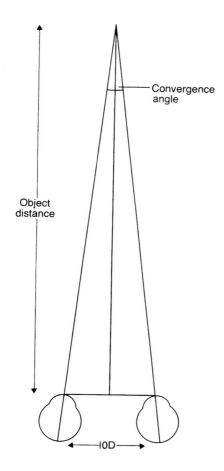

Figure 4.10 The geometry of ocular convergence and distance. The physical distance to the point on which the eyes are converged can be found from
the ratio of the interocular distance (IOD) to the angle by which
each eye deviates from the straight-ahead position. More precisely,
the distance is equal to the IOD divided by two times the tangent of
the convergence angle. This equation is only approximate if convergence is to a point which is not straight-ahead; beyond around
6 m the optic axes are effectively parallel for all points of fixation.

from convergence, which has determined the perceived size, indicates the
opposite.

Vergence movements change the state of convergence to different egocentric distances. Vergence movements are approximately equal in extent, but
opposite in direction, in the two eyes. In addition, as discussed earlier, the
eyes may move so as to change the point of fixation to a different egocentric

direction. Such version movements cause the eyes to move through equal extents in the same direction. Both vergence and version obey Hering's law, which states that the eyes act as a single functional unit, whose movements are always of the same extent—in the opposite direction for vergence, and in the same direction for version. Hering's law applies independently to vergence and version, which seem to be controlled independently. This can be seen clearly if fixation is shifted from one target to another at a different distance and in a different direction, which requires a change in both vergence and version. There is a shorter delay before the vergence movements start than is the case for version, so there is an initial change in vergence towards the distance of the new target. However, vergence movements are relatively slow compared to version, and before the new state of convergence has been reached, a rapid change in version takes place, appropriate to the direction of the new target. The vergence movement then continues until the target is imaged on the fovea in each eye. In each phase, eye movements obey Hering's law, although the overall result may be that each eye has moved by a different amount in order to change fixation.

Information which is geometrically equivalent to convergence can also be obtained by viewing an object from different directions, for instance when the head is moved from side to side. The change in an object's egocentric direction when viewed from two positions could be used to find the object's distance, if the extent of the head movement is known. There is some evidence that this cue of egocentric motion parallax can be used by human perceivers.

It is also possible that we are sensitive to the differential vertical magnification of images in the two eyes. When an object is beyond about 6 m, it projects images whose vertical size on the retina is effectively the same for both eyes. However as an object is brought closer, the eyes must converge if the object is to be imaged on the foveas of both eyes. As a result there is a difference between the vertical extent of the retinal images in each eye. Imagine that the object is an outline square, perhaps drawn on a piece of paper. If the eyes are appreciably converged, the retinal images will be trapezoidal, with the vertical nearest the nose shorter than the vertical nearest the temples. As can be seen from Figure 4.11, however, the nasal and temporal lines represent opposite sides of the square in each eye. Thus the nasal vertical in the left eye corresponds to the temporal vertical in the right eye. This difference between the vertical extent of images falling on corresponding regions of each eye increases as an object is brought closer. This is a purely optical source of information about distance, in that although it arises as the result of convergence, its interpretation does not require information about the positions of the eyes (Howard & Rogers, 1995).

One question raised by the above discussion is how we are able to see the distances of objects beyond around 6 m. Conventionally, rays of light emanating from a source at 6 m or more are said to lie at optical infinity, because they are effectively parallel to the optical axis. There will therefore be no appreciable convergence of the eyes when viewing an object at or beyond this

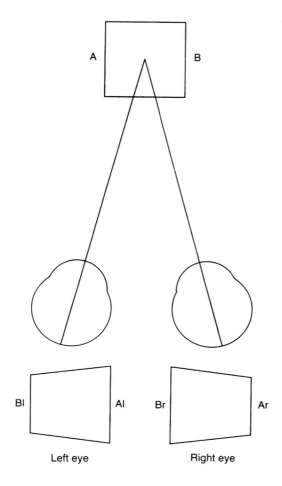

Figure 4.11 Vertical disparity produced by convergence. The stimulus is a square with equal sides, but its optical projection to each eye is unequal. The trapezoids represent the left and right retinal images of the square, and show that the temporal vertical sides are longer than the nasal ones. Binocular fusion takes place between Al and Ar, and between Bl and Br. The difference in the projected lengths of these pairs constitutes the vertical disparity. This provides a cue to the distance of the stimulus, since it varies with convergence.

distance. Clearly, the world does not appear to collapse into two dimensions as cues to egocentric distance are reduced, so there must be additional processes at work. One possibility would be the familiar size of objects. If the things we see at a distance are familiar from past experience, such as people, buildings, or vehicles, then we might base the perception of their distance on our knowledge of their true physical size. This would require that the perceived size of the object is compared to some representation in memory of how big the object actually is. The ratio of perceived size to remembered physical size could then be used to derive the distance. The role of familiar size in distance perception has been the subject of many experiments. What seems to be the case is that the perceived size of objects, whether or not they are familiar, is based on their retinal size and their perceived distance. This gives a perceived size which may or may not correspond to familiar, remembered size. If there is a discrepancy between the size that a familiar object appears to be, and the size which we know it to have, then we may alter what we *say* we think its distance is. If you look down from a tall building towards people on the ground, there is very little distance information available. The people below will look small, despite our knowledge that they are not likely to be abnormal in this respect. Thus our perceptions will not be altered by our past knowledge, but our verbal interpretations and possibly our actions may be (Gogel, 1993).

Relative distance

The various cues that indicate the relative distance between objects enable us to extend the perception of distance in the environment beyond the range of egocentric cues, and also to obtain information about the three-dimensional structure of objects. In themselves these cues cannot give an egocentric scale of distance or depth; they can indicate the relative separations of objects and parts of objects, but the scaling of the separation is ambiguous. Given three points at different distances, relative cues would enable an observer to state that the distance from A to B is twice that from B to C, but not to give metric information about these separations. If the points A, B, and C lie on the surface of a solid object, relative cues will correctly specify its shape, but not its overall size. That is, it would be possible to recover the three-dimensional shape of a car, and recognise it as such, but not to say what size it was, or even whether it was a real car or a toy. However, if the egocentric distance to any one point is known, perhaps from convergence, then this allows relative distances to be scaled unambiguously. This means that relative cues can provide distance information extending out to a greater range than is possible with egocentric cues alone. All that is needed is the egocentric distance to one nearby point, to act as a stepping-stone for the rest of the visual scene. In principle the relative distances between objects could be obtained from a series of egocentric distances; if the distances to A and B are known independently, the distance from A to B could be given by subtraction. In practice, as we have seen, egocentric distance information is not available much beyond the range of physical action, and its primary role seems to be to provide a metric for interpreting the cues that specify relative distances directly.

The first people to understand the importance of cues to relative distance were painters, rather than scientists. The problem is to establish how far such pictorial cues to distance are important for normal perception. Clearly, to the extent that they work in pictures, they are able to influence perception. What is more doubtful is whether we should regard the perception of pictures as representative of normal perception. This might be reasonable if the retinal image were a single static "snapshot" of the external world, like a picture, but in fact it is not. Not only does perception derive, in those with two eyes, from the combination of two different images, but these images are in constant motion as the result of eye movements and head movements. Many textbook descriptions of distance and depth perception are primarily accounts of the perception of pictures, and this leaves out all the information that is available to an active, moving perceiver.

In principle, the effectiveness of a relative cue to distance can be measured by presenting it in isolation, and assessing the extent to which it creates a perception of depth. In practice, experimental techniques cannot eliminate all information about depth other than the cue being studied. There is therefore a cue conflict, and the actual perception of distance is a compromise between the various sources of information, depending on their strength. A good example of this is the perception of depth in pictures. A picture may incorporate a number of cues to relative depth, such as overlap, height in the picture plane, perspective, and shadowing. All these cues can indicate consistent depth, and need not conflict with each other. However they do conflict with other information that specifies a flat plane, arising from the picture surface, its frame, and surroundings. The depth that we see therefore depends on a compromise between the various cues. Cues to the flatness of a picture can be reduced, for example by creating an image on a surface without a visible texture and without a clearcut frame. If so, the impression of depth in a picture can be markedly increased, as is the case with large screen projections in the cinema. Picture perception will be discussed further in Chapter 7.

Stereoscopic depth perception

A compelling cue to relative depth arises when the images of an object fall upon different retinal areas in the left and right eyes (Figure 4.12). As described previously, stimulation of corresponding retinal locations gives rise to single vision, and perception of a single visual direction. If the stimulated locations are very different, double vision results. Between these two extremes, there is a range where stimulation of noncorresponding points causes single vision and the appearance of depth. The process that gives rise to depth in this way is called stereopsis, and it is probably the most intensively investigated phenomenon in the history of vision research.

The geometry of binocular disparity was described long before the function that it serves was appreciated. In fact, the link between disparity and stereopsis was not described until 1838, when the physicist Charles Wheatstone published his account of the stereoscope and the experiments he had

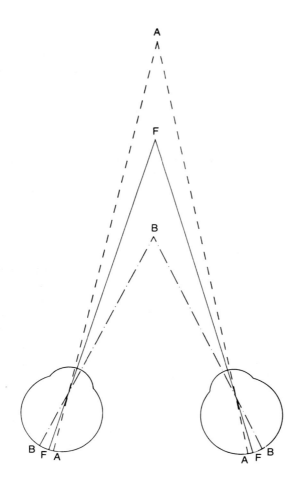

Figure 4.12 The geometry of retinal disparity. Both eyes fixate on point F, so that
its image falls on the fovea of each eye. The images of points A and
B, which are respectively further and nearer than F, fall on noncorresponding points. These differences in the projections from the two
points are referred to as retinal disparities. If the disparities are not
too great they can be processed in the visual system to provide
information for relative distance, called stereoscopic depth perception or stereopsis. The sign of disparity depends on whether the
nonfixated point is nearer or further than the fixation distance. Disparities can be described in terms of visual directions. Point A
appears to the right of F when viewed by the right eye alone, and to
the left with the left eye; this is called uncrossed disparity. Conversely, point B appears to the left of F when viewed by the right eye,
and to the right with the left eye; this is referred to as crossed disparity. These differences in visual direction can easily be demonstrated.
Hold both index fingers straight ahead of the egocentre, with one a
few centimetres higher and further away from the other. If you fixate
on the nearer one the far one will have uncrossed disparity, whereas
fixation on the further one will result in crossed disparity for the
nearer one.

conducted with it (see Wade, 1983). A stereoscope is an instrument that permits presentation of slightly different figures to each eye independently. If the figures have the characteristics of the left and right eye views of an object, then the impression obtained is of a solid or three-dimensional figure rather than a flat one. There are several ways in which this can be achieved optically. Wheatstone's stereoscope consisted of two plane mirrors, at right angles to one another, which reflect figures mounted appropriately on the side arms (see Figure 4.13a). An alternative model based on lenses was devised in 1849 by a Scottish physicist, David Brewster (see Figure 4.13b), and it was this type of stereoscope that graced many a Victorian parlour. The popularity of the stereoscope in the nineteenth century was based not only on the impression of depth derived from two flat pictures, but also because it could be married to the newly invented art of photography.

In addition to systems based on lenses or mirrors, there are other ways of viewing a stereogram in order to obtain stereopsis. The basic requirement is that a different pattern of stimulation can be presented to each eye independently. Some people can voluntarily alter their ocular convergence so as to fuse the two halves of a stereogram, and thus see the represented depth. This free fusion becomes easier with practice, and it can be tried with Figure 4.14. Anaglyphs are stereograms in which the left and right eye images are superimposed, but printed in different colours, such as red and green. When seen with a red filter over one eye and a green one over the other, the combined image is separated into a red and black image to one eye with a green and black image to the other, and binocular fusion may take place between the disparate black images. This method is also effective with projected images, and has been the basis of so-called 3-D films. Although stereopsis in moving images is impressive, the anaglyph method is not entirely satisfactory because of the instability of binocular fusion with monocular images of different colours. The same result, but without the colour separation, can be achieved with polarizing filters. The left and right eye images are projected through vertically and horizontally polarised filters, and are viewed with corresponding filters in front of the eyes.

Wheatstone was able to free-fuse easily, but he made the mirror stereoscope so that those who had difficulties with free fusion could still experience stereoscopic depth from paired pictures. An even earlier description of depth perception without any optical device is called the wallpaper illusion (see Wade, 1998), because regularly patterned wallpaper is an ideal stimulus for inducing it. If similar, but laterally displaced, patterns are combined binocularly (by convergence at a depth plane in front of or behind the wall) then the surface is seen either in front of or behind the actual wall. This effect has been manipulated with great subtlety by Tyler and Clarke (1990) to produce autostereograms consisting of a multitude of small elements. Rather than having all the elements evenly spaced, autostereograms have some repeated at regular horizontal separations and others varying by precisely computed extents. When the repetitive elements are combined by over- or under-convergence

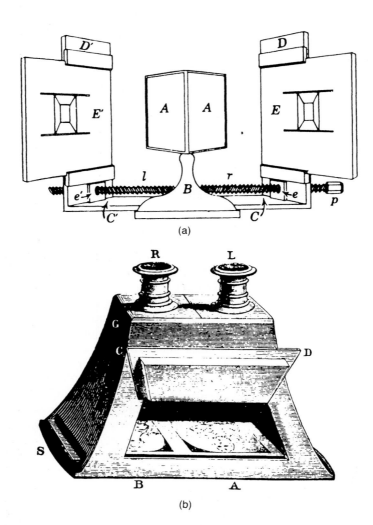

(a)

(b)

Figure 4.13 (a) Wheatstone's mirror stereoscope. The two slightly different perspective drawings of a solid object are placed on the side panels and their images are reflected to each eye via the mirrors (A). (b) Brewster's lenticular stereoscope. Half-lenses are located in the viewing tubes and act as magnifiers and prisms, so that the two pictures (A and B) appear to be straight ahead. This type of stereoscope was particularly popular in the latter half of the nineteenth century for combining stereophotographs.

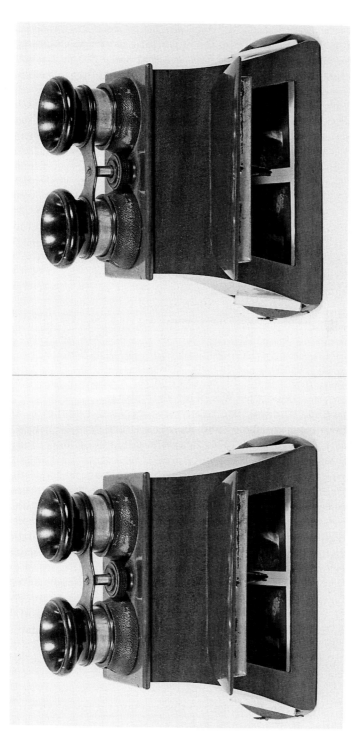

Figure 4.14 Stereophotograph of a stereoscope. The method for combining images in different locations, described in the caption to Figure 4.8, can be used to fuse this stereopair. The left and right images have been arranged so that the one on the left should be viewed by the right eye, and the one on the right by the left eye. If these photographs were combined with a stereoscope, so that the left one went to the left eye, then the disparities would be reversed, as would the perceived depth.

then particular patterns emerge in depth. Like their close cousins, random dot stereograms, autostereograms are easy to see by some people but others require considerable time and practice to see the depth that they can express.

The geometry of binocular projections, as shown in Figure 4.12, was known and illustrated in the sixteenth and seventeenth centuries, but binocular vision was considered solely in terms of visual directions (see Wade, 1987). An object that was further away than the point of binocular fixation appeared directed to the right side when using the right eye alone, and to the left side when using the left eye alone. This is now called uncrossed disparity. Conversely, a nearer object is said to have crossed disparity, because it appears directed to the left of the fixated point when using the right eye and to the right when using the left eye. Prior to Wheatstone, the principal problem in the study of binocular vision was that of singleness of vision: How is the world seen as single when we have two different views of it? The generally accepted answer was that only objects with the same visual directions would be seen as single. In the terminology of the previous section (pages 155–159), only objects stimulating corresponding points (or falling on the Vieth–Müller circle) would be seen as single, all others would be double. Wheatstone demonstrated experimentally with the stereoscope that this was false: The stimulation of slightly noncorresponding points can yield singleness of vision, but it also results in the perception of depth. Accordingly, Wheatstone established for the first time that binocular vision is concerned with distance as well as direction, and it is for this reason that the instrument he invented and the experiments he conducted with it are so important.

Binocular or retinal disparity is a relative cue, because it applies to situations where one object is fixated (and therefore stimulates corresponding retinal points) while one or more other objects at different distances project to different regions of each eye. As can be seen from Figure 4.12, disparity can be produced either if an object is nearer than the plane of fixation, or further away. For an object of fixed size the disparity will vary with egocentric distance. Wheatstone described the changes that occur when an object approaches the eyes (or when an observer approaches an object): There are increases in retinal size, retinal disparity, convergence and accommodation. Despite these changes the object appears to remain the same size. Wheatstone conducted experiments to manipulate these cues independently, and of particular interest was the relationship between disparity and convergence. When retinal disparity was kept constant and convergence increased, perceived depth decreased. Conversely, when convergence was held constant and disparity was increased perceived depth increased. Therefore, under normal circumstances there is a trade-off between increasing retinal disparity and increasing convergence which serves to maintain the constancy of perceived depth.

These points can be emphasised by means of an example. Suppose that an object such as a pencil is held at a slant so that the point is towards you, and that you are fixating on the point. There is a disparity between the retinal images of the other end of the pencil, which alters as the whole pencil is moved towards or away from you. The relationship follows an inverse square law; the disparity is proportional to the inverse of the egocentric distance squared. Thus if the egocentric distance to the point of the pencil is doubled, the disparity of the far end will be a quarter of its original value. Because of this, in order to perceive that an object is a constant length in depth, it is necessary to scale the disparity with the perceived distance. Errors in perceived distance will produce errors in the perceived depth from disparity. The IOD also determines disparity; for any given physical depth interval, the disparity will be larger if the eyes are further apart. As with egocentric distance from convergence, the IOD must be available to the visual system.

Motion parallax

Although it is obviously necessary to view the world with two eyes in order to detect disparity, there is a functionally similar cue available to monocular vision, if the head moves from side to side. This cue is relative motion parallax, and its geometrical basis can be seen from Figure 4.15. This figure is identical to Figure 4.12, except that the two eyes have been replaced by a head, moving sideways through some distance. It is evident that the successive projections of objects on a single retina carry similar information about relative depth as does binocular disparity. If you move your head to the right so that your left eye is located in exactly the position previously occupied by your right eye, then the successive retinal projections to your left eye are identical to those that were available to your left and right eyes, with your head in its original position. Experiments have shown that the depth produced in this way is very similar, if not identical to stereopsis, and it is possible that both patterns of stimulation activate the same cortical mechanisms. For example, prolonged viewing of a stereogram of a corrugated surface produces an aftereffect in which a flat surface appears to be corrugated in the opposite direction, and this also occurs with depth due to motion parallax (Howard & Rogers, 1995).

Motion parallax consists of relative motion between the retinal images of objects at different distances, and is created by lateral motions of the observer's head. The kinetic depth effect shows that relative motion may also act as a cue to depth even if seen by a stationary observer. Suppose an object is placed behind a back projection screen, and illuminated by a source of light such as a projector. If the object is stationary, its two-dimensional shadow projected on the screen will convey little or no information about the three-dimensional form of the object. However, if the object is rotated, an observer will report the appearance of a solid object, rather than relative motions between parts of a flat shadow.

If one eye is covered, and the head is kept still, the visual world does not suddenly cease to appear three-dimensional. The cues available in this situation are primarily those which were referred to above as pictorial, because of

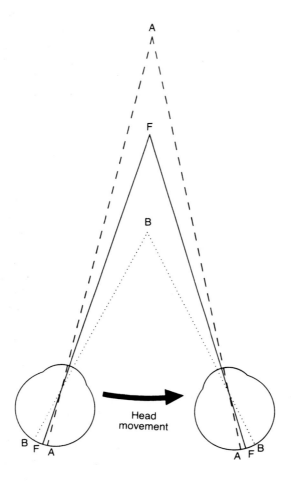

Figure 4.15 The geometry of relative motion parallax. The observer maintains
    fixation on point F, while moving his head from left to right through
    the distance shown by the arrow. The images of points A and B,
    which are respectively further and nearer than F, are displaced across
    the retina, by an amount which depends on the extent of the move-
    ment and the distance of the points relative to the plane of fixation.
    The distances AF and BF can be recovered if the egocentric distance
    to F and the extent of the movement are known. The pattern of
    stimulation, and the necessary sources of information, are analogous
    to the binocular disparity produced by static observation with two
    eyes (compare Figure 4.12).

their use in graphical representations. Despite the term, however, they are also present in natural scenes, which is why they are also effective in pictures. Several such cues have their origin in the fact that the retinal projection of any object or surface decreases in angular size with increasing distance. This fact of geometry means that natural scenes contain perspective due to differences in relative retinal size between similar objects at different distances. Also, more distant objects on a ground plane are located higher in the visual field than nearer ones. Most natural surfaces have a visible texture, and artificial ones commonly have either decorative patterns or a regularly repeating structure. When seen at a slant such surfaces therefore display a gradual change in the density of the texture. Such texture gradients provide information not only about relative distance between the nearest and furthest parts, but also about the rate of change of distance; that is, edges, steps, corners, and other surface features. Relative size may also change over time. If an object approaches you, its retinal projection increases in angular size. That this can act as a cue to relative distance is shown by the fact that observation of images undergoing expansion and contraction produces a compelling perception that the represented object is moving in depth, towards and away from the observer (Swanston & Gogel, 1986). The constraints of optical geometry also ensure that opaque objects obscure more distant ones where they overlap, or modify the colour or brightness of the transmitted light if they are transparent. If the observer moves, different portions of obscured objects become visible, and this revealing or obscuring of texture can itself function as a cue to distance.

Over very long distances in the natural environment the colour of surfaces tends to become bluer. This effect, known as aerial perspective, is due to the absorption and scattering of shorter wavelengths by dust and moisture particles in the atmosphere, and gives a sense of receding panorama to a landscape. In very dry or clear air aerial perspective is reduced, and it may be hard to judge the distance and size of landscape features. Aircraft pilots and mariners report problems with navigation as a result. The importance of the various cues to distance in the natural environment is shown when they are reduced or eliminated; the perception of space then becomes very uncertain. In the absence of strong cues to distance, adjacent areas of the field of view tend to take on similar apparent distances, a phenomenon which is called the equidistance tendency (Gogel, 1978). This effect can be quite pronounced if a distant scene is observed through a nearby frame, like a window. The strong cues available for the distance of the frame tend to make the whole scene appear to be at the same distance.

It is common for textbooks to include an illustration showing the various cues to relative distance. We feel that this may be misleading, since the impression of depth in pictures is complex, and invariably based on a number of conflicting cues. Alternatively, the cues mentioned earlier can all be seen by observing your own visual environment. If you look at a nearby object, such as a pen held at arm's length, you can note the difference between the views of the object available to each eye, by opening and closing each eye alternately. Using both eyes, converge on a surface about 1 m beyond the pen, and you will see the double images of it, since they have too great a degree of crossed disparity to be fused. If you reduce the distance between the pen and the further surface, the double images will disappear and you should see a single pen and the background separated in depth. Now observe with one eye only, but move your head from side to side through about 10 cm. The depth should reappear, this time from motion parallax. With a stationary head and with one eye covered, look at the room you are in, or out of a window if possible. If there is enough distance, you can observe the presence of perspective in the texture of walls, floors or ceilings, and in the convergence of actually parallel contours. If there are a number of objects in view, some will partially obscure others, providing the cue of interposition. Note the presence of shadows; we generally tend to ignore their presence, but they carry information about the shape of the objects that cast them, or the surface on which they fall, if the location of the light source is known. Paradoxically, the fact that you can see these effects with monocular observation and a stationary head means that they are at best partially effective as cues to distance. If they were wholly effective, then they would cause the modification of perceived size to correspond to the actual physical distance, and no differences in relative size would be apparent.

NAVIGATION

The issues discussed in this chapter have concerned determining our location in space—deriving a geocentric representation of the locations of objects in the surrounding environment relative to us. This provides the coordinates to control our behaviours like reaching, writing, and ambulation. Crossing the road engages all the processes already discussed as well as those for motion and recognition (Chapters 5 and 6). However, these actions are often undertaken to accomplish tasks that can be beyond the scope of perception; that is, the goal or end point is not available to the senses. When we cross the road we can see the other side that we wish to reach, but when we go to catch a bus we may be far away from the route that the bus takes so that we need to navigate through the environment to get to the bus stop, detect the appropriate bus, and alight. We typically use mental maps of the environment to navigate successfully, and such cognitive tasks are beyond the scope of this book. None the less, a little will be said about navigation.

There is much debate about the form these mental maps take and how we use them. Are they comprised of landmarks that we link, do we have formal internal lists of directions that we follow, or do they conform to the layout of a geographical chart? Charts or graphs have similar features because they represent arbitrary two-dimensional surfaces on which distances are compressed in some convenient way. For maps this is determined by the scale, for example 1 km on the earth's surface could be scaled down to 1 cm on a map. Locating a position on a map can be given by the values of latitude and longitude, both of which have to be derived from other measurements for those travelling by air or sea. It is somewhat easier to determine positions on graph paper because the position of the axes (with respect to the earth's surface) are themselves arbitrary so that any point on the graph can be given a vertical and horizontal coordinate. We tend to take maps and graphs for granted, although they are of relatively recent invention, and have afforded enormous advances in geography and geometry. Mercator devised the system of map projection that bears his name in the sixteenth century, and Cartesian coordinates (named after Descartes) were described in the following century.

It would seem clear that the characteristics of navigation might differ greatly from the geocentric perception that we achieve, but the concepts used to describe them are similar. Howard (1993) has made a distinction between frames of reference based on the observer's position (what we have referred to as geocentric) and those adopting an origin outside the observer (which he calls exocentric). Such an exocentric map would typically be two-dimensional and would include the position of the observer within it, so that navigation between various features of the environment could be achieved. One of the tasks for applied vision research is to determine the type of exocentric map that assists active observers in complex tasks, such as flying (see Wickens, 1999).

5 Motion

We need to locate objects not only in space but also in time. Without the temporal dimension spatial location alone would be of little use to us. Of course, change in spatial location over time is motion. Retinal image motion can be a consequence of displacement either of an object relative to a stationary environment or of an observer relative to a stationary object. In addition both object and observer could move together. All these conditions result in changes in the pattern of stimulation at the eyes, but despite these we retain an appropriate representation both of our position in space and that of the object. Occasionally, errors do occur in our perception of motion, and these can be very instructive in understanding the nature of motion perception.

One example that most people have experienced is the false allocation of motion that can occur when seated in a stationary train as a neighbouring train pulls slowly away from the station. We initially perceive the carriage in which we are seated to be moving, and this false allocation is only later replaced by the veridical percept when the other train is moving faster. Why does this happen? In order to understand it we need to examine the frames of reference that are present. First consider the situation when the train in which we are seated moves out of a station. There is a relative displacement of the platform with respect to the windows of the carriage. Some aspects that were initially visible disappear from view and others that were previously occluded become visible. The rate of these changes increases as the velocity of the train increases. Any stable environment will produce such an optic flow (to use one of Gibson's terms) with respect to a moving vehicle, and so it is this characteristic that usually defines vehicular motion. In the case where the neighbouring train starts to move the optic flow produced is ambiguous—it could be a consequence of either train moving, but it is more common for the motion of the whole visual field to specify self motion rather than motion of the environment. The illusion of motion only occurs if the neighbouring train is close enough to occupy most of the view visible through a large window; if it is several tracks away, so that other parts of the station are visible, then there is no illusion. One of the reasons that we cease to experience motion of our own carriage after some seconds is that the illusory motion is not accompanied by the slight carriage motions that do occur when our train is actually moving. We can register these via receptors in the inner ear (in the vestibular system) that signal body motion through space. There is, then, a conflict between visual information signalling self motion and vestibular information signalling that the body is stationary; initially vision is dominant but it is later modified by the vestibular signals for stability. However, the situation is rather more complicated than this, because the eyes rarely remain fixed with respect to the surrounding environment. During the illusory motion we can look around the carriage and perceive that it is stable. Thus, some image motions over the retina (due to eye movements) result in perceptual stability of the carriage whereas others (due to motions relative to the window frame) produce an illusion of motion.

It is clear from this example that there are many aspects to motion perception—motion with respect to the eyes due to eye movements, motions of the head, and relational motions within the visual field. It is for this reason that we will treat motion perception in a similar way to that adopted for the perception of location, namely by starting with simple situations and building up to more complex ones that more typically reflect our normal perception in a well-structured environment. The first stage will be to consider motion with respect to a single, stationary eye, then eye movements will be introduced, and finally head and body motions will be included. The resulting perception is of motion with respect to the stable frame of reference of the earth's surface. Our representation of location and motion is with respect to this stable frame of reference, which we refer to as geocentric. It might not appear so from many experiments concerned with motion perception, because they are often conducted under unnatural conditions involving a fixed head, and sometimes with stimuli that are presented for such short intervals that the eyes cannot move over them.

The example that we have chosen to illustrate an illusion of motion is also unnatural. Our species, like all others, has evolved to process motions that occur in the natural environment and to compensate for the consequences of our own biological motions. These latter involve rotations of the eyes, and translations of the head produced by walking, running, jumping, and turning. We have not evolved to compensate for the vagaries of vehicular travel, although we do so successfully most of the time. Similarly, we have not evolved to process briefly presented sequences of still pictures, like those produced on television and in films, although we do derive a compelling illusion of motion from them. Many experiments on motion perception have focused on this type of apparent motion, to the detriment of research on what is called real motion. We will try to redress the balance a little by concentrating on object and observer motions.

SOURCES OF MOTION STIMULATION

One of the paradoxes of visual motion perception is that movement over the retina is not a necessary condition for its occurrence. This has been established most clearly in laboratory experiments, but it can also be demonstrated in a number of naturally occurring phenomena. When the moon is observed on a cloudless night it appears to be stationary. However, when clouds pass near or over the moon it appears to move, even when we maintain fixation on it. This is called induced movement, and it is a clear instance of visual motion without retinal displacement. We will return to the phenomenon of induced movement later in this chapter, but for the moment it suffices to indicate that we need to consider more than retinal motion if we are to understand the perception of motion.

Motion over the retina can be produced in a wide variety of ways, because of the complex motions that observers can make with respect to a stationary environment, as well as the motions of objects in that environment. In this section we will outline the major sources of motion stimulation that follow from observer and object motions, and we will also describe some of the motion phenomena that are studied by visual scientists.

Observer motions

Observer motions can be considered in terms of the principal articulations that change the position of the eyes in space. The most basic level is that of eye movements. All eye movements relative to the orbit are rotations. The centre of rotation is located about 13.5 mm behind the cornea, and rotations can occur around a vertical axis (towards and away from the nose), around the horizontal axis between the eyes (elevation and depression) and around the optical axis of the eye (torsion). The rotations can be slow and smooth, as when pursuing a moving object, or they can be very brief and ballistic.

Many eye rotations occur as a consequence of head movements, and their function is to maintain fixation on environmental stimuli despite the change in head position. Such compensatory eye movements result from stimulation of receptors in the vestibular system, and they take place both quickly and with precision; they are referred to as vestibulo-ocular reflexes. Amongst these are the "doll's eye reflexes"—when the head rotates upward and backward about a horizontal axis the eyes retain the same direction with respect to the environment. That is, they rotate in the opposite direction to the head, as occurs with many dolls which have movable eyes. There are similar compensatory eye rotations for the other rotations of the head in space.

The head undergoes translations as well as rotations in space. The translations can be very complex because of the many articulations that are possible with other body parts—the head on the trunk, rotations of the torso, and bending at the hips and knees. Many of these articulations are a function of locomotion, and the motion of the head during walking and running is more uniform than that of other body parts. This can be seen most clearly in animals with lateral eyes: If you watch the head of a bird, like a seagull, when it is walking, its head remains relatively fixed in space and then moves rapidly forward, remaining there until another rapid forward movement is made. When we walk the head motion follows a path that is more nearly horizontal, despite the appreciable vertical movements of other parts of our body. We do not have the jerky head movements that are common in birds because both our eyes are pointing in the direction of motion. We can fixate on some distant object straight ahead and maintain fixation during locomotion.

The optical consequences of head movements can be distinguished from those produced by eye movements. When a single eye rotates all objects in a scene that are aligned in one eye position remain aligned following a rotation. You can easily ascertain that this is so. Keeping your head still, and closing one eye, look at some objects that are in the same direction but at different distances from you; when you rotate the eye they will remain aligned. Another characteristic of eye rotation is that some parts of the scene that were formerly visible disappear, and others that were not initially visible are disclosed. This occurs symmetrically for elevations and depressions, but not quite so symmetrically for rotations about a vertical axis. The visual field is not evenly bounded on the nasal and temporal sides, and so turning the eye in a nasal direction results in the nose obscuring a larger part of the visual field than is the case when the eye rotates temporally. All these features are unique to rotations of an eye, and they can be contrasted to the consequences of head rotations and translations.

Head rotations, as in turning to the left or right, involve translations of the eye as well as changes in direction. This results in the relative displacements of objects at different distances. Again, you can easily demonstrate this for yourself. Try to keep the position of the single open eye constant in the orbit and rotate the head: Objects no longer retain the same alignments, and near objects can occlude parts of more distant ones that were formerly visible or, conversely, disclose parts that were formerly hidden from view. Moreover, the occlusion and disclosure at the left and right boundaries of the visual field does not change the proportion of the field occupied by the nose. Thus, the pattern of visual stimulation can serve to differentiate between rotations of the head and of the eye.

Head movements can also be translations in the three dimensions of space. Forward movement results in a radial expansion of the visual field; if the gaze is straight ahead, then objects at the extremities of the visual field are lost from sight, and distant ones are enlarged. Movement towards a large object results in it occluding more of the background, and the optical expansion increases greatly with impending contact. Sideways movement produces a horizontal optic flow, and upward movement results in a vertical flow. In each case there is a symmetrical change at the extremities of the field, and objects at different distances undergo relative displacements.

Object motions

All the retinal motions described above have been considered with respect to a stable and stationary environment. Additional retinal displacements follow from object motion. When a rigid object moves with respect to a stationary background certain transformations in the optic array occur which can be used to determine the path of object motion. Suppose a rectangular object moves in a frontal plane, then parts of the background will become occluded by the leading edge, other parts will be disclosed by the trailing edge, and there will be shearing along the edges parallel to the motion. You can produce such motion with this book, by holding it at arm's length and moving it horizontally and vertically; note the displacements of the book with respect to objects in the background. This pattern of relative displacements will apply whatever orientation the book is held in, as long as its motion path is in the frontal plane. If, however, the book is rotated in the frontal plane a different pattern of transformations will ensue. Some small part of the background remains occluded continuously, whereas other parts (those in close alignment to the edges of the book) are systematically and symmetrically occluded and disclosed. Yet other transformations follow from varying the angle of the book to the line of sight (rotating it about a vertical axis). The maximum amount of background is occluded when the book is in the frontal plane and the minimum amount when it is in the median plane (with its spine either towards or away from you); between these two extremes, the approaching edge expands optically and the receding edge contracts. Thus, there is optical information available in the patterns of transformation for the paths along which rigid objects move (Gibson, 1979). These three situations are illustrated schematically in Figure 5.1.

In these examples of object translations and rotations we have considered the transformations with respect to the visible background. What would be seen if the background was not visible? This situation is difficult to examine if an object like a book is visible, but it can be studied by attaching points of light to the four corners of the cover of a book and observing them in an otherwise dark room. Motion of the four points in a horizontal direction would not produce any changes in their relative position nor in their relative orientation (see Figure 5.2a). Under these circumstances the motion might not even be detected at all. If it was, it would be due to information from the eyes derived from pursuing the points. This is a situation that we refer to as uniform motion, and it will be discussed in more detail in the following sections. Rotation of the points in the frontal plane would not change the relative orientation of the points—they would remain in a rectangular configuration—but their orientation with respect to gravity would be changed (see Figure 5.2b). We can perceive motion accurately under these conditions, which indicates how important object orientation is in determining our perception of location and motion. The third transformation, rotation about a vertical axis, modifies both the relative

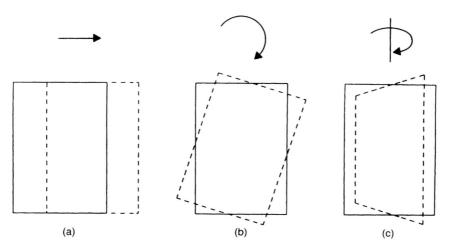

Figure 5.1 Optical transformations produced by a rectangular object (a) moving horizontally in the frontal plane, (b) rotating in the frontal plane, and (c)
rotating about a vertical axis. In addition to the optical transformations of
the object itself, different aspects of the background are occluded and
disclosed by each one.

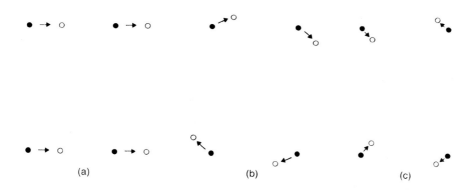

Figure 5.2 Optical transformations produced by four lights at the extremities of a
rectangular object (a) moving horizontally in the frontal plane, (b) rotating
in the frontal plane, and (c) rotating about a vertical axis.

separations and the relative orientations of the points. The lights on the
receding edge would remain vertical but their separation would decrease
while those on the approaching edge would increase and remain vertical;
the separations of the upper and lower points would decrease as would
their relative orientations (see Figure 5.2c). These complex transformations

are typically seen as a surface changing its bearing with respect to the observer.

The Swedish psychologist Gunnar Johansson has examined these conditions experimentally (see, for example, Johansson, 1973, 1975). Rather than attaching light points to the corners of a book he has simulated the transformations on a flat screen, so that only the four points are visible. He even made more subtle transformations than the ones described earlier. If just one of the points moves with respect to the others observers report that a surface, like a sheet of paper, is bending. As a consequence of these and many other experiments Johansson has proposed that the visual system spontaneously abstracts relational invariances in the optic flow and constructs percepts of rigid objects moving in three-dimensional space. Similar rigidity assumptions lie at the heart of computational approaches to motion perception. That is, transformations over time between imaged points will be interpreted as changes in the orientation of a rigid surface with respect to the position of observation.

Support for the rigidity assumption derives from research Johansson initiated on biological motion. These experiments are just like the situation described previously with placing lights on the extremities of a book. However, lights were placed on the joints of moving humans so that the many articulating parts would change the relative positions of the lights. Figure 5.3 illustrates a static view of lights placed on the shoulders, elbows, wrists, hips, knees and ankles of a walking person; not all 12 light sources are necessarily seen because some are occluded by the body. Without some prior knowledge (such as you now have) it would be difficult to discern the nature of the object so illuminated. As soon as the array undergoes movement the object is recognised as a person, and the nature of their movement can also be discriminated—whether running or walking, dancing, or drinking. It is unfortunate that this dramatic conversion from a static jumble of dots to a coherent perception of action cannot be illustrated in a book.

Our ability to make fine discriminations of biological motions has received considerable experimental attention (e.g., Kozlowski & Cutting, 1977; Mather & Murdoch, 1994; Runeson & Frykholm, 1981). With film sequences, human motion can be recognised in as little as $\frac{1}{10}$ s, that is, from just two frames of film. Reliable estimates of the gender of the lighted subject can be made, largely on the basis of differences in the centres of moment (the point in the body relative to which all movements are related); it is higher in females than males. With lights on the hips, knees, ankles and toes it is possible to distinguish between a walking male or female from a single step. Observers can estimate the weight of unseen objects on the basis of the relational dynamics of the points on the lifter. Thus, not only is the optic flow to a moving observer transformed in systematic ways, but the articulations of observed humans can be readily perceived. These examples demonstrate the perception of biological motion based on the detection of particular transformations in the optic array. In general, there is now a large body of work

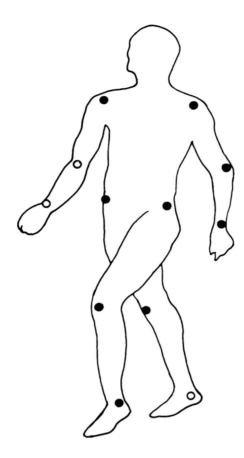

Figure 5.3 Six pairs of lights attached to the major articulations of the body; the filled dots would be visible and the unfilled ones would not be seen in the posture shown here. When a single static array is seen it is not recognised, but as soon as movement is added the lights are recognised as being attached to a person. (After Johansson, 1975)

which shows that the perception of many sorts of environmental events and the control of appropriate behaviour can be related to dynamic patterns of visual stimulation, in both humans and animals.

MOTION PHENOMENA

It is evident from the above discussion that motion over the retina can be produced in a wide variety of ways, many of which are a consequence of eye and head movements. These complex and dynamic patterns of stimulation might be thought of as making motion perception incredibly complicated, but we do not experience it as such. We perceive the world as stable despite all these perturbations; in fact, we are not usually aware that a problem exists. Psychologists hold differing views about both the nature of and the solution to the problem of perceiving moving and stationary objects. The description of optic flows above reflects Gibson's approach to motion perception. He has drawn attention to the lawfulness of the transformations that take place with eye and object motions and he suggests that we use them to determine both our posture and the motion of objects in the world. In spite of the promise of this approach, relatively little research has been addressed to it. Instead, the history of research on motion perception has focused mainly on simple phenomena that can be studied in the laboratory. Several nineteenth-century accounts of motion phenomena, like Addams's description of the waterfall illusion and Silvanus Thompson's list of "Optical illusions of motion", are reprinted in Dember (1964). Boring (1942) outlines the early experiments on visual persistence and apparent motion using instruments like the stroboscopic disc, as do Wade and Heller (1997).

Motion thresholds

Motion phenomena have a longer history than many other phenomena in visual perception. This is probably because certain aspects of motion perception in the natural world are paradoxical. One was mentioned earlier, namely, the induced motion of the moon when clouds pass near it. It was only when the laws of planetary motion were properly understood that a physical explanation (i.e., that the moon was actually displaced by the clouds) could be ruled out. Another phenomenon relates to visual vertigo: When the body has been turning and stops suddenly objects appear to continue moving. This is now known to be a consequence of involuntary eye movements which occur after rotation. Yet another motion phenomenon relates to the apparent movement of stars at night. In 1799, during his voyage to South America, the great German naturalist, Alexander von Humboldt, recorded that a certain star appeared to wander about haphazardly in the night sky. He even called the phenomenon "Sternschwankung" or star wandering. Other observers were able to see the phenomenon, too, though they did not all describe the haphazard movements in a similar way. A debate arose about the precise nature of the star movements, and it was decided that a particular star should be observed independently by several astronomers at the same time, and the reports of the motion paths could then be compared. When there was no consistency in the motions of the same star seen at the same time, it became clear that they were dealing with a perceptual rather than a physical phenomenon. The German physiologist Hermann Aubert called this the autokinetic phenomenon, and it is not confined to stars. If you look at a stationary and very dim light (like a glowing cigarette end) in an otherwise totally dark room it will appear to wander about haphazardly, like the star that von Humboldt observed.

Aubert (1865) imposed some degree of order on a wide range of visual phenomena, particularly those involving motion. For example, he measured the thresholds for detecting uniform and relational motions. When a target moved in isolation its motion could be detected when it reached a velocity of about 0.3°/s. When a patterned background was visible the threshold was approximately 0.03°/s. Isolated stimuli should therefore only be seen to move when they undergo quite large displacements. In the autokinetic effect there is no stimulus motion, so the perceived movement must be caused by some internal process, probably related to actual or suppressed movements of the eyes (Post & Leibowitz, 1985).

Motion aftereffects

The first half of the nineteenth century was a particularly rich period for describing novel motion phenomena. One that has been examined almost continually since its description in 1834 is the waterfall illusion. The phenomenon must have been seen countless times, but it was described initially by Robert Addams, a London chemist, during a tour of the Scottish Highlands. Addams observed the Falls of Foyers (Figure 5.4), located near Loch Ness, from a platform located on a level with the centre of the waterfall (Addams, 1834, quoted in Swanston & Wade, 1994, p. 1108):

> Having steadfastly looked for a few seconds at a particular part of the cascade, admiring the confluence and decussation of the currents forming the liquid drapery of waters, and then suddenly directed my eyes to the left, to observe the face of the sombre age-worn rocks immediately contiguous to the water-fall, I saw the rocky surface as if in motion upwards, and with an apparent velocity equal to that of the descending water, which the moment before had prepared my eyes to behold that singular deception.

Thus, rocks that were initially seen as stationary could appear to ascend following observation of descending water. We now call this a motion aftereffect, because it is not confined to waterfalls. It can be produced by prolonged inspection of almost any uniformly moving surface, but it is frequently studied in the laboratory with stimuli like those shown in Figure 5.5. Adaptation to motion is restricted to the area of the retina exposed to the real motion and it decays relatively quickly (Mather et al., 1998). Following inspection for around 30 s, motion in a stationary stimulus can be seen for up to 20 s; initially the velocity is high and then it decreases until the stimulus appears stationary once more. The motion seen as an aftereffect is itself somewhat paradoxical—the stationary stimulus appears to move but not to change position! For example, the rocks by the waterfall seem to ascend but they

Figure 5.4 A nineteenth-century engraving of the lower Fall of Foyers; Addams would have observed the waterfall from the observation point shown.

remain in the same position with respect to neighbouring rocks that are not subject to the apparent motion. The motion is termed paradoxical because any real motion of objects involves changes in location over time. The motion aftereffect is a negative aftereffect, like that for tilt described on page 138; that is, the appearance of motion in the stationary field is in the opposite direction to the real movement previously observed.

Motion interactions

Induced movement can also be studied with a wide range of stimuli, like those illustrated in Figure 5.6. The motion can be linear or circular, and the induced motion of a stationary stimulus is always in the direction opposite to the inducing movement. It is possible to move the inducing component so slowly that it cannot be detected, but it can still induce motion in the stationary component, provided that the inducer encloses the induced. This provides a powerful example of the operation of frames of reference in visual perception. If the induced component is itself moving then its path or velocity of perceived motion can be modified by motion of the inducer. Induced movement is a simultaneous disturbance of motion perception, rather than a

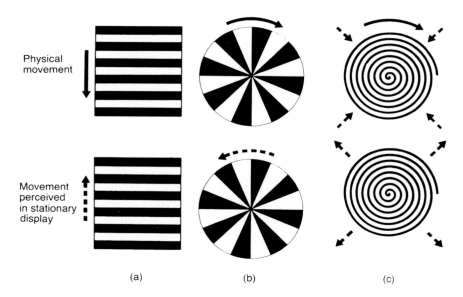

Physical movement

Movement perceived in stationary display

(a)　　　　　　　(b)　　　　　　　(c)

Figure 5.5 Laboratory stimuli that are used to produce motion aftereffects. (a) Linear motion of a grating, (b) rotation of a sectored disc, and (c) rotation of a spiral. The physically stationary patterns are initially seen as stationary. During the physical motion the movement is perceived as shown by the solid arrows, but the spiral also appears to contract. Following about 30 s adaptation the stationary patterns appear to move in the directions indicated by the dashed lines.

successive one like the motion aftereffect. It can operate over considerable distances, but is most effective when the inducer both surrounds the induced component and is close to it (see Wade & Swanston, 1987).

Another type of motion interaction, between a moving field and its fixed surround, is called the barber-pole illusion. The sign for a barber's shop is traditionally a pole with a white and red helix painted on it; when it rotates the stripes appear to be moving along the pole rather than rotating. This is because we cannot detect the motion within the white or red areas, but we can detect the motion of the contours defining their boundary. Suppose a field of random dots moves horizontally within a rectangular frame. The direction of motion will be seen unambiguously, and will not be altered if the frame has different orientations or shapes. There is a different outcome if the random dots are replaced by a pattern of black and white stripes oriented at an angle to the surrounding frame (hence the term barber-pole illusion, although in a real barber-pole the stripes are usually red and white). Now, the direction of motion is usually seen as aligned with the longer side of the frame, no matter what the physical direction of motion of the stripes may be.

With a barber-pole the stripes appear to move along its length, although

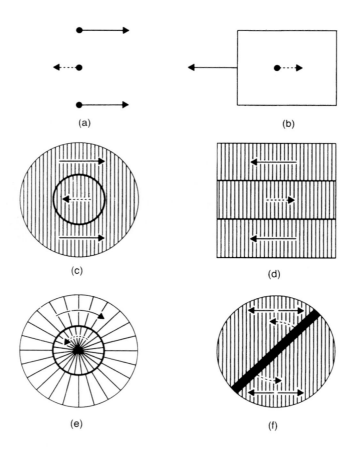

Figure 5.6 Laboratory stimuli that are used to induce movement in a stationary
target. In all cases the physically moving parts are shown by solid lines
and the dashed lines indicate the induced motion of the stationary
components. (a) Two moving dots, (b) dot and rectangle, (c) annular
movement of a grating, (d) flanking movement of gratings, (e) rotary
motion of a radial annulus, and (f) line rotation induced by optical
expansion of a grating. Linear induced motion is produced by (a)–(d),
rotary induced motion by (e), and a combination of linear and rotary
induced motion in (f).

they are painted as a helix, which is rotating. This represents a specific
instance of the general influence of visible frames on perception, and it is
referred to as the aperture problem. If the stripes behind a rectangular aperture were oriented vertically, and moved vertically, an observer would not be
expected to see any motion: In the absence of any texture in the stripes, there
is nothing to indicate physical displacement, and the retinal stimulation does
not change. When the stripes are oblique and are moved vertically, there is

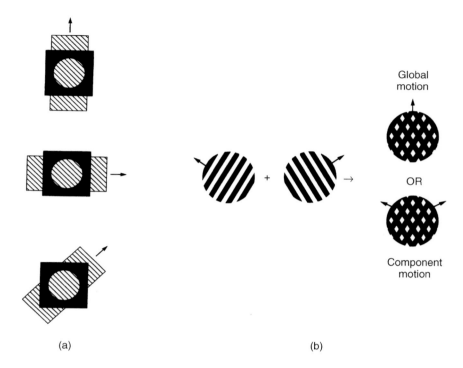

Figure 5.7 The aperture problem. (a) Different motion paths of gratings behind a circular aperture result in the same perceived motion. (After Kandel, et al., 2000) Alternatively, the same motion path can be perceived as moving in different directions if rectangular apertures are used; the contours appear to move in the direction of the long axis of the frame. (b) Plaid motion: The combination of two gratings moving in orthogonal directions could result in perception of their global motion or of their independent motions. (After Tovée, 1996)

now information that they are moving, but only by an amount equal to their horizontal vector of motion. The set of different motions shown in Figure 5.7a, when viewed through a circular aperture, would all appear as equivalent motions—upwards and to the right. The interesting perceptual observation is that this essentially ambiguous motion stimulus can be influenced by the shape and orientation of the frame. The perceived motion tends to be aligned with the long axis of a rectangular frame (Wallach, 1976). The stimulus is ambiguous because there is a large number of possible physical motions that could give rise to the motion of the stripes.

There has been considerable experimental and theoretical interest in the analysis of the perceived motion of gratings moving behind an aperture. Pairs of gratings inclined to each other and seen through an aperture are termed plaids (Figure 5.7b). The conditions under which their motion seems to be in a single joint direction, rather than remaining independent, has been studied intensively, in part because a retinal receptive field is in principle itself an aperture and will therefore give the same motion signal for many physical stimulus motions (see Bruce et al., 1996).

Stroboscopic motion

The extension of the range of novel motion phenomena described in the early nineteenth century was not solely a consequence of a growing interest in motion perception, but also because of the invention of instruments to present stimuli in novel and artificial ways (see Wade & Heller, 1997). Prominent amongst these was one, invented independently by three visual scientists around 1833, which forms the basis of modern motion pictures. It presented stimuli discretely, briefly, and in succession; that is, a sequence of drawings differing slightly from one another were viewed successively through slits in a rotating disc (Figure 5.8). To the astonishment of the observer, the represented figures appeared to move: Perceived motion was synthesised from a sequence of still pictures.

The apparent motion seen with the phenakistoscope (or stroboscopic disc as it was also called), and in films, is based on two phenomena—visual persistence and stroboscopic motion. Visual persistence has a very long observational history (see Wade, 1998). It was described and even measured by Newton: He noted that a glowing ember at the end of a stick could be seen as a circle if the stick was rotated with sufficient speed. That is, the visual response to light outlasts the duration of physical stimulation. Much of our artificial lighting is intermittent rather than continuous, but we are generally unaware of this because of visual persistence; fluorescent tubes flicker with twice the frequency of the alternating current supply, but we only notice the intermittency when they become faulty. In the nineteenth century stroboscopic motion was a novel phenomenon: When two successive stimuli are presented in slightly different locations motion is seen, within certain temporal limits. If the blank interval between the briefly presented stimuli is too short then they appear to be visible simultaneously; if it is too long they appear to be successive, and at around 100–200 ms motion appears. It is possible to satisfy the conditions for stroboscopic motion independently of those for visual persistence. This is what happened in the early days of the cinema. Films were taken and projected at 16 frames per second; this satisfies the criteria for stroboscopic motion, but it is rather slow for visual persistence, and so the pictures appeared to flicker—hence "the flicks". The problem was overcome by both increasing the frame rate to 24/s, and illuminating each frame with three pulses of light, so that the flicker rate is 72/s, which is well above our flicker threshold.

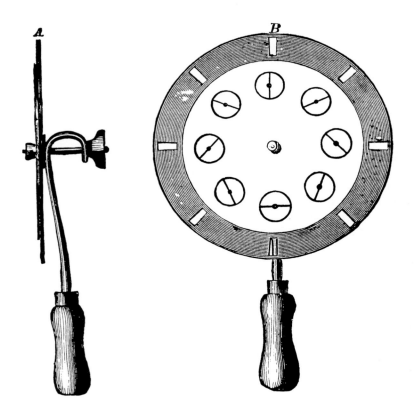

Figure 5.8 A phenakistoscope or stroboscopic disc. A side view is shown on the left, and the disc could be rotated by turning the central knob. The front face is shown on the right. The disc is rotated while facing a mirror. Its reflection is observed through the slits around the circumference. Each slit is opposite a slightly different drawing—here a set of diameters—which are seen in succession, creating an impression of a rotating diameter. (From Helmholtz, 2000)

Kinetic depth effects

There are various situations in which motion may be perceived as depth and structure in the moving object. Wallach and O'Connell (1953) set up a wire frame shape behind a screen and illuminated it so that its shadow was seen by the observers. When the object was stationary, its shadow appeared as a two-dimensional pattern of lines. When the object was rotated, the shadow was seen as a solid three-dimensional shape in motion. There are many possible interpretations of the pattern of motion of such a shadow, but the one most readily seen corresponds to the rotation of a rigid object. There are many examples of this process of the recovery of structure from motion (Ullman, 1979, 1996) and it is remarkable how little information is needed to produce perception of stable three-dimensional shape.

Figure 5.9 illustrates patterns that may be used to create another type of depth perception from motion. If patterns like these are spun about their centres, for example by placing them on a rotating disk like the old-fashioned record turntable, a shape like a cone may be seen to emerge. Usually the apex appears to point to the observer, but it may also seem to be concave and receding. The apex of the cone appears to "wobble" along a circular path. The effect is striking, and can be observed by photocopying the figures, cutting out the shapes and mounting them on a turntable.

The phenomenon of motion parallax, described in the previous chapter, provides a further example of perceived depth from motion. In this case the depth is most clearly and reliably perceived when the relative motion in a display is contingent on lateral movements of an observer's head. However, depth may also be seen by a stationary observer, in a similar manner to that obtained with the shadow-caster described earlier.

Vection

The rail system was also developing rapidly in the early nineteenth century, and rail travel exposed people to patterns of visual motion that were outwith the natural range. It is not surprising, therefore, that there are phenomena, like those mentioned in the introduction to this chapter, particularly associated with vehicular stimulation. The false motion that is attributed to the carriage in which we are seated is, again, one case of many that can be studied in a laboratory. The experience of self movement as a consequence of visual movement is called vection, and it can occur in the three dimensions of space. That is, we can experience forward body motion when the optic flow is artificially modified to mimic this, or forward tilt or sideways rotation if the visual environment is appropriately manipulated. Howard's (1982) book has an extensive treatment of vection, the impression of self motion when the

Figure 5.9 Patterns that, when rotated, produce a strong kinetic depth effect.

visible surround is actually moving, as well as a detailed treatment of eye movements and the factors that influence them.

These effects are not confined to vehicles and laboratories, as they have a venerable history in the fairground. Many fairground attractions involve abnormal patterns of motion, both vestibular and visual, and so it is not surprising to find that the desire for abnormal stimulation should have exploited vection, too. There is a venerable and fiendish device called the witch's swing, on which an individual stands and experiences considerable self motion although little occurs. The visible room surrounding the person is not anchored to the ground, but swings about. This induces the impression of self motion in the opposite directions to those of the room; such impressions are intensified when allied with an unstable platform on which the hapless individual stands.

The phenomena of motion perception, like those in other areas of vision, tend to be those cases where errors are made in the allocation of motion. These errors occur under natural conditions as well as artificial ones, and we can learn a lot from studying them. They should not, however, deflect us from examining the wider range of instances in which our perception does correspond to the physical motions in the environment. In the following sections of this chapter we will outline an approach to motion perception that builds on the concepts described in the previous chapter for the perception of direction and distance. That is, we will commence by considering motion with respect to a retinocentric frame of reference, and then proceed through the pattern-centric, egocentric, and geocentric levels.

RETINOCENTRIC MOTION

The physical definition of motion is the change of position over time. Position is a relative term and its measurement requires the specification of a frame of reference, as was described in Chapter 4. The first frame of reference we will examine is that of the retina itself. Visual motion is mediated by stimulation of the retina, but motion perception is not synonymous with retinal motion. Initially, we will examine the simplified situation of a single eye that is stationary with respect to the head, which in its turn is stationary with respect to the environment. If the eye is fixed in space then object motion would produce motion over the retina. We will consider two conditions of object motion—with and without any background visible. When an object moves in isolation (without any visible background) the only source of information for its motion derives from the displacement over the retina; this is called uniform motion. When a background is also visible, there is information for its uniform motion and also for its displacement relative to the background; this is referred to as relational motion. It was noted earlier that the threshold for relational motion is much less than that for uniform motion. We will, however, consider uniform motion initially.

Uniform motion

When a target, like a point of light, moves over the retina it stimulates a sequence of receptors, whose local signs provide information about where the stimulation has occurred. In order for the sequence of stimulation to be registered as motion there would need to be some temporal integration between the neighbouring local signs. Visual persistence provides evidence that such temporal integration does occur. That is, if the neural effects of stimulation at neighbouring local signs outlast the duration of stimulation, then they will be active at the same time even though the physical stimulation is successive. Temporal integration only operates within certain limits: If the motion is too slow it will be registered as successive; if it is too fast it will be registered as simultaneous. The same retinal motion signal would be produced by different motion paths of objects in the external environment, provided that the angular velocity with respect to the eye was the same. For example, two objects might be at different distances, but the nearer one could be moving more slowly than the farther one. If the distances and velocities are chosen appropriately, the retinal images of both would move across the same distance on the retina in the same time. The retinocentric motion signal is the information available to the visual system about the displacement of retinal images, with respect to the retina.

The retinocentric frame of reference is not confined to the retina, but is constrained by the retinal coordinate system. Neurophysiologists have demonstrated that the cells in the visual cortex are coded retinocentrically; that is, they respond when particular regions of the retina are stimulated, regardless of the direction the eyes are pointing. Many cells in the visual cortex are specifically responsive to motion in a particular direction and also at a particular velocity (see pages 127–134). For example, one cell might respond to a horizontally oriented edge moving downwards over a particular region of the retina; it would also respond to a stationary horizontal edge in the same region, but not as strongly as to the downward motion; upward motion of a horizontal edge over the same region would have very little influence on the cell's activity. Another cell can have the opposite pattern of activity. In this way, different cells will respond to all orientations and directions of motion. Cortical cells could only respond in these ways if there is temporal integration over retinal local signs.

Considerable attention has been directed to understanding the ways in which the visual system might implement retinocentric motion detection. Accessible and thorough reviews can be found in Bruce et al. (1996) and Papathomas et al. (1995). A key question concerns what is, or could be, detected. Under normal circumstances, when a real object moves, all its properties move with it. Its shape, colour, distance, and luminance displace together, because these are all properties of the object as a single physical entity. Similarly, the object's retinal image, which carries information about these physical properties, moves in a coherent manner. It is, however, a matter of empirical investigation to determine which of these properties is used by the visual system to detect motion. The most fundamental property is luminance. Consider a simple luminous square against a black background. Its retinal image will produce a response from the area of retina on which it falls. If it moves to another location in space, and the eye is stationary, then there will be a change in the location of retinal stimulation. Another way of expressing this is to say that there has been a change in the spatio-temporal distribution of light energy on the retina. Various systems have been proposed that could pick up this change. The simplest sort of motion detector would link the luminance detecting elements at the areas of retina stimulated during the motion. If the output from the luminance detectors activated by the square at its initial position were to be delayed, and subsequently combined with the signal from the square at its final position, then when both coincide, motion has taken place between the two retinal locations. A cell that received the delayed and concurrent inputs of such luminance detectors would function as a simple motion detector. Of course, the delay would have to correspond to the retinal velocity of the stimulus, so motion detectors with different delays and/or separations would be tuned to detect different velocities. This simple scheme can be improved and elaborated on by various sorts of additional processing, but the principle of operation is unchanged. It is noteworthy that such a motion detector has a side-effect: It will signal motion if there is no continuous movement between two retinal locations, but instead a stimulus is briefly presented at one point and then briefly presented at another. This is the basic requirement for the perception of apparent movement in a series of briefly presented static scenes, as described previously.

This type of motion perception is often termed "first-order" or "Fourier" motion, because of the presence of spatio-temporal luminance change. As with the perception of depth from retinal disparity, there is evidence from random dot displays that object recognition is not necessary to detect first-order motion. A random dot cinematogram, in which an area of texture is displaced with respect to a textured background (Julesz, 1970), is the logical equivalent of a random dot stereogram. When the textured area is moving, it is seen clearly as a distinct shape. When the movement stops, no shape can be seen. This corresponds to the perception of a shape separated in depth from the background in a random dot stereogram. In this case, one eye sees an area of texture which is displaced with respect to the equivalent area seen by the other eye, but no shape can be seen using either eye alone. There are very interesting parallels between motion and stereo perception, perhaps reflecting the evolutionary derivation of the latter from the former. All visual systems detect motion, but only some animals have stereoscopic vision. Possibly, as is often the case in evolution, a pre-existing system became adapted for a new purpose.

However, there is also good evidence that we can see motion when there is no displacement of a luminance boundary on the retina. This is termed "second-order" or "non-Fourier" motion. Suppose that a random dot field consists of dots which are constantly changing from black to white and vice versa; that is, the whole field appears to twinkle. If a portion of the field is displaced, the mean luminance is everywhere the same, and there is no moving luminance boundary. Nevertheless, observers can see motion in the field. The same is true of moving boundaries defined by colour or contrast instead of luminance. Simple motion detectors could be used to drive systems which apply transformations to the first-order signals, and in theory second-order motion perception could be explained in this way. Alternatively, observers may pay attention to features defined by colour or contrast, and this attentive tracking has been the subject of much research (see Cavanagh, 1992). Probably both these processes play a part in such motion perception, but natural circumstances which might involve non-Fourier motion are quite difficult to imagine.

Some visual motion phenomena have been interpreted in terms of processes like simple first-order motion detectors. One such is the motion aftereffect mentioned previously. Consider what happens when an observer initially looks at the rocks by the side of a waterfall: The stationary rocks will have many contours that will stimulate physiological edge detectors. Many of these edge detectors will respond more strongly to motion in one direction than in the opposite. For example, horizontal contours will excite motion detectors for downward and upward movement, but the net effect of these would cancel. Thus, the perception of stationariness is dependent upon the balanced activity of motion detectors coding opposite directions of motion (Figure 5.10). When the waterfall is observed the downward motion detectors will be strongly stimulated; if this stimulation is prolonged, the motion detectors will adapt or fatigue. Subsequent observation of the stationary rocks will produce a different net effect: The fatigued downward motion detectors will exert less influence than the unadapted upward motion detectors. Therefore, the signal from the stationary rocks would be similar to one produced by contours moving slowly upwards, and that corresponds to what is seen. The effect is considered to be retinocentric because the motion aftereffect is confined to the region of the retina that has been exposed to the motion.

There is evidence that second-order motion can give rise to a motion aftereffect, and also that the first-order (luminance change) type is influenced by quite complex features of the surrounding configuration. The latter are discussed later. It seems likely that there are many motion aftereffects, not one, and that they reveal different motion detecting processes, together with the influencing factors to which each is subject (Swanston, 1994).

The recordings from single cortical cells fulfil the requirements for retinocentric stimulation because the experimental animals are anaesthetised and the eye is immobilised. Therefore any stimulus motion will have a geometrically corresponding retinal image motion. This rarely occurs with natural vision because of the eye movements that will be described in the next section. However, stroboscopic motion does come close to meeting the require-

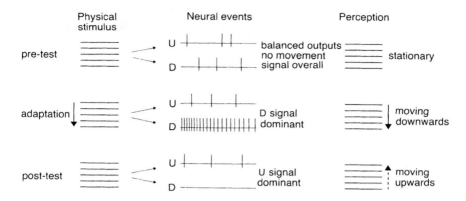

Figure 5.10 An interpretation of the motion aftereffect based upon adaptation of
cortical motion detectors. In the pre-test a stationary grating will excite
motion detectors for upward (U) and downward (D) direction equally, and
so the net activity will favour neither, resulting in its stationary
appearance. During adaptation the downward direction detectors are
strongly excited resulting in a neural signal for that direction, which is
reflected in perception. In the post-test the stationary grating is presented
again. The downward direction detectors have been adapted due to prolonged stimulation and so are not responsive. The upward detectors signal as before, but since there is no balancing output from the downward
detectors the net activity signals upward motion, and the stationary
grating is seen as ascending. (After Frisby, 1979)

ments for retinocentric stimulation: Apparent motion can be seen between
two brief, stationary, and spatially distinct pulses of light, if the temporal and
spatial separations are appropriate. Two different types of stroboscopic or
apparent motion have been described (Braddick, 1974). One is called the
short-range process because it is confined to spatial separations between the
stimuli of less than 15 min of visual angle, and temporal intervals of about
100 ms. The short range process can only be activated if both stimuli are
presented to the same eye. This distinction has been questioned by later
workers (e.g., Cavanagh, 1991), and it may not reflect genuinely different
underlying processes. Nevertheless, it has been very influential in the development of ideas about motion detectors, and in determining the type of
experiments on apparent movement carried out over many years.

Relational motion

Returning to the motion aftereffect, waterfalls are not seen in isolation; they
occur in a wide variety of terrains. Accordingly, waterfall illusions in the
natural environment involve relational motion. The water descends with
respect to the "age-worn rocks immediately contiguous", and so there is

available an alternative visible frame of reference—a patterncentric one. Motion adaptation examined in the confines of the laboratory is similarly dependent upon relational motion (Wade, Spillmann, & Swanston 1996). Rotating sectored discs and spirals present relational motions between their individual parts, but aftereffects based on linear motion require a patterned background relative to which the motion can be allocated. Therefore, even one of the phenomena that was thought to be dependent on uniform motion is in fact using patterncentric signals, too. It might be expected that a large uniformly moving display, like a vertically striped cylinder rotating around an observer, would be the ideal stimulus for generating a motion aftereffect. In fact it is not; rather than producing a visual motion aftereffect it results in the observer's apparent self motion. It is an example of vection, similar to the situation in the train mentioned earlier in the chapter.

Patterncentric signals register the relational motions between stimuli, rather than the retinocentric motions. One of the targets is adopted as a frame of reference relative to which the motion of the other target can be registered, and vice versa. Thus, patterncentric frames of reference are confined to interactions within the pattern projected onto the retina. The patterncentric signal remains the same even if the eyes move, because this does not alter the object separations. Eye movement simply adds a constant amount to the displacement of all retinal images, leaving differences in displacement unchanged. There are as many patterncentric frames of reference available as there are independently moving objects. Although this might sound a dauntingly complex process for the visual system to undertake, it is not so in practice because many of the patterncentric frames of reference are equivalent. Consider the eye fixed in space and viewing the waterfall. The patterncentric frame of reference could be taken as the descending water or as the rocks. In the former case the water would be taken as stationary and the rocks would be registered as moving upwards, or the rocks could be taken as stationary and the water descending. We do not need to use knowledge of the world to adopt the latter frame of reference, because there is much more correlated patterncentric information for the stability of the rocks rather than the water. Many other objects projected onto the retina, like trees, grass, or the river bed, yield the same outcome as that for the rocks, namely that the water is descending and the other features remain in the same relation to one another. Under normal circumstances, the environment provides a stable patterncentric frame of reference relative to which object motions can be allocated.

The night sky is somewhat unusual in this regard, and the induced movement of the moon provides us with a phenomenon that can be used to emphasise the points made earlier. Induced motion can be studied in the laboratory with displays like those shown in Figure 5.6, which allow us to study the uniform and relational components in retinocentric motion. One of the simplest displays consists of three points of light in an otherwise dark room; the central point remains stationary and the outer two move in the same direction at the same speed. Under these circumstances observers report that the central point appears to move in the opposite direction: Motion is induced in it. The two moving points provide a more powerful patterncentric frame of reference than the single stationary one. On the one hand, if the patterncentric frame was the only factor operating then the two outer points would not appear to move at all; on the other, if uniform process operated alone the central point would appear stationary and the outer points would appear to move. However, what typically happens is that motion is seen in both components of the display. This outcome indicates that both uniform and patterncentric processes are implicated in induced movement. The same outcome applies to the other displays shown in Figure 5.6.

Up to this stage we have considered motion with respect to a single eye. Relational motion can also be considered to operate between the eyes. That is, different patterns of retinocentric stimulation can occur with respect to each eye. This can be illustrated in terms of the second type of stroboscopic motion, which is called the long-range process because it can occur with longer temporal intervals and greater angular separations between the stimuli (Braddick, 1974). It is possible to present the first stimulus to one eye and the second to the other and apparent motion still occurs. This technique of splitting the stimulation between the eyes is widespread in vision research. It is called dichoptic presentation, and it can be used to indicate whether a particular phenomenon is based upon neural processes at or before the stage of binocular combination or at or beyond it. The signals from the two eyes are first combined at the level of the visual cortex (see pages 127–134). Therefore, if a phenomenon (like short-range apparent motion) cannot be elicited when the components are presented dichoptically, it is likely that it is due to neural processes occurring before the visual cortex. Alternately, when the phenomenon (like long-range apparent motion) does occur with dichoptic stimulation, it is suggestive of a more central site for its occurrence, at or beyond the level of binocular combination.

Induced motion has also been examined dichoptically. That is, the inducing stimulus can be presented to one eye and the stationary stimulus to the other. The results from such experiments are not easy to interpret because some have shown dichoptic effects and others have not. The situation is difficult to examine experimentally because there is no common stimulus to keep the eyes in alignment. When induced motion has been produced under dichoptic conditions it is possible that the eyes moved with respect to one another, and so the motion seen could have been due to uniform motion alone.

Another popular technique that addresses a similar question is interocular transfer. The motion aftereffect can be elicited if one eye is used for observation and if both eyes are used. What would be the outcome if one eye observed the moving display and the other eye viewed the stationary test? The aftereffect still occurs, but it does not last as long as when the same eye is used for both inspection and test. If the effect was confined to monocular processes alone it would not show interocular transfer; since it does, this suggests that binocular processes are also implicated in the motion aftereffect. Typically, the magnitude of interocular transfer in aftereffects is around 50% (Wade, Swanston, & de Weert, 1993). The value is about the same for the tilt aftereffect as it is for the motion aftereffect, which suggests that it might represent a fairly general feature of the way spatial information is coded in the visual system. The involvement of binocular processes in spatial aftereffects is supported by the finding that individuals lacking stereopsis (usually as a consequence of an uncorrected squint in childhood) also fail to experience any interocular transfer of aftereffects. It has been found that much larger values for IOT of the motion aftereffect (up to 100%) can be obtained when the test field is flickered at 2–3 Hz (Nishida & Ashida, 2000). The reason for this remains unclear, but the finding is hard to relate to existing theories and opens up new experimental approaches to this long-standing issue.

EGOCENTRIC MOTION

Human eyes are only stationary when they are paralysed or damaged. As a result, by far the most common cause of retinal image motion is the movements of the eyes themselves. Retinocentric motion information is therefore ambiguous, since it could arise from any combination of object movement and eye movement. In order for the visual system to allocate the retinal image displacement between object movement and eye movement correctly, there must be a source of information about eye movement. Only when both image displacement and eye movements are considered together is it possible to recover changes in the egocentric direction of an object in the environment. The outcome is a representation of object movement with respect to the self; that is, egocentric motion, which is independent of the motions of the eyes in the head.

Types of eye movement

Eye movements and their control have been studied intensively, because they offer the possibility of understanding in detail the link between a visual stimulus and a behavioural response, and of relating these to neurophysiological processes. Various methods have been devised for measuring eye movements, which vary in complexity and precision. The simplest procedure is observation of someone else's eye movements as they read, carry on a conversation, or look around the environment. The most common type of movement is called a saccade, which consists of a rapid displacement of the gaze to a new location. Saccades can reach very high velocities, approaching 800°/s at their peak. The size of a saccade is typically around 12–15°, but with significant numbers of both larger and smaller amplitudes. When a stimulus appears away from the fovea, there is delay of between 150 and 250 ms before a saccade starts. Therefore, stimuli can be presented for such short intervals (less than 150 ms) that saccades cannot take place while the stimulus is exposed. This technique of brief stimulus presentation enables experimenters to control the locus of stimulation on the retina, and perceptual phenomena can be examined without interference from retinal displacement due to eye movements. Most people maintain their gaze in one direction for a second or two at most, so saccadic movements are constantly producing image motion over the retina. A good way to elicit saccades is to ask someone to read a passage of text.

With the aid of Figure 5.11 you will be able to observe your own saccades, through the effect they have on the apparent position of an afterimage. After fixating on the white dot for about 60 s, move your gaze to the black dot. You will find that the afterimage appears to jump about at irregular intervals, or to drift slowly in one direction. Each jump reflects the occurrence of a saccade.

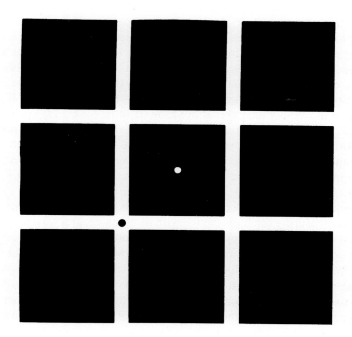

Figure 5.11 A pattern suitable for producing afterimages. Fixate the central white dot for about 60 s, under good illumination, then look at a blank surface. The afterimage will appear to be opposite in contrast to the pattern. Note how afterimages of the squares appear to be different sizes when seen against surfaces at different distances. As you move your eyes, the afterimages appear to move also. If you fixate the black dot after the white one, you will be able to see the effects of small involuntary eye movements, in the form of rapid displacements of the afterimage squares. You will need to generate afterimages several times in order to see all these effects.

When the slow drift has led to a significant fixation error, it is corrected by a saccade back to the target. These movements are easier to see because the afterimage is seen against the contrasting squares of the original figure. Although saccades can be readily observed, there are also much smaller movements that are harder to detect. Microsaccades with an amplitude of around 5 min occur constantly, as does a high frequency oscillation of the eyes, known as tremor. The latter two types of movement probably reflect instability or noise in the nerves and muscles which control the positions of the eyes.

Pursuit eye movements occur when a moving target is followed with the eyes. They serve to stabilise the image of the tracked target on the retina. While a pursuit eye movement is taking place, the image of the rest of the visual scene is displaced over the retina in the opposite direction to the eye movement. Pursuit eye movements vary in velocity according to that of the target, although there is an upper limit to target velocity of around 30°/s if the eyes are to keep up with it. A characteristic pattern of eye movement known as opto-kinetic nystagmus (OKN) occurs when the whole visual scene moves. This happens when looking out of a window in a moving vehicle, and OKN was once known as railway nystagmus for this reason. OKN has two components, called the fast and slow phases. In the slow phase there is smooth pursuit of the moving field, which stabilises the retinal image. If the velocity of field movement increases above around 30°/s, the eyes lag progressively behind, and the stabilisation is less effective. The slow pursuit phase alternates with fast, saccadic eye movements that return the eyes to the straight-ahead position. OKN seems to be a primitive form of eye movement control, designed to prevent displacements of the retinal image during head movements.

Detailed information about eye movements requires some means of recording and measuring the movements, with as much accuracy as possible. Film or video recordings of the eyes can be made under magnification, and a human or a computer program can analyse the movements. This is not the most sensitive technique, but it does not require attachments to the observers' eyes or head. As a consequence, recordings can be made during relatively normal behaviour. If the video camera is attached to a helmet, the observer can move around in the environment. Such studies of natural eye movements are giving important insights into the role of vision in everyday activities. For example, Land, Mennie, and Rusted (1999) have reported the pattern of fixations associated with boiling a kettle and making a cup of tea. They found that almost all fixations were relevant to the task, and that although the behaviour was carried out in an almost automatic and unconscious manner, eye movements indicated that all the component actions were closely monitored by vision.

Electrical potentials can be recorded from electrodes placed around the orbit, which alter as the eyes move; this technique is known as electrooculography. Another technique involves small infra-red emitters and detectors which can be mounted on spectacle frames, and aligned so as to pick up the change in the infra-red light reflected from the boundary between the iris and the sclera, as the eyes move. Other methods make use of contact lenses. A small mirror mounted on a contact lens can reflect a narrow beam of light whose displacements follow those of the eye, and can be recorded with suitable detectors. Contact lenses have also been made with a coil of fine wire implanted in them. If the observer sits inside a strong magnetic field, any movement of the eye causes an induced current in the wire, which can be picked up. These procedures require trained observers, and usually interfere to some extent with natural viewing. They require very careful calibration if the measurements are to be accurate, but in principle eye position can be resolved to within less than one degree of angular rotation. Figure 5.12 shows typical recordings of the main types of movement that can occur.

The same methods can be used to interfere with the normal relationship between eye movements and image displacements. For example, the image can be made to remain on the same part of the retina no matter how the eyes move. The earliest attempts to do this in the 1950s used miniature projectors mounted on a thin stalk attached to a contact lens, to produce an optically stabilised image. Provided the lens was firmly attached, observers reported some striking perceptual effects. Most notably, after a few seconds, any pattern would fade completely from view. Before this, complex patterns typically fragmented into a number of components, which sometimes appeared to be related to the meaning of the pattern. For example, a figure consisting of the two letters "H" and "B" joined together might be reported to fragment into one or other letter, rather than a random selection of the component lines. It is now thought that reports of meaningfulness in the fragmentation of stabilised images probably reflected the verbal categories available to observers to describe what they saw, and not a perceptual mechanism as such. Similar effects can be observed during steady fixation or with afterimages (Swanston, 1979). The latter are also a form of stabilised image, in that the locus of retinal stimulation remains the same regardless of eye movements.

Afterimages undergo complex patterns of fading and reappearance, until they finally cease to be visible. Coloured afterimages in particular produce striking changes, since the colours alter as fading proceeds. Even voluntary fixation of a low-contrast pattern will suffice to produce disappearance; although the eyes still continue to move, this may not be enough to maintain the visibility of poorly defined contours. The fading of steadily fixated patterns is known as the Troxler effect (see Wade, 1998). The effects of stabilisation demonstrate the importance of continual shifts in the pattern of stimulation on the retina. Prolonged and unchanging stimulation causes fatigue and loss of sensitivity at various levels in the visual system, and this leads to subjective disappearance and fading.

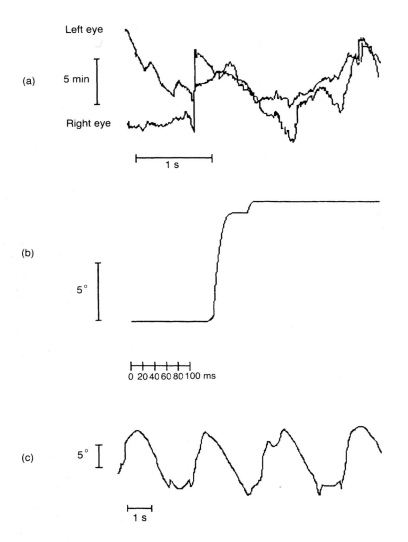

Figure 5.12 Typical examples of eye movement recordings. (a) slow drift and tremor, during attempted binocular fixation on a point. As fixation error builds up, a corrective saccade brings fixation back on target. Note the absence of strong correlation between the drift in the two eyes, which is essentially random. (b) a refixation saccade. The trace shows an initial undershoot of the target, followed by a second saccade to correct the error. (c) pursuit of a moving target. The target has a pendulum motion, which is followed by the eyes. Errors give rise to saccades which return the eyes to the target.

Compensation for eye movements

Eye movements are an inevitable counterpart of normal visual perception, whether to fixate on a different part of the visual field, to keep a moving target on the fovea, or to maintain visibility. Recovery of egocentric movement therefore requires information about both image movements over the retina and the movements of the eyes. In practice, it is only pursuit movements that create a significant problem. Saccadic movements are so fast that retinal stimulation is smeared out, during which there is little possibility of detecting any information. In addition, there may be a suppression of visual signals during a saccade. Image displacements during pursuit are by contrast similar in extent and velocity to those which occur with object movement. This process of compensation of the retinocentric signal for eye movements was described by Helmholtz, and has since been examined experimentally. In principle, to derive egocentric motion, the requirement is for compensation of retinocentric image motion for pursuit eye movements.

What sources of information are available to the visual system regarding pursuit eye movements? There has been much discussion of this issue, generally focusing on the role of feedback from the extra-ocular muscles. Muscle groups, such as those that move the limbs, have sensors that respond to being stretched, and can signal the state of contraction of the muscle. This information provides feedback as to whether a movement is taking place as planned. The eye muscles might work in a similar way, and signal their state of contraction, and thus the movements of the eyes to which they are attached. In fact this does not seem to occur, at least as far as movement perception is concerned. A demonstration of this is that when an eye is moved passively, for example by gentle pushing, stationary objects in the environment appear to move. If there was information available from the muscles themselves, this would not happen. The major source of eye-movement information is referred to as the efference copy, which means that the signals sent to the eye muscles are stored and also used to represent how the eyes will in fact move. Evidently this can only work if the eyes actually move as they are commanded to do, and it may be faster than an afferent feedback loop. The role of efference in motion perception can be seen with afterimages; when the eyes are moved voluntarily, the afterimage appears to do so also. In this case the absence of retinal motion together with the efference copy corresponds to an object moving at the same speed and in the same direction as the eyes. However, if the eye is moved passively, the afterimage does not appear to move, since there is no voluntary command, and the efference copy therefore specifies that the eyes are stationary. You can confirm this with an afterimage obtained from Figure 5.11. Eye movements can in principle also be signalled by optical cues, as was pointed out earlier. When there is a pursuit eye movement, the whole retinal image displaces with equal velocity and by the same extent, apart from the stimulus that is being pursued. This pattern of change could not normally occur for any other reason, and could provide reliable information about eye movements. To be used, there would have to be some means of detecting and comparing image motion across the whole visual field. At present, we have little information as to whether there is such a system, and how it might work.

The account of egocentric motion so far has been based on the assumption that image motions and eye movements are represented correctly in the visual system. Clearly, there might be many reasons why this would not be so. Detection of image motion, like any other sensory process, will depend on the stimulus exceeding a threshold value, and this may vary across the retina. Wertheim (1994) has comprehensively reviewed the evidence relating to this issue and compared models of how egocentric motion may be recovered.

Sensitivity to motion is better in the fovea than in the periphery, although motion is more likely to attract attention in the latter case. Similarly, the signal representing eye movements may not correspond to the actual value. When such mismatches occur, then there should be predictable errors of motion perception. Some examples were given above for active and passive eye movements, but these represent extreme cases. In general, if the extent of eye movements is under-represented, a visible object will appear to move by more than it actually does, and the converse applies to image motion. Illusions like this can be observed. If a moving object, like a pencil, is pursued by eye movements across a patterned background, the background appears to move in the opposite direction. This can be explained if the internal value for eye movement is too small, so that subtracting it from the image motion of the background gives a non-zero result. If so, it would be predicted that people should underestimate the velocity of the pursued target. This underestimation does occur, and is known as the Aubert–Fleischl effect after its first investigators.

GEOCENTRIC MOTION

The discussion of egocentric motion was concerned with displacements of the retinal image due to movements of the eyes in the head. Such eye movements are rotations, and can therefore be directly related to the angular extent of image motion. Compensation for the effects of eye movements can be based on simple representations of the extent of rotation of the eyes, and the extent of image displacement on the retina. However, retinal images may move as the result of head movements, which also change the location of the eyes in space. Eye movements occur with respect to a frame of reference provided by the head, but movements of the head occur in three-dimensional space. The head may turn with respect to the shoulders, but the centre of rotation is not the same as that of the eyes. A more common situation is that the head, and the eyes, move to different spatial locations as the result of movements of the whole body. These may be active, as in locomotion, or passive, as in travelling in a vehicle. These sorts of movement take place with respect to the physical environment, which therefore provides the frame of reference. Movement expressed with respect to the environmental frame of reference is geocentric. A change in egocentric direction as the result of a head movement cannot be interpreted unambiguously unless the extent of both the head movement and of object motion in three dimensions are known. A further stage of analysis, incorporating information for both self movement and perceived object distance, is therefore required. The geocentric representation which results is the basis for motion perception.

Perceived distance and motion

As an example of a phenomenon which demonstrates the interrelation of distance and movement perception, try folding a strip of paper into the shape illustrated in Figure 5.13. Note that the illustration is not the basis for the effect; it is necessary to observe the folded paper itself. It is usually called the Mach card, and once it is prepared, place it on a table top in front of you

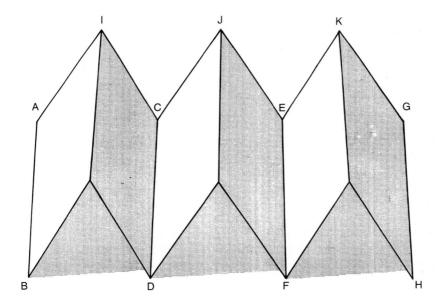

Figure 5.13 How to fold the paper strip for the demonstration described in the text. The paper should be placed on a flat surface so that all the labelled points are touching it. Observe with one eye, and a stationary head. After a time you should see a change in the apparent orientation of the strip. Points A, C, E, and G will appear to be in the air, and I, J, and K on the surface. AB, CD, EF, and GH will appear vertical and nearest to you. Small movements of your head will create striking deformations of the shape of the strip. Mach's (1866) folded card demonstrates the interplay between perceived distance and motion, although Mach was concerned principally with variations in perceived brightness rather than motion.

under even illumination, and look at it with one eye, by covering the other eye with your hand. After a minute or so you should find that a striking perceptual change occurs, and that there is an inversion of the shape of the folded paper. The peaks become troughs, and vice versa, which means that their perceived distances no longer correspond to their physical distances. Once you have seen this configuration it will be easier to obtain in future, so it is worth persevering. You may notice changes in the apparent brightness of the illuminated and shaded surfaces, indicating that the interpretation of surface luminance is also dependent on distance information. More obviously, if you move your head slightly from side to side (large movements will destroy the inversion) you will see large shifts in the position of the folds. They will probably seem to move as if the paper is elastic, and being flexed from side to side, with the apparently nearer edges moving in the same direction as your head, and the apparently further ones in the opposite direction.

This perplexing interaction between perceived distance and motion has been exploited by the artist Patrick Hughes (see Wade & Hughes, 1999). He has produced paintings in reverse perspective; they are painted on protruding planes (like truncated pyramids and wedges) so that the parts that are physically close to the observer are pictorially distant. That is, the lines that would converge on a flat picture plane to allude to distant objects are physically closer in these works. They appear as flat paintings until the observer moves whereupon they undergo a plastic motion that is beguiling. The pictorially distant (but physically closer) parts move in the direction opposite head movement. This is the outcome that would be predicted on the basis of Gogel's (1982) experiments on concomitant head movement and perceived distance: If the perceived distance is greater than the physical distance then a retinally stationary stimulus will appear to move in the opposite direction to the head. When standing close to the works they can switch between the two states, which could be called pictorial and veridical, and equivalent lateral head movements produce dramatically different apparent motions. In the pictorial state the corners appear fluid and in motion whereas in the veridical state there is little apparent motion. If the eyes have retained the same convergence during these two states then the apparent change cannot be attributed to the pattern of retinal motion during lateral head movement.

The same effects can be seen in Mach's card when it is constructed, but not in a drawing of it as in Figure 5.13. They are more immediate and compelling with a painted model. Wade and Hughes (1999) provide detailed instructions and a downloadable construction set at www.perceptionweb.com/perc0999/wade.html. Also available on the same internet site is an animated sequence made from camera movements with respect to one of Patrick Hughes's paintings.

Similar interactions between perceived distance and motion can be observed with stereograms, since they also appear to move when the observer does. Points which are seen with crossed disparity, nearer than the image plane, will move with the head, whereas points with uncrossed disparity, that appear further away, seem to move against the head. These examples show that perceived distance directly influences the perception of motion. The explanation lies in the processes required to recover geocentric motion from egocentric motion. Consider a stationary object located at a constant egocentric distance. For a stationary observer, the egocentric motion will be zero, if changes in retinal stimulation due to eye movements are fully compensated for. But if the observer's head moves, there will be a shift in egocentric direction, whose extent depends on the distance of the object. Thus, a given head movement produces different retinal motions, and therefore egocentric motions, depending on how far away the observed object is. If the object is to be correctly seen as geocentrically stationary, despite head movements, then a representation is needed of its position in three-dimensional space. This can be obtained from the egocentric motion by scaling it according to perceived distance. If the perceived distance matches the physical distance, the scaled change in egocentric direction will match the extent of the head movement. However, if perceived distance is in error geocentric motion perception will also be in error. Figure 5.14 shows the effects of underestimation and over-estimation of perceived distance on the apparent motion of a physically stationary object. The object may appear to move either left or right, and by varying amounts, depending on the error in perceived distance. Clearly, stimulation on the retina is wholly inadequate to predict what will be seen.

The same analysis can be applied if an object is also moving during observer movement. As with a stationary object, its geocentric motion can only be obtained if its egocentric angular motion is scaled by its perceived distance. Errors in perceived distance could cause an object which is moving to the left being seen to move to the right, and vice versa. The various cues to perceived distance have been discussed in Chapter 4, and there are many situations where errors can occur. A good example is provided by looking out of a window that has marks or dirt on the glass. These are nearby, and there are good cues to their distance. Because of the equidistance tendency, objects seen through the window will appear to be in the same plane as the marks, and therefore appear to be nearer than they are. Consequently, if the head is moved laterally, objects beyond the window appear to move in the same direction as the head.

Perceived self motion

Our discussion of perceived distance in motion perception makes clear that information is also required about self movement. The egocentric motion signal with respect to a subordinate frame of reference (the head) needs to be compensated for the effects of head movements if geocentric object motion is to be obtained. Since head movements are three-dimensional, egocentric object movement must be expressed as a displacement in three-dimensional space before the two can be combined. An internal value for the extent of self movement plays the same role at the geocentric level as does the value for eye

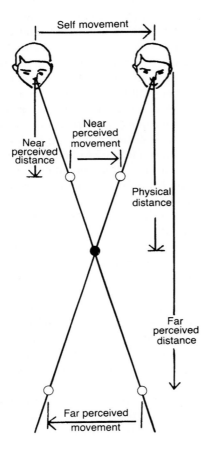

Figure 5.14 The relationship between the perceived position of an object, perceived distance, and self movement. An observer moves his head
through a distance towards the right, while observing a stationary
object, represented by the filled circle. If the object is seen at its
physical distance, it will not appear to move. However, if there is an
error of perceived distance (open circles), then the object will be
perceived as moving. If it is seen as nearer than it really is, it will
appear to move in the same direction as the head; if it is seen as
further away, the perceived movement will be opposite to the head
movement. The extent and direction of apparent movement during
self movement can therefore be used as an indirect measure of perceived distance. The same relationships apply if the object is physically moving; it will only be seen correctly during self movement if it
is seen at the correct distance. (After Gogel, 1982)

movement at the egocentric level. As might be anticipated, if perceived self motion differs from that which actually takes place, errors in perceived object motion will result. There are a number of sources of information which contribute to the sense of self motion. The vestibular system in the inner ear detects acceleration in each of the three spatial axes. The three semi-circular canals are fluid-filled tubes oriented at right angles to one another, so that a change in velocity of the head results in a movement of the fluid within the canals most nearly aligned with the direction of motion. Fluid movement is detected by the displacement of hairs embedded in cells in the canals. This system detects only angular accelerations, and does not respond to a constant velocity of movement. Associated structures called the otolith organs detect the static orientation of the head with respect to gravity, as well as other linear accelerations. Sensory systems in the muscles, tendons, and joints provide information about posture and limb movement. It is also likely that there is an efference copy of motor commands to the limbs which functions similarly to the efference copy of eye movements.

The function of the vestibular system, and its role in motion perception, is shown by the effects of prolonged stimulation. If you spin round on the spot, or are spun round on a rotating chair, there is strong stimulation of the vestibular system from the rotary motion. As is well known, there are marked aftereffects of rotation. These may include nausea, and you should only try to experience the effects yourself with care. The fluid in the semi-circular canals continues to circulate for a time after rotation has ceased, giving rise to a stimulus which corresponds to continuing rotation in the opposite direction. This causes observers to feel as if they are continuing to rotate, even though stationary. This illusory self motion is associated with an illusion of object motion called the oculo-gyral illusion. Stationary objects seen in isolation appear to be moving in the same direction and at the same speed as the observer's body. In addition, there is a characteristic pattern of eye movements, referred to as postrotary nystagmus. This is similar to OKN, and consists of alternating fast and slow phases of eye movement, as if the visual scene were actually continuing to move. It is an interesting historical fact that the characteristics of postrotary nystagmus were clearly demonstrated before the function of the vestibular system was understood (see Wade, 2000).

Vision itself also contributes to the perception of self motion. This process, which Gibson termed visual proprioception, depends on the detection of characteristic transformations in the optic flow, such as the radial expansion associated with approaching a stationary surface. If the whole visual field, or a large part of it, changes in a defined manner, then this can be used to derive changes in posture. In effect, the motion of the visual field with respect to the observer is interpreted as motion of the observer with respect to a stationary environment. This is almost certainly correct if the transformation affects most of the visual field. We, and many animals, seem to make this assumption automatically, as is shown by the witch's swing example mentioned earlier. The advantage of visual proprioception is that it can signal constant velocities within the range of biological motion, which the vestibular system is unable to do. In laboratory studies of vection, the sense of self movement takes some time to build up. The initial rotation of the surrounding drum involves an acceleration from rest, and the visual signal conflicts with the vestibular signal. The latter takes precedence, and the drum is seen as moving. However, when the drum has reached a constant velocity, there is no sensory conflict. The signal from the vestibular system will be that there is no acceleration of the self, and this is compatible with moving at a constant velocity. Hence the observer experiences moving at a velocity determined by the visual motion. This is an illusion, in that the observer is actually stationary. As a result, if an image which is stationary with respect to the environment is superimposed on the rotating drum, the stationary image is seen to move in the opposite direction to the drum. The geocentric motion of the stationary image is obtained by compensating the egocentric motion signal (zero) for perceived self motion (positive but incorrect).

When we travel in moving vehicles, the landscape outside often appears to be in motion. The cause of this is probably the lack of sufficient kinaesthetic information for self movement. Most vehicles have some form of cushioning or suspension, so vestibular stimulation is limited except when there is marked acceleration or deceleration. The optic flow may contribute some sense of motion, but perhaps because the velocity is higher than could occur from self-produced motion, this is not sufficient to override the vestibular signal for being stationary. Consequently, the egocentric motion of the landscape is mostly perceived as geocentric motion, and the world appears to be moving. The fact that we know that this is not the case may allow us to act appropriately, but does not change the perceptual experience.

Our discussion of motion perception has reviewed some of the many visual phenomena associated with motion, and a model for understanding how we perceive veridical motion despite the movements of our eyes, heads, and selves was proposed. Although there have been clear advances in understanding the early stages in motion perception, there is still much to be added. There is a great deal of evidence that the displacement of an image over the retina, whatever its qualitative or quantitative spatio-temporal energy distribution, is not enough to specify what motion we will actually perceive. Retinal image displacement can be reduced, nulled or even reversed in perception by manipulating the perceived distance of the moving object. The pattern of retinal stimulation could therefore vary greatly and still produce the same perceptual outcome. Our present neurophysiological models of retinal motion detection will need considerable elaboration, or even replacement, if a full understanding of motion perception is to be achieved.

6 Recognition

In Chapter 1 we introduced the example of the dog guiding a blind human across the road. The guide dog must perceive its environment geocentrically in order to behave in the manner it does; it must respond to the edge of the pavement, the width of the road, and to the approaching vehicles in much the same way as a sighted human would. Both guide dogs and sighted humans respond to objects in terms of their visual locations and dimensions in three-dimensional space, rather than the projective aspects of these (the locations and dimensions on the retina). That is, objects are normally seen as having constant dimensions despite changes in the retinal projections of their sizes and shapes. This is called perceptual constancy, and it is the prerequisite of more complex perception like recognition.

The subject of perceptual constancies is treated in virtually every book on visual perception, and in most psychology textbooks. However, it is not generally considered as a precursor to object recognition, as we do here. The frequency with which constancy is discussed is unfortunately not correlated with the clarity or accuracy of the discussion. Several of the sources cited for earlier chapters contain good general discussions of constancy, for example, Gregory (1997), Kaufman (1974), and Rock (1984, 1997). Gibson's argument that the problem of constancy is easily understood when perception occurs in normal environments is expressed in most of his writings and those of his followers (see Gibson, 1966; Michaels & Carello, 1981). Also, many of the references for Chapter 4 are appropriate here, especially Epstein (1977).

In the preceding chapters we have described how geocentric perception of the environment is obtained from the patterns of stimulation reaching the eyes. An important feature of this approach has been the emphasis on a moving, active observer. By moving our eyes and our heads we gain information about new aspects of the world that would otherwise not be available. This information has to be extracted from the complex changes in stimulation that are caused by our own movements. As a result we obtain a geocentric representation of the direction, distance, and movement of objects with respect to the environment. Without this, we, and other animals, would be unable to carry out the co-ordinated activities necessary for survival. In addition, a geocentric representation provides the basis for recognition, because it also conveys the defining properties of objects, like their size, shape, orientation, and location. In this chapter we will first discuss the perception of stable object properties, and then consider how these may be used for recognition.

PERCEIVING OBJECT PROPERTIES

Perception of object characteristics needs to conform to the frame of reference within which behaviour takes place, which will normally be the surface of the earth. We refer to such perceptions as geocentric. An active perceiver, whether human or animal, must recover the geocentric properties of objects, despite self motion. In the previous two chapters, we have described the frames of reference relative to which information can be represented, and from which geocentric information can be derived. The first, retinocentric, level is the one that is studied by neurophysiologists as described in Chapter 3: Information is coded in terms of the coordinate system of the retina. Retinocentric information describes image characteristics with respect to retinal coordinates, but it is not necessarily localised in the retina. The fact that a response occurs in the visual cortex, or elsewhere, need not preclude it from being retinocentric in character. The term retinocentric expresses the nature of the information, and not its anatomical site. As was discussed in Chapter 4, information about the location of objects can only be expressed in terms of a particular frame of reference. The retina generates neural signals that carry information about the location of stimulation with respect to a retinal frame of reference. Such information is then potentially available at any later stage in the visual system, and remains retinocentric unless transformed into another frame of reference.

This retinocentric level is essential for vision but it cannot serve as a basis for object perception or recognition because we have two eyes and both of them move. The next frame of reference uses an integrated binocular signal from the two eyes together with their movements to provide an egocentric frame of reference, the coordinate origin of which lies between the eyes. We perceive the directions of objects with respect to the egocentre. Visual direction alone would not enable us to locate objects in space; in order to do this we also need to determine the distance objects are away from us along the line of visual direction. There are many sources of information for the relative distances between objects—which is nearer or further—but these need to be anchored by information for egocentric distance before objects can be adequately located in space. If information for the observer's own movement is incorporated, then objects can be represented in the geocentric frame of reference. When we have derived a geocentric representation of objects, we are in a position to behave appropriately with respect to them. In the next section, the operation of these frames of reference will be illustrated in the context of motion perception, but as will be made clear, the principles apply equally to other object characteristics, such as size, shape, and orientation.

PERCEPTUAL CONSTANCIES

In this section we will examine the phenomena known as the perceptual constancies, together with some of the explanations that have been proposed to account for them. The term perceptual constancy refers to the fact that we normally perceive objects as having constant characteristics, like size, shape, or colour, even when there are changes in the information about these characteristics that reaches the eye. However, the issue is really broader than is implied by this definition. A fundamental requirement for perception is that both the changing and constant characteristics of the environment should be accurately represented. This has to be accomplished despite changes in the pattern of stimulation reaching the eye due to an observer's own activities. We can perceive that objects with a constant physical size are not changing in size when we move towards or away from them or they move towards or away from us, and we can perceive an object's shape correctly even if it is seen from different directions. Without such abilities, recognition and identification would be impossible, as there would be no consistent description of an object to remember and make use of on subsequent occasions. It is equally necessary to perceive changes when they do occur. An object may move between locations in the environment, or undergo changes in orientation, but it must still be possible to recognise it correctly. Perhaps the most characteristic property of living things is that they can change both their shape and their location. A tree may be blown by the wind and alter its shape considerably. Animals can move about in the environment, and adopt a wide variety of postures. Biological shapes are highly variable, but our capacity for recognition is most striking for just these sorts of patterns, like those which define an individual's identity. Thus, an account of how we are able to perceive objects as constant when they are constant must explain how we can perceive changes in objects as well.

Location and motion constancy

One fundamental object property is its location, whether this is changing (i.e., the object is moving) or fixed. If behaviour is to be appropriately directed in the environment, then it must be guided by veridical information about the location of objects within some stable frame of reference. If the object is moving, then its velocity will need to be recovered. As we have seen in earlier chapters, this presents problems for biological visual systems, since the motion of an object's image on a retina may be caused by object movement, movements of the eye in the head, movements of the head on the body or movements of the whole body through the environment.

Consideration of retinal stimulation alone cannot account for geocentric visual perception. Many other sensory systems are involved in the recovery of the location and movement of objects in space. For example, information from the vestibular system is used to determine accelerations of the observer's head in three dimensions, and this is essential if the pattern of retinal change arising from a head movement is to be interpreted unambiguously. The integration of these sensory systems constitutes visual perception, and it would be wrong to suppose that visual perception can be understood solely in terms of light reaching the eye. Figure 6.1 summarises the process of achieving geocentric perception (Wade & Swanston, 1996). Initial registration of retinocentric location and motion in each eye gives rise to a single binocular (cyclopean) retinocentric signal. This expresses location and motion with respect to a point located between the eyes. Since the two eyes move by equal amounts when vision occurs, a single signal for eye movement can be combined with the binocular retinocentric signal to give an egocentric representation. This carries information for changes in angular direction with respect to the observer, despite movements of the eyes. If the observer's head moves (either with or independently of the rest of the body), then the eyes necessarily move too. This causes displacement of the retinal image, in a way that cannot be interpreted unless the extent of self motion and the distance of the object are known. Scaling the egocentric information by perceived distance gives the three-dimensional location of objects with respect to the observer. This can be corrected for the effects of self movement, since both are expressed in terms of three-dimensional displacements, to produce a geocentric representation of the position and movement of objects in the environment. Information for eye movement, self movement and distance may be derived from a number of sources, including visual ones. For example, when there are several objects at various distances, their relative displacement during self movement may provide information for their relative distance. At this level of analysis, the nature of the information required is defined, rather than its sources. The concern is with the rules and relationships that permit a geocentric representation of the external world by observers who can move in the environment, and whose sense organs can move with respect to the body. A geocentric representation is required for effective action in the environment, and if a geocentric representation is stored in memory it can be matched to the same object when encountered on a subsequent occasion. There may of course be errors in the process of recovering a geocentric description. Eye movements, self movements or distance may not be accurately detected, and image displacements on the retina may be more or less than the signal to which they give rise. If so, then there will be errors in the perception of shape, size, or movement, and object may not be recognised.

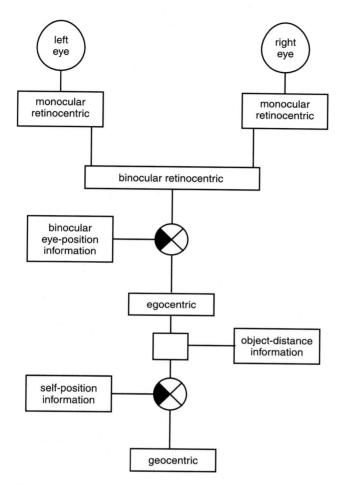

Figure 6.1 A schematic diagram of a model for the perception of space and motion in the absence of a patterned background. The retinocentric signals provided by the left and right eyes are integrated to yield a binocular retinocentric signal. This can be combined with information for the direction of both eyes, to give an egocentric representation. A three-dimensional, or geocentric, representation of space is derived from the egocentric signal scaled for object distance and head or body movement. (After Wade & Swanston, 1996)

Size constancy

Size constancy is easily observed, although we seldom notice that it takes place. In order to see this for yourself, hold up one hand with your palm facing you about 25 cm from your face, and the other with your arm extended. Separate your arms by an angle of about 30°, so that you need to turn your head to look from one hand to the other. When you do this, do your hands appear different in size? It is likely that they do not, in which case you are correctly perceiving their constant size despite large differences in the angles they subtend at your eyes. How can size constancy be explained? One possibility is that you see your hands as a constant size because they are familiar objects, and you already know from experience what size they are. This view, which might be the explanation suggested by common sense, cannot be correct. It would mean that size constancy would only apply to objects we recognise, and whose size we know about from past experience. Clearly it would also mean that recognition of objects precedes perception of their characteristics, and this presents logical problems. An alternative approach could be to argue that we are mistaken in supposing that constancy is a problem to be solved by the visual system. This view was strongly argued by Gibson (1950, 1966, 1979), who pointed out that size constancy may be given by invariant features of the optic array.

Suppose that an object like a car is seen at various distances. If only the optical projection of the car is considered, then our ability to see it as a constant size seems in need of explanation. The angle subtended at the eye by the car is apparently ambiguous, since the same angular subtense could represent a wide range of different-sized vehicles, at different distances. However in practice we would not rely only on the visual angle of an object in order to determine its size. Other sources of information may be available in the retinal image that remove the ambiguity, and determine the perceived size. One suggestion made by Gibson was that the amount of adjacent background texture obscured by an object remains constant, despite changes in its distance and angular size. This would then constitute an invariant property of the optic array, which directly specifies size. Although there is relatively little information available about which optical invariants are significant, and how they may be detected, the general point made by Gibson about the lack of real ambiguity in the retinal projection is a very important one.

Size–distance invariance

There are other sources of information that determine an object's apparent size, as well as purely optical invariants, and the most important of these is perceived egocentric distance. Cues to egocentric distance were discussed in Chapter 4, and there is good empirical evidence, reviewed by Gogel (1993), that perceived size is linked to perceived distance.

The relationship is known as size–distance invariance, and it can be expressed by the statement that perceived size is proportional to the product of visual angle and perceived distance; or, equivalently, that the ratio of perceived size to perceived distance is proportional to the visual angle. Gogel (1993) has provided a comprehensive analysis of the perceptual consequences of size–distance invariance. The geometry of this relationship is illustrated in Figure 6.2. Since visual angle is the ratio of physical size to physical distance,

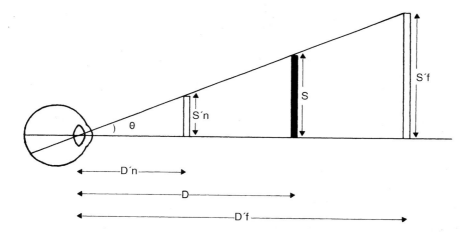

Figure 6.2 The relationship between perceived size, perceived distance, and visual angle, as expressed by size–distance invariance. An object of a given physical size (S), at a given physical distance (D), subtends an angle of θ° at the eye. Such a visual angle could correspond to an infinite number of different-sized objects at different distances, all of which have the same ratio of size to distance, and therefore the same visual angle. By size–distance invariance, the perceived size of an object (S′) depends on its visual angle and its perceived distance (D′). Thus, if the object is incorrectly seen as nearer than D (D′n), then it will appear to have a size of S′n; similarly with too large a perceived distance (D′f), the perceived size is S′f, so that the ratio of S′ to D′ is constant. In general, S′ = (D′.S)/D, or S′ = D′.tan θ, since tan θ = S/D.

another form of the equation is that perceived size is proportional to the product of physical size and the ratio of perceived distance to physical distance. Therefore, if perceived and physical distance are the same, their ratio is one, and perceived size will be constant if physical size is constant, even though distance varies. For an object of constant physical size, the product of visual angle and perceived distance is a constant (invariant) characteristic, despite changes in distance. If angular size increases and perceived distance decreases, as would happen with an approaching object, then perceived size will remain constant (Swanston & Gogel, 1986).

Size constancy can be regarded as a special case of size–distance invariance, which can also account for situations where errors in perceived size occur. Suppose that the perceived distance of an object is increased by a change in the cues available for perceived distance, such as a decrease in the convergence of the eyes. Its visual angle remains the same, because its physical distance has not altered, so the product of visual angle and perceived distance will be larger. That is, the perceived size of an object with a constant visual angle should increase if its perceived distance increases, and decrease if perceived distance decreases. This outcome can readily be observed and is termed Emmert's law, although it has been reported several times in recent centuries (Wade, 1998). An afterimage can be produced by fixating, for a minute or so, on the white dot in the centre of Figure 5.11 (see page 203). The afterimage of the grid pattern can then be observed against a close surface like your hand, or a further one, such as the ceiling. You should find that the apparent size of the afterimage changes, so as to appear larger when seen against the further surface. Clearly, there must be good cues to the distance of the surfaces. The retinal area stimulated necessarily remains a constant size, and is seen at the apparent distance of the background as a result of the equidistance tendency.

The Ames room (named after the American ophthalmologist Adelbert Ames II (1880–1955) who devised it) demonstrates size–distance invariance very clearly. Ittelson (1952) has described the principles of its construction, together with a number of Ames's other striking demonstrations of the illusory perception of real objects. Figure 6.3 illustrates the geometry of an Ames room. Although the far wall is at an oblique angle to the observer, all the internal features, such as the skirting boards and window frames, have been shaped to appear as if on a front-parallel surface. With monocular observation, the effective cues to distance (principally linear perspective) correspond to a rectangular room, and the perceived distance of the far wall differs from its physical distance. As a result there are remarkable effects on the perceived size of objects placed within the room. Two identical objects placed in each corner look to be very different in size. If the objects change places, they seem to grow and shrink. It is not necessary to suppose that this has anything to do with knowing that rooms are generally rectangular, because the effects are exactly as would be predicted on the basis of size–distance invariance, given the available cues to distance (Gogel & Mershon, 1968). The apparent sizes of objects in the room are appropriate to the product of their visual angles (which depend on the physical size and the physical distance) and the perceived distance. Perhaps the most striking aspect of the Ames room is that knowledge about the objects within it has little or no effect on perception. Even if people are observed moving around in the room, they still appear to shrink and expand. It is often stated (e.g., Bruce et al., 1996) that if these people are of special significance to the observer, they may be seen veridically and the room as non-rectangular. However, following initial reports (Wittreich, 1959), there has been little evidence to confirm this influence on perception of knowledge about the actual sizes of such familiar objects (Pylyshyn, 1999).

The account of geocentric perception given earlier was based on a similar principle to size–distance invariance. The scaling of changes in egocentric direction by perceived distance is equivalent to the scaling of visual angle by perceived distance in size–distance invariance. The equivalence is apparent if you think of a difference in the egocentric direction between the edges of an object as defining visual angle, and a difference in egocentric direction of a

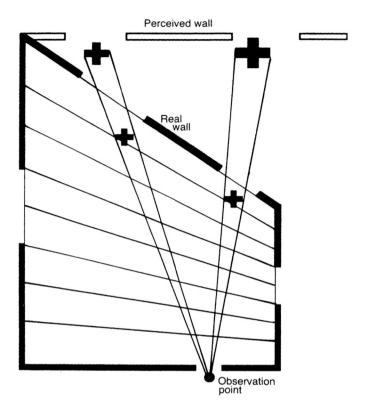

Figure 6.3 The layout of an Ames room. The actual shape of the room is trapezoidal, with the far wall sloping at an angle towards the observer.
However all the available cues from linear perspective, texture gradients, etc. are adjusted to indicate that the far wall is at right angles to
the observer. For example, window frames are trapezoidal, but give
rectangular projections at the eye due to the slope of the wall in
which they are set. The far wall is therefore seen in the position
shown, and as a result objects placed in the room appear to be distorted in size. Equal-sized objects appear much larger when seen on
the right than on the left. These perceived sizes are what would be
expected from size–distance invariance, given the errors in perceived
distance.

single point over time as defining movement. Our account of geocentric perception (Wade & Swanston, 1996) predicts both size constancy and location
constancy; that is, our ability to see stationary objects as stationary despite
observer movement. Location constancy is a special case of a more general
process of geocentric motion perception. An adequate explanation of spatial
perception will account for both location and size constancies, as well as the
systematic ways in which they break down.

Shape and orientation constancy

The same principles can be extended to explain shape constancy. Consider a rectangular object like this book. When closed and face on, the retinal projection of the book is rectangular, and corresponds to the physical shape. If the book is rotated about a vertical axis, the retinal projection of the cover is altered to a trapezoid, because the far edge now subtends a smaller visual angle than the near edge. The principle of size–distance invariance is sufficient to account for our ability to continue to see the cover as rectangular even when it has been rotated. If there are adequate cues to distance, the perceived size of each edge will correspond to its physical size, and thus the overall perceived shape will correspond to the physical shape.

In orientation constancy we compensate for changes in our orientation with respect to gravity so that objects appear to retain the same orientation despite their changing retinal orientation. This can be demonstrated under the reduced conditions of the laboratory (Howard, 1982; Wade, 1992). When only a single line of light is visible we can judge its orientation quite accurately even when the head or the whole body is tilted to the side. This is possible because of information provided by the otolith organs in the vestibular system; they signal the orientation of the head with respect to gravity and these signals are used to modify the information for orientation relative to the retina.

Outside the laboratory there is ample visual information to specify the vertical: Our environment has been constructed to comply with the demands of gravity, and so buildings and their constituent parts tend to be vertical and horizontal. These conditions can be contravened in the laboratory. If observers are placed in a rectangular room that is artificially inclined, then their judgements of orientation will be biased by the tilted room. Objects will appear vertical when they are tilted in the same orientation as the room, and the observer will feel tilted: If they remain vertical with respect to gravity they will feel to be tilted in the opposite direction to the room. Similar situations do occasionally occur in the natural environment. Some years ago there was an earthquake in Japan that resulted in the buildings in one district being inclined by a few degrees. Thus there was conflicting information from the visual and vestibular systems. One of the consequences of this was a dramatic increase in the number of people who consulted their doctors with postural problems like dizziness and nausea.

An alternative view of how we achieve perceptual constancy suggests that it is based on assumptions about the structure of physical objects. The best known is called the rigidity assumption (Papathomas et al., 1995), because it consists of interpreting retinal changes in terms of the rotation and translation of rigid three-dimensional objects. For example, the changes in the contours of a book as it rotates about a vertical axis could be produced by a large set of environmental events, in which the book itself undergoes changes in physical size and shape. If it is assumed in advance that objects are rigid and unable to change shape, then the retinal transformations allow only one interpretation. The difficulty with the rigidity assumption, and other sorts of a priori principles in perception, is that it constrains what can be seen. Objects can in fact change shape, since some are elastic. We can evidently see non-rigid transformations when they occur. A rigidity assumption may not be necessary if sufficient information is available about an object, in addition to its retinal transformations.

Underlying much discussion of perceptual constancy is the conception of a retinal image that is intrinsically ambiguous (Rock, 1997). The same optical projection on the retina can arise from many different physical structures, and yet our perception normally corresponds to the one which is actually present. This point of view has led to the development of various explanations of how we may resolve the ambiguity. It is unarguable that the retinal image of a given object considered in isolation provides ambiguous information for its size, location and shape. Like any ambiguity, this can be resolved if other information is available. The major theoretical approaches to this have been to incorporate past knowledge, prior assumptions, other concurrent sources of visual information such as distance, or other information in the retinal image like texture and perspective. However, objects are seldom seen in isolation outside the laboratory, and if they are, they may well be perceived incorrectly. The appearance of an object can be changed by the visual background against which it is set, and there is little doubt that the visual system interprets the retinal image of an object in the context of other retinal patterns, although we know little about how this comes about. As has been demonstrated, information about egocentric distance is critical in determining perceived size, motion, and shape. These perceptual characteristics can best be understood as aspects of spatial perception, which must be geocentric if behaviour is to be appropriately directed. In addition, a geocentric representation provides a description of objects in terms which would permit subsequent recognition.

Colour and lightness constancy

Two further perceptual constancies may be less closely related to the processes of spatial perception. Colour constancy refers to the fact that we see objects as being a constant colour even when the wavelength of ambient illumination changes. Under white light, an object will reflect a part of the total spectrum, which determines its colour. If the ambient illumination is restricted to, say, the longer wavelengths (so as to appear red), the object will continue to appear the same colour as before, even though it now reflects a quite different range of wavelengths. In effect we are able to compensate an object's apparent colour for any bias in the colour of the prevailing illumination. In order for this to happen, there must be sufficient information about ambient illumination. Thus, if an object is illuminated by a narrowly focused source of coloured light, which does not impinge on the rest of the scene, then colour constancy will fail, and the object will seem to be a colour deter mined by the fraction of the incident wavelengths which it reflects (Land 1977; Zeki, 1993).

A similar process, known as lightness constancy, occurs with changes in th intensity of ambient illumination. A piece of coal will appear black and sheet of white paper will appear white, even when the intensity of the ligh they reflect is changed over a wide range. Even more strikingly, if the paper i in shadow, it may reflect less light than the coal, but the coal will still appea darker than the paper. Again, this is dependent on being able to perceive th intensity of the ambient illumination. If the paper and the coal are place side by side and the coal is illuminated by a hidden spotlight, it can be mad to appear whiter than the paper. These constancies are also influenced b perception of the three-dimensional space in which illuminated objects ar placed. Gilchrist (1977) found that the perceived lightness of a surface wa altered if its apparent distance (and thus the shape of the object of which i was a part) was perceived to change. A similar effect can be observed wit a shape made as shown in Figure 5.13 (see page 209) when it undergoes ; perceived depth reversal.

RECOGNISING OBJECTS

All animals need to respond appropriately to aspects of their environmen that are important for their survival—for their sustenance, shelter, and repro duction. Such aspects are three-dimensional, and so the general rul advanced above is that perception is geocentric. This applies to guide dog before their specialised training. They can avoid objects, bite them, paw them or climb onto them without any training by humans. Guide dogs requir extensive training before they are assigned to a blind owner because they nee to behave unnaturally. They are trained to stop at small steps that they coul easily negotiate and to avoid projecting objects that they could easily rui under. In effect, they are trained to respond as if the space they occupy i equivalent to the dimensions of a human. It is rather like starting to drive a car, when we gradually learn to control a vehicle that occupies a greate volume of space than we do. Guide dogs are trained to discriminate feature of their environment that are not intrinsically important to their behaviour For example, a dog can be trained to discriminate between steps that are toc low to interfere with the blind person's gait, and steps that are higher and might be tripped over. The dog is trained to respond differentially to twc different states of the world (not to two different retinal projections), and sc there will be some stored internal representation of these against which any present state can be compared. That is, the dog can recognise the distinction between the heights of steps. This behaviour is not restricted to the particulai steps for which training occurred, as the guide dog would be expected to respond appropriately to examples of steps not previously encountered.

Therefore, recognition involves two complementary aspects—discrimination and generalisation.

Discrimination and generalisation

Discrimination concerns assigning different behaviours to specific objects or object properties, like two different heights of step. In addition, these discriminatory behaviours can be generalised to instances of the same properties in other objects, as when a guide dog responds correctly to a different road from those on which it was trained.

The points about discrimination and generalisation can be illustrated further with an example more readily to hand. If the copy of this book that you are reading was to be placed with a number of different books, you could no doubt recognise it correctly. As was discussed previously in connection with perceptual constancies, you would see the shapes, sizes, and colours of the books correctly, even if they were at different distances, oriented at random with respect to the surface on which they were placed and illuminated with different intensities or wavelengths of light. You would therefore have a perceptual representation of each book that could be compared to a stored representation of previous perception. You could of course recognise this particular book on the basis of the text on the cover, but even if any words were hidden you would probably still be successful. The information you would use would relate to the size, shape, and possibly colour of the book. Evidently we must have this sort of information available in order to discriminate. If another copy of the same book were put in the place of this one, the task would become much more difficult. You might well suppose that the replacement copy was the original, and incorrectly recognise it. This would be an instance of generalisation, in which there is sufficient similarity between the characteristics of two objects for the response to both to be the same. In order to pick out this particular copy, it would be necessary to store some information about it that was sufficiently specific to allow discrimination between copies, like marks or damage to the cover. Generalisation gives an indication of the nature of the representation that has been stored, by comparing the characteristics of objects that are confused. It demonstrates the occurrence of recognition, and shows the basis on which this has taken place. For instance, you would be likely to recognise this book if it was upside down. Your response would generalise to different orientations of the same object, which means that the stored representation does not include the particular orientation in which the book was first seen. None the less, you would also perceive that its orientation had changed.

Both generalisation and discrimination are indications that recognition has taken place. In studying recognition in animals and human infants, behavioural measures of recognition are necessary. With normal adult humans, recognition is more usually assessed by the seemingly simpler method of asking an observer for a verbal response. Although this has been the basis of much research on recognition, the issues addressed by this research often concern the linguistic rather than the perceptual representation of information about the world.

The investigation of recognition and identification has a very long history. The early philosophers of China and Greece confronted the issue of how we can recognise an object as a member of a general class, and also as a particular instance of that class. Whereas philosophers concentrated their thoughts on the problems of knowing about real objects, psychologists have tended to study recognition in terms of simplified laboratory tasks, generally involving two-dimensional pictorial patterns. Would you mistake a picture of this book for the book itself? Would you expect a guide dog to do so? Much research on recognition has been based on supposing that this would be the case. Since pictorial images are so widespread in both research and everyday life, it is important to know how the recognition processes that apply to real objects may generalise to pictures. This issue, and its consequences for the misinterpretation of picture perception, will be taken up in the next chapter.

Many animals, besides humans, have well-developed capacities for discrimination and generalisation. These abilities have been the subject of extensive investigations, usually in the context of studying the mechanisms of learning. Although a full understanding of recognition would involve consideration of the processes responsible for learning, the initial step is the acquisition of perceptual information necessary for recognition. The processes responsible for perceptual constancies provide a geocentric description of objects which capture their unchanging, intrinsic characteristics. These processes also convey information about changes in objects that do not alter their identity, such as their location and orientation, and the representation they provide is therefore a suitable basis for recognition.

Matching representations

Recognition, however it may be measured, requires that some representation of a currently perceived object is matched to some stored representation of a previously perceived object (see Tarr & Bülthoff, 1999). This seems simple but deceptively so. In particular, what is the nature of the perceived and stored representations, and by what means are they matched? It is generally achieved very quickly, so the process is clearly efficient. Failures and errors do occur, but they are usually indicative of abnormal neurophysiology (Humphreys & Riddoch, 1994). To recognise an object in the natural world we have argued that it is necessary to have access to geocentric perceptual information, which is independent of the articulations and movements of the observer. Current work on recognition, discussed later, is generally supportive of this position, although there are a number of different theoretical approaches.

One widely used concept is that of an "object-centred" representation, as a basis for both perception and recognition. Essentially, this refers to a description of an object which is entirely independent of the observer. An object would be defined in terms of its dimensions with respect to a frame of reference defined by itself. Thus, a cylinder would be represented by the distance of its external surface from an implicit central axis. The use of this idea by Marr and Nishihara (1978) will be described later in the chapter, but it is worth noting at this stage that a geocentric and an object-centred description are not the same. The former does not include any information other than that which is perceived. The latter is a form of idealised representation, in that it incorporates information about parts of objects that are not currently perceived. Consider, once again, this book. At the moment, you are not perceiving the spine or the outside covers. A three-dimensional object-centred representation of its shape would incorporate information about all its surfaces, seen and unseen. It is possible that object-centred representations in memory may be built up from a number of geocentric perceptions, but there is little theoretical or experimental basis for any such speculations. However, it will be important to bear in mind the distinction between these two types of representation.

Parts and wholes

Two main strands of theorising can be identified, reflecting a dichotomy that runs widely throughout psychology. On the one hand, an object can be thought of as a collection of parts, or features, which are independently detected. The nature of these features and how they may be identified has been the subject of much experimentation and theorising. In general, such theories constitute an analytical approach to perception, in which a complex process is reduced to a set of simpler elements that can be studied in isolation. Although this is eminently suitable for the design of experiments in the laboratory, it also necessarily raises important questions as to what the relevant elementary features are and how they may be recombined to give an integrated perception. By contrast, a global or holistic approach stresses the importance of the overall pattern of stimulation and its priority in determining the recognition of the object. The statement that the whole is more than the sum of its parts, which is often used to summarise Gestalt psychology, exemplifies this viewpoint. The difficulties here are concerned with explaining how a complex pattern of stimulation is detected as a whole, and how similarities can be identified between members of a class that are the same in some respects and different in others.

Consider our metaphorical guide dog. Recognising it as a member of the general category of animals called dogs involves matching its appearance to some stored representation that includes the common characteristics of all dogs, which can be extremely variable. Recognising it as a particular, individual dog requires identification of its familiar distinguishing characteristics. A more subtle, and difficult, act of recognition would be to identify its breed.

This category is quite unstable, and dependent on arbitrary definitions by dog breeders, so there is a predictably high level of disagreement amongst untrained observers.

In recent years the analytical, feature based approach has been the most influential. In part this has been due to neurophysiological studies of the organisation and response specificity of single cells in the visual pathway and visual cortex. As described in Chapter 3, cells display properties that can be described as feature detection (Barlow, 1972; Blakemore, 1990). That is, they are organised in groups, or maps, which respond to one particular characteristic of visual stimulation, such as direction of movement, retinal disparity, colour, or orientation. This sort of organisation could be interpreted as a mechanism for identifying and measuring elementary properties of any arbitrary pattern. Such a pattern would produce simultaneous activity in those maps which are able to detect its particular features. Colour, movement, and orientation would be determined at the same time, in parallel.

There is psychophysical evidence to support the existence of a process like this (Treisman, 1988). For example there are circumstances under which a target is immediately discriminable from other patterns presented with it. The target seems to "pop-out" from the rest, provided it differs in respect of a simple feature. A single horizontal black line in a background field of vertical black lines is detected very quickly, as is a red horizontal line amongst green horizontal lines. This rapid segregation of visual information is not affected by the number of background patterns, which suggests that the process is based on simultaneous evaluation of all visible patterns. It is not necessary to examine each one successively to see if it is the desired target. However, if the target is defined by a conjunction of two features, then it takes much longer to find, and the time needed increases with the number of background patterns. A red horizontal line in a background of red verticals, green horizontals, and green verticals is not readily visible, and can be found only by a successive, serial, examination of each element. These experimental results may shed light on camouflage strategies found in nature, because the purpose of camouflage is to prevent immediate visibility in the natural environment.

How might recognition be achieved from an initial stage of feature detection? One approach, from which computer-based pattern recognition schemes have been derived, is to apply a decision process to the outputs of the feature detecting stages. Suppose that the letter E is to be identified. A number of features in this pattern could be found, such as the presence of three parallel horizontal lines meeting another line at right angles. The decision process would examine this set of features, and compare it to a stored description of letters of the alphabet expressed in the same terms. Various other letters, like F or B would partially fit the input, whereas others, like O or W would not fit at all. A decision as to which letter has been presented would be based on the best fit between the input and the stored descriptions. Selfridge (1959) proposed an influential system called Pandemonium, which worked in this way (Selfridge, 1959; Selfridge & Neisser, 1960). Simple feature detectors (e.g., for vertical and horizontal lines) fed into detectors of more complex combinations of features, such as a cross. In turn, these activated letter detectors, whose responses would vary in strength. A letter like E would activate the E detector (or "demon") most strongly, but also, less strongly, letter detectors for F and T. The outputs of all the letter detectors are compared by a decision process, which chooses the strongest signal. A system like this can work reasonably well for a small, well-defined set of patterns, like letters or numbers, and it can even be used to recognise single spoken words. However it has little success when the patterns to be recognised are subject to distortions and ambiguity. In this case, the recognition system needs to be provided with extensive information in advance about the patterns that are likely to occur; in effect, a database of world knowledge that gives a context for events. It seems unlikely that perception in animals with nervous systems less developed than a human's could operate in this way.

Although recognition could be based on activation of complex feature detectors, the number of such special purpose high level units would have to be enormous. There would need to be distinct units for every possible object that could be recognised, from yellow Volkswagens to your grandmother, to use the examples that are often cited. The problem is known as the combinatorial explosion, and it is hard to see how it could be solved in biological systems. A similar objection can be raised against what is known as a template theory of recognition. In such a theory it is proposed that the visual system compares the pattern of retinal stimulation against an exact copy of previous perceptions of objects. Thus, if you are looking at this book, it would be recognised by rapidly comparing what you see now with stored copies (templates) of previous perceptions. Recognition is achieved when a match is found. The scope of the search for a match could be narrowed down by means of contextual information, but even so it would require the storage of almost inconceivable amounts of information about all possible appearances of all recognisable objects.

One of the principles that emerges clearly from studies of the brain, perception, and recognition is that we use many strategies to reduce the amount of information that needs to be processed and stored. However, it is possible that hierarchical feature detection (in effect, a template process of recognition) plays a part in recognition of some biologically important patterns, like faces. Single cells have been reported in monkey inferotemporal cortex which are selectively responsive to particular individuals, such as the monkey's keeper. Some cells may be even more selective than this, and respond only to certain types of action by an individual, like approach (Perret et al., 1992).

Structural descriptions

It is useful, but not essential, to be able to relate psychological theories to neurophysiological discoveries. Many theories of recognition are based on purely psychological data, and concentrate on specifying what processes occur, without making any claims about how they could be carried out in the brain. One such approach is to postulate that recognition depends on deriving an abstract structural description of objects. A structural description makes use of perceptual information, but converts it into a number of propositions about the perceived object. For example, a square could be described as "a space enclosed by four equal length lines joined at right angles". Such a description is independent of any particular instance of a square, and any pattern that matched this requirement would be recognised. The difficulty with this sort of process is that structural descriptions are very difficult to define for real three-dimensional objects.

The relationships between the contours of an object vary greatly in the retinal image, depending on where the observer is looking from. These relationships are therefore described as viewpoint-dependent. What is needed is a description that is independent of uninformative variations in the retinal image, for example due to changes in egocentric distance or movements of the observer.

Volumetric primitives

Marr and Nishihara (1978) proposed a theory of recognition based on object-centred descriptions of the type described earlier in this section. The basic principle was that a complex object could be described in terms of a set of simple three-dimensional geometric shapes. Such components are called volumetric primitives, of which many instances such as cylinders, can be considered as various examples of a cone. Thus, "generalised cone" is the term used to describe the most fundamental volumetric primitive.

The first step was to establish a major axis for the object, with respect to which its general dimensions could be defined. For example, a human body would have a major axis running from the head to the feet, and it would be represented as a generalised cone (in this case a cylinder) of suitable height and width. Within this, various parts of the body, such as the arms and legs, would have their own axes identified and then in turn represented by suitable cylinders. The overall representation of the body and its parts would then be a hierarchical set of connected elements, each defined by a volumetric primitive. The fingers on the hand, the arms and legs on the body, and the whole body would make up such a descriptive hierarchy. Although there is some evidence that a system like this can provide a mechanism for analysis and recognition of objects that can be realised for simple situations in computer programs (Marr & Nishihara, 1978), there is little to support the existence of such processing in human perception (Gordon, 1997). It is, however, clear that artists have used the technique of decomposing three-dimensional forms into simple geometric elements for many centuries, as is illustrated by Figure 6.4. The early twentieth-century artistic movement known as Cubism was based on a belief that paintings should explicitly reveal the representation of

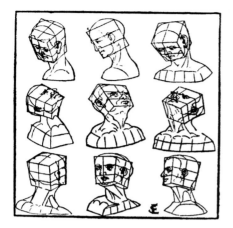

Figure 6.4 Diagrams of body parts defined by rectangular blocks, as illustrated by Erhard Schön in the sixteenth century.

objects by simple geometric shapes such as cones, spheres, and cubes. Although this might be advanced as evidence for the existence of processes in the visual system designed to identify such shapes, it may only demonstrate the desire of artists as well as scientists to reduce complex real experiences to simpler imaginary elements.

Recognition by components

Biederman (1987, 2000) proposed a theory which drew on the concept of volumetric primitives, and elaborated the way in which these may be detected. The theory identifies a number of basic elements called geons (geometric ions) that could be used to provide a description of any object. This description is then available for matching against stored representations and thus recognition of the object. Geons are conceptually similar to Marr and Nishihara's generalised cones, but Biederman's theory does not necessarily require a viewpoint independent object-centred representation of an object. He has pointed out that geons could be identified in a two-dimensional projection if certain assumptions are allowed. For example, if the image contains parallel lines, it can be concluded with reasonable confidence that this is due to the presence of parallel edges in the object itself. The general principle is that the critical cues for identifying geons can be found in the retinal image, and although these could arise by chance, it is very unlikely that they would in fact do so. Some situations, like those created by Adelbert Ames and described earlier, may elicit perceptual misinterpretation because assumptions about the presence of geons in the retinal image are false. One advantage of Biederman's theory is that it is relatively straightforward to instantiate in a computer vision system. Since analysis is carried out only on contours identified in the retinal image, there is no need to draw on other sources of information, such as for egocentric distance or observer movement, or prior knowledge about the object that is to be recognised. However, evidence for the theory is based on studies with outline drawings of objects (Biederman & Cooper, 1991), and its application to the recognition of real three-dimensional objects with an actual rather than implied spatial location is unknown. It is possible that Biederman's theory is most likely to be applicable to the human perception of pictures of objects.

Neural nets

Another development in the field of object recognition is based on the study of the properties of interconnected nets of nerve cells, nowadays usually simulated by computer programs (see Quinlan, 1991). These neural nets receive information through an input system, essentially equivalent to one or more of the senses. The output, which corresponds to a decision about the nature of the input, develops over time. Inputs are fed into the net, and spread through it by means of the interconnections between the elements. These interconnections can be weighted, in that they can be set to transmit more or less activity to the next element. If the weights are altered as the result of the output of the system, a form of pattern recognition can be achieved. The net is "taught" the connection between a particular pattern of input activity, and a particular response. Models of neural nets have become very complex and, although they have very few components relative to the brains of any vertebrate, can display properties of generalisation and discrimination that would be difficult to achieve by any other means.

Theories based on neural nets have a long history. Wilkes and Wade (1997) have assessed the work of Alexander Bain (1818–1903) in the late nineteenth century, and shown that in many respects he anticipated ideas that are often thought to have been developed over half a century later. The Perceptron, described by Rosenblatt (1959) and using concepts of cell assemblies advanced by Hebb (1949), was an early (but in practice inadequate) specification for a pattern recognising neural net. The WIZARD system (Aleksander, 1983) is a working mechanism that can recognise patterns such as pictures of faces, but requires quite strong constraints on conditions such as illumination. A detailed understanding of the design and properties of neural nets has required the availability of computer systems in which they can be simulated and studied. Although the study of neural nets in biological and computational systems is in its early stages, it may provide an indication of how a holistic pattern recognition system could operate.

It has to be borne in mind that there has been very little investigation of the recognition of real, three-dimensional objects, rather than arbitrary symbolic patterns like line drawings or photographs of objects. Such patterns play an important role in human activity, in the form of alphanumeric symbols and pictures of all sorts, but are not encountered in the natural environment. The next chapter considers pictorial representations and their relationship to reality in more detail.

7   Representations and vision

Throughout this book we have emphasised the applied, functional character of vision. Vision exists in humans and other animals because it is an aid to survival. The properties of vision are those needed to carry out significant activities such as seeking food, shelter, and sex, so that individuals can survive and reproduce. In the case of humans, significant activities are not necessarily restricted to the primary demands of survival and reproduction. We may seek a variety of sources of visual stimulation, many of which are cultural products nowadays. Some of these, like painted pictures, may be as old as the human race itself. Others, such as photographic or television images, are more recent. Writing and printed text are visual stimuli of particular complexity, because the shapes bear little visual relationship to the objects or meanings they convey.

Human survival seems to depend on intellectual as well as nutritional sustenance, and in the case of the former pictures appear to satisfy a universal appetite. The use of created patterns of visual stimulation as representations of other things is one of the most characteristic features of modern culture. Of course, pictures may sometimes be abstract, and appreciated for the shapes they contain, but it is very hard not to attribute meaning into anything we look at. Pictures can be both objects in themselves (a surface with marks on it like a painting or computer screen) and representations of objects. One consequence of this is that pictures are likely to be more complex stimuli to process than solid objects.

How might animals, such as our guide dog, respond to pictures? What does a dog see when it is looking at a television programme? Little experimental evidence exists, despite a plethora of anecdote. We might expect a response on the basis of stimulus generalisation; that is, in terms of the extent to which a pictorial pattern has common features with the thing it represents. Certainly, pictorial stimuli are often used to study animal vision, but these pictures are usually quite abstract, and the animal learns to associate a particular visual feature (such as the number of dots or the orientation or colour of lines) with a particular response. It is much harder to know if an animal's perception of a pictorial representation in any way resembles ours. There has been much research on the possibility of animal language (a different type of representation of reality) and there are reports of the production of pictures by higher primates and even elephants, but this does not help to answer the question. The issue is unresolved at present, but perhaps deserves future study.

In this chapter we will focus on the perception by humans of pictures as representations, because we now derive so much of our information about the world through pictures. We will also discuss some of the difficulties of perceiving and working with these sorts of stimuli. In addition, we will consider the perception of pictorial representations that have some of the three-dimensional properties of real objects—so-called "virtual reality". We begin by considering the principles underlying the relationship between pictures and the objects they represent.

PICTURES AND OBJECTS

Most experiments on object recognition use pictures of objects rather than the objects themselves. Accordingly, we know quite a lot about picture recognition. In order for this knowledge to be of use in furthering our understanding of object recognition we need to appreciate the relationship between pictures and objects. This was discussed on pages 43–46, particularly with respect to a painting by René Magritte (Figure 2.4), in which a curved pipe was pictured above text stating that it was not a pipe.

Magritte was contrasting two different forms of representation—pictorial images and written text. Both are in fact pictorial representations, but one concerns the spatial aspects of the particular object and the other the conventional description of the class of objects—pipes. Magritte exploited this distinction with skill because the pictorial representation of the curved briar pipe was readily recognisable. The orientation he chose for its representation was not arbitrary; had he painted it from other orientations its recognition would not have been as rapid. For example, the four pictures shown in Figure 7.1 are photographs of the same pipe as was used for producing Figure 2.4, but they were in different orientations with respect to the camera. Some might not even be recognised as representing a pipe if they were to be presented in isolation and without any context. You could try this out by showing someone the picture in the lower left quadrant on its own, by covering up the others, and asking them to say what object it would correspond to. We would not have the same difficulty in recognising an actual pipe in a number of orientations, because we would have information for its orientation in space and its dimensions. More pictorial variations on this theme can be found in Wade (1990). Therefore, if we are dealing with pictures of objects we need to consider the viewpoint from which the pictures are taken, and the orientation in which the picture itself is presented.

Pictures and their perception have often proved a fascination for visual scientists. Pictures have an advantage over objects in so far as we can

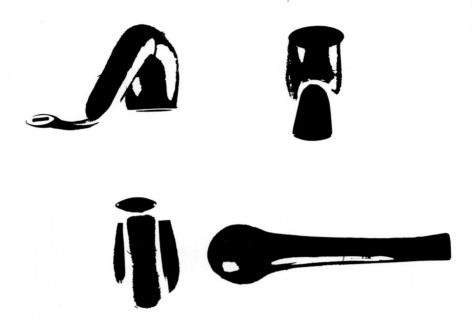

Figure 7.1 Four photographs of the same pipe from different viewpoints.

manipulate their characteristics much more readily than we can those of objects. Therefore, experimental studies are much easier to conduct with pictures, although there are many reasons for concluding that perception of a picture of an object is not the same as perception of the object itself. Gibson (1966, 1979) has been especially critical of experiments based solely on two-dimensional representations of objects and he has argued that the relation between such indirect perception and the direct perception of objects is a complex one. Gibson's essays on this topic have been collected by Reed and Jones (1982), and his ideas are evaluated by Gordon (1997). Wade (1990) presents a model of the imaging stages in vision and relates these both to the development of styles of representational art and to the allusory perception of depth in pictures. The possible relationships between visual neurophysiology and art are explored by Zeki (1999).

Orientation and bearing

It is clear from the example above that some pictures of the same object can be recognised more easily than others, according to the viewpoint from which they are imaged. Clearly this only applies to asymmetrical objects: Different views of a sphere would be the same, but almost all objects in our environment are asymmetrical. Even a symmetrical object like a cube can be pictured in many different ways, depending upon the orientation of the faces with respect to the viewpoint. With a camera mounted on a tripod, imagine photographing a cube with its near face in the frontal plane and the centre aligned with the optical axis of the camera. The outline of the photographic image would be a square (see Figure 7.2a), and the same configuration would result from any rotation of the cube around the optical axis of the camera. Figure 7.2b shows another view, with the face of the cube rotated by 45° with respect to the camera. The only difference between these two pictures is their orientation, but this is a critical one for our perception. We can discriminate differences based upon orientation alone, so that even though we can recognise that the configuration is a square in both instances, we can also discriminate the difference between them. In fact in this example we are likely to give different names to the same configuration, based solely on orientation: (a) would be called a square whereas (b) would be described as a diamond.

We will discuss the perception of pictures of a cube in more detail, in order to make clear some basic principles of representation. Changes in the orientation of pictorial images can be achieved in two ways: The cube could be rotated with respect to the stationary camera, or the camera could be rotated with respect to the stationary cube. The resulting photographs would be indistinguishable if the rotations had been equivalent. This projective equivalence would also apply to an observer but the two states would not be perceptually equivalent. If a square is presented vertically and at 45° we can discriminate the difference with ease. On the other hand, if we view a square with the head vertical and then with the head rotated so that the square is at 45° with respect to the retina, the two will not be easy to discriminate because of orientation constancy. That is, we make compensations for the inclination of the head to gravity.

The photographs of a cube we have considered so far have shown only one of its faces, and its rotations have been around the optical axis of the camera. In order to picture two faces of the cube it is necessary to rotate it around a vertical or horizontal axis, and three faces are imaged with rotation about both (see Figure 7.3). When all three faces are pictured there is a wide range of viewpoints that can be adopted to display varying proportions of each. Only when a diagonal axis of the cube is in the optical axis of the camera will the area and configuration of the three imaged faces be equal.

Parallel sides on a face of a cube converge in the photographs shown in Figure 7.3. The degree of convergence depends upon the characteristics of the lens used in the camera, the size of the cube and the distance from the camera. The photographs of the same cube shown in Figure 7.4 were taken with different lenses, and they have been enlarged to the same pictorial dimensions. The focal length of the lens in a conventional 35-mm camera is about 50 mm; Figure 7.4a shows a photograph taken with such a lens; the parallel sides converge by a moderate amount, and much more than in the case of a long focal length (200 mm) telephoto lens (Figure 7.4b). The convergence is considerable with the wide angle lens used to produce Figure 7.4c.

(b)

(a)

Figure 7.2 Photographs of a cube (a) with its sides vertical and (b) with its sides inclined by 45°.

(b)

(a)

Figure 7.3 Two photographs of a cube (a) with two faces imaged, and (b) with three faces imaged.

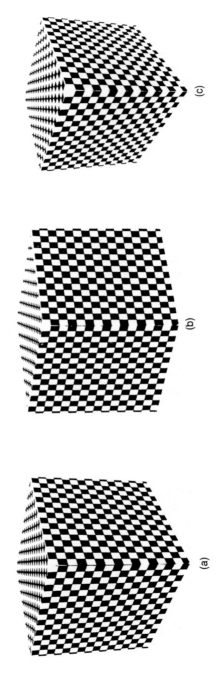

Figure 7.4 Three photographs of the same cube taken with (a) a 50-mm lens, (b) a 200-mm lens, and (c) a 20-mm lens.

If the eye is to be likened to a camera, then we should try to compare like with like. The focal length of the eye varies from around 14–17 mm, according to the state of accommodation. A lens with these characteristics in a camera would produce an image with massive distortions—straight lines would appear curved and the convergence of parallel lines would be considerable. Clearly, what we see does not correspond to the image formed in a camera with similar optical properties to the eye.

Stereotypical viewpoints

No photograph of a cube can be said to represent adequately a cube as an object, because they can, at best, only show three of the cube's six faces. The object pictured can only be a cube if it is assumed that the unseen faces correspond to those that are imaged. Exactly the same set of photographs to those shown earlier could have been produced with an object having only three connected faces rather than six—it could have been an empty shell. Despite this shortcoming we are remarkably good at recognising pictures of objects as representations of the objects. However, as was hinted previously, not all pictures of the same object are treated equivalently. Returning to Magritte's pictured pipe, some viewpoints are more readily recognised than others. These have been called canonical, typical, or stereotypical views of an object, and they apply principally to asymmetrical objects like pipes and people. What are the features that the stereotypical view has, that render it more readily recognisable? Magritte's pipe provides a good vehicle for considering this issue. All the photographs of pipes shown in Figure 7.1 are in accurate central perspective, as is that in Figure 2.4. Therefore, accurate representation is not the feature that distinguishes the stereotypical view from others. Many objects have a fixed polarity; they have a defined orientation with respect to the surface of the earth. This applies to people, who maintain a fixed posture with respect to gravity, and it applies to pipes, because tobacco will be retained in the bowl more readily in a particular orientation. Therefore, the stereotypical view needs to retain the normal orientation of the object. The normal orientation is retained in several of the photographs in Figure 7.1, but they are not stereotypical views because they foreshorten a critical dimension of the pipe—that along the stem.

   The structure of any object can be described in terms of a set of three-dimensional coordinates of all points on its surface. This set of coordinates would enable its surface structure to be reproduced. Another way of achieving such a structural description would be to take three projections of the object from three orthogonal directions. This is rather like taking a silhouette of an object from three viewpoints at right angles to one another, and this has been done for a pipe in Figure 7.5. One silhouette corresponds to a view from the side, another from the front, and a third from above. (Note that this is treating the pipe as though it has a clearly defined side, front, and top.) Each silhouette maximally foreshortens one of the dimensions of the pipe. Of the

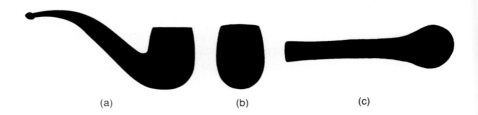

(a)   (b)   (c)

Figure 7.5 Silhouettes of a curved briar pipe viewed from (a) the side, (b) the front, and (c) the top.

three silhouettes one is more readily recognisable than the other two as representing a pipe, and that is the side view. The most difficult silhouette to recognise is that from the front, and that from above does not distinguish between a curved and a straight-stemmed pipe. Accordingly, the stereotypical view corresponds to the most recognisable silhouette of an object. It also corresponds to the viewpoint that minimally foreshortens the most asymmetrical dimension of the object (see Wade, 1990). It will be noted that in Figure 7.1, as in Magritte's painting, the viewpoint was shifted slightly from the side view, so that the circularity of the bowl could be represented as an ellipse. Thus, the three dimensions of the pipe are represented in the picture, but the most asymmetrical dimension is least foreshortened.

This analysis is easier with pipes than with people, because the surfaces are generally smoother with pipes. There is a great deal of significance attached to the patterning of features on people's heads, and so rather than take silhouettes we could take normal photographs from three orthogonal viewpoints. If we consider only the head, then it could be photographed from the front, the side, and from above, as is shown in Figure 7.6. Here it is not so obvious from which viewpoint the face can be recognised most easily. It is clear which is the poorest—the view from above, but the other two seem equally informative. Thus, it seems as though there are two stereotypical views for the human head. It is not coincidental that criminal "mug shots" are taken from profile and full-face views, and that most portraits are in three-quarter profile, so that dimensions of the protruding facial features are not lost.

Faces have often been considered to be special stimuli (see Bruce, 1988; Farah, 2000), and a vast amount of research has been conducted examining the facility which humans have in discriminating between them. Experimental work initially used simplified stimuli, like schematic faces, but the power of computers has revolutionised both the ways in which pictures of faces can be presented and the transformations of them possible (see Wade & Bruce, 2001).

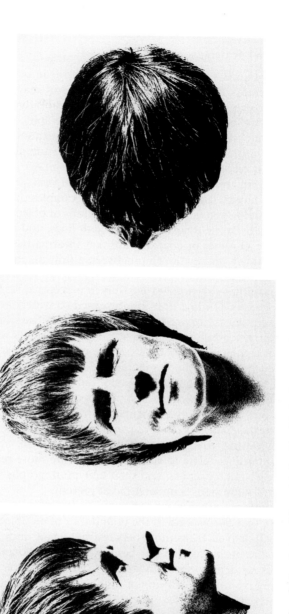

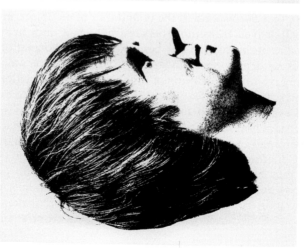

Figure 7.6 Three photographs of a head viewed from (a) the side, (b) the front, and (c) the top.

Photographs and drawings

Cameras are designed to produce pictures that are in central perspective; most of the pictures that we see in newspapers and magazines have been derived from a camera and so are in perspective. The situation is somewhat different when we consider drawing and other graphic arts. Perspective arrived rather late on the scene in Western art, and cannot be considered in any way as universal. Paintings were made in caves from about 30,000 years ago, and we can recognise the objects (usually animals) that are depicted. These are nearly all represented in the stereotypical view—outline profiles of bison, deer and horses. Thus, from the earliest examples of art outlines have been used to describe and delineate representations of objects. When we draw objects we initially define their boundaries with lines, and often do not proceed any further. Outlines or contours are very informative, and they can be sufficient to establish the relationship between a drawing and the object it is intended to represent.

Drawings or outlines are used extensively in perceptual research, far more so than photographs. Outline drawings are used so widely because, in large measure, they are so easy to produce and manipulate. The situation has been compounded by the onset of interactive computer systems which enable an observer to manipulate characteristics of the outline display. This is one of the factors that has led to the burgeoning of research on visual illusions—they can readily be drawn and manipulated. Indeed, simple outline drawings have even been used to determine complex perceptual dimensions, like the facial expressions, as in the experiments illustrated in Figure 7.7. There are consistencies in the emotions observers attach to these simple outlines, but it is difficult to know how to interpret them. In order to do so, we would need to know how the outlines relate to static views that are more representative of actual faces (e.g., photographs), and then how photographs relate to actual faces. Neither of these steps is understood at present.

Contours in drawings are abrupt changes in the amount of light reflected from a surface; they correspond to the boundaries of an object, but there are rarely such well-defined transitions between light and dark in the original scene. One of the problems that has beset workers in the area of computational vision is to define the boundaries of an object in a well-structured scene. Therefore, an outline drawing of an object is an abstraction that does not correspond readily to any features of the pattern of light projected from a scene. We are exposed to such simplified representations from a very early age, and so we learn how to interpret them. Experiments have established that we extract information not only from contours but also from the regions of a drawing where contours change direction or intersect (Attneave, 1954).

It is clear that humans have produced pictures for much longer than recorded history, and a variety of styles can be discerned. Linear perspective is amongst the most contrived because it requires picture-makers to forego their perception of space and to record visual angles from a single station

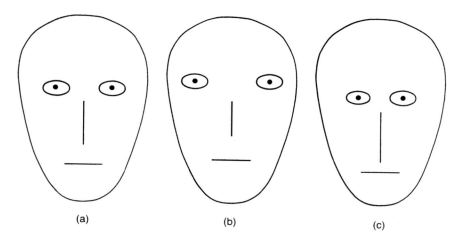

Figure 7.7 Examples of schematic faces. Brunswik and Reiter produced nearly 200 schematic faces, all within the same oval outline, by manipulating: the height and separation of the eyes, the height and length of the nose, and the height of the mouth. Of the three examples shown here (a) corresponds to the neutral standard, (b) was rated by observers as young, good, likeable, and beautiful, whereas (c) was rated as sad, old, ugly, and unlikeable. (After Brunswik, 1956)

point. Unlike the art forms that preceded it, linear perspective set out specific rules for representing the sizes of objects on the picture plane and, more importantly, the dimensions of texture on the receding ground plane. These were determined by the distance of the station point from the picture plane and the height of the station point from the ground plane (see Figure 2.5 on page 46). Thus, all the "painter's cues" to distance, described on pages 166–167, can be enlisted to increase the allusion to distance on the flat surface of the picture. Artists have to learn to draw in linear perspective and similarly observers have to learn to interpret pictures so produced. The drawing can be assisted by all manner of aids, the simplest of which were suggested by Alberti and Leonardo in the fifteenth century (see pages 44–48). If the picture plane is replaced by a pane of glass then, with a single eye at a fixed position (the station point), the contours in the scene can be traced on the glass surface: The tracing will be in accurate linear perspective.

The rules of linear perspective provide a consistent way of treating the dimension that the picture itself lacks—depth or distance. When three dimensions are reduced to two it is possible to play tricks with the transition, and to create worlds on paper that could not exist in three-dimensional space. Figure 7.8 illustrates two "impossible figures" that employ perspective capriciously. The impossible triangle is in accurate perspective at all the corners, but the connecting lines create the impossibility. The "devil's pitchfork"

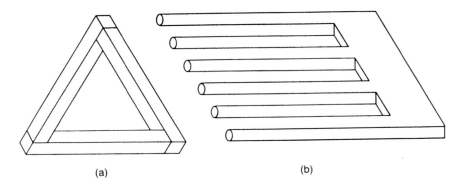

(a)   (b)

Figure 7.8 Impossible figures: (a) an impossible triangle, and (b) the "devil's pitchfork".

is another example that is based upon the minimum requirements for representing a cylinder and a rectangular bar: The twelve horizontal lines are connected to six ellipses on the left, representing six cylinders, but they constitute only four rectangular bars on the right.

Allied to these impossible figures are others that are not sufficiently specified to be perceived unambiguously. Perhaps the most famous of these is called the Necker cube, after the Swiss crystallographer Louis Necker who first described it in 1832. He was observing a crystal under the microscope and noted that its structure appeared to alternate in depth. Necker actually observed a rhomboid rather than a cube (see Figure 1.6c on page 28), but subsequent illustrations used a cube, and that is the structure with which he is eponymously linked. The Necker cube is an outline figure that is equivalent to a skeleton cube imaged with a telephoto lens so that the sides remain parallel (see Figure 7.9). The figure appears to fluctuate in orientation, at one moment it seems to be pointing down and to the right, then it flips to appear pointing up and to the left. Note how the fluctuation is less pronounced for a representation of a skeleton cube that has converging sides (Figure 7.9b). Some artists have manipulated a related form of perceptual ambiguity in which the same outline can be seen as representing two different objects, only one of which is visible at once.

Perceiving pictures

We perceive pictures in the same way that we perceive other objects in the environment: They are flat, mostly on paper, but occasionally in frames. There is nothing peculiar about pictures as objects. However, this is not what is usually meant by picture perception. The term refers to the interpretation of the marks on the surface of the picture—to the recognition of the marks as

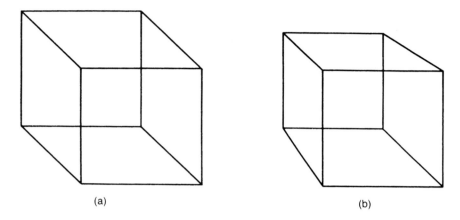

Figure 7.9 Necker cubes drawn with (a) parallel and (b) converging sides.

referring to objects that are not actually there. Thus, pictures have a dual reality: They exist as objects and, in addition, the marks signify other objects and spaces than those they occupy. In the first sense, pictures pose the same problems as pipes and people; they have locations and dimensions that need to be resolved by the perceiver. In the second sense, they are paradoxical because they allude to another space or to other objects.

It is possible to arrange conditions such that a picture is not seen on the surface it occupies. Such works are called trompe l'oeil because they "fool the eye" (see Wade & Hughes, 1999). Successful trompe l'oeil paintings are very rare, and they are exceedingly contrived. One example can be found in the National Gallery, London; it is a perspective cabinet painted by the seventeenth-century Dutch artist, Samuel van Hoogstraten. The scene represented is an interior of a house with many interconnecting rooms, which can be seen through open doors. The interior of the cabinet can only be viewed through a peephole. What is of interest is that the surfaces upon which the various parts are painted are complex and do not correspond to those in the scene: A chair, for instance, is painted on three surfaces at right angles to one another! The painting achieves its aim (i.e., not to appear distorted) because of the constraints placed on the observer: It can only be viewed from the fixed station point with one eye, and the viewing angle is such that the extreme edges of the painted surfaces cannot be seen. Neither of these conditions apply to the pictures we normally see: We use both eyes, look at them from many different positions, and we can see the borders that separate the picture from its surroundings.

It would seem, from this discussion, that pictures are very complex stimuli. Because we can recognise the objects represented from such a wide range of viewpoints we cannot be processing a pattern of stimulation like that from the original scene. It is more likely that we apply shape constancy to the border of the picture before processing the contents and interpreting the cues to depth. If this is the case then processes involved in picture perception must occur after those for object recognition. One consequence of this conclusion is to question whether the insights derived from picture recognition can be of any utility in furthering our understanding of object recognition.

COMPUTER-GENERATED DISPLAYS

Many of the pictures we now look at are presented on computer screens. Indeed, the technology of computer graphics is advancing so rapidly that attempts to simulate scenes are within our grasp. That is, the picture on the screen can mimic the view of a scene and it can change with movements of an observer in the way the view of a scene would. Furthermore, artificial environments can be generated by computers and presented to observers to induce the impression of exploring a virtual space. The experience from systems which seek to simulate real or artificial scenes so that they will be seen as three-dimensional is referred to as virtual reality.

Virtual realities

We think of virtual reality as a modern engineering enterprise, made possible by the power of computers, because they are associated with dynamic stereoscopic displays. However, the issues at the heart of virtual reality address some ancient questions of visual perception. One of these is the contrast between monocular and binocular vision, which Leonardo da Vinci repeatedly struggled with (see Wade, Ono, & Lillakas, 2001). He made many drawings of viewing with one and two eyes, and realised that the perception of depth is deficient in a painting or any other two-dimensional representation. Alberti's window, described on pages 44–48, provides a monocular match between a picture and a view from a single point, but what happens when two viewpoints are adopted? It is clear that Leonardo came close to representing binocular disparities, but he was unable to do so because he had no adequate theory of image formation in the eye. As was stated in Chapter 4, Wheatstone (1838) supplied this want with his invention of the stereoscope. It was the first apparatus for matching binocular incoming messages and can be considered as satisfying Leonardo's desire to imitate nature binocularly.

Neither Leonardo's painted imitation of the world from a single vantage point nor Wheatstone's paired pictures entertained the possibility of a moving perceiver. That is, the projected images themselves change as a consequence of observer movements, and the technology for capturing such changes did not then exist. It is now possible to present paired and disparate images to the two eyes on small screens mounted in a helmet. The location of the head-mounted device can be monitored so that the two images can be

rapidly and appropriately transformed, as can sounds presented to each ear. The visual and auditory changes can be augmented by sensors which apply pressures to the surface of the skin. With such devices it is possible to present artificial or virtual worlds for observers to explore and become immersed in. Thus, the head-mounted displays that are used in creating a virtual reality today enslave the paired pictures to eye and head movements, so that incoming messages of a more complicated nature can be matched to a mobile observer. Even with this addition, however, the incoming binocular messages of the simulated space cannot be matched perfectly from two flat screens, because the differential defocusing of the retinal image is not yoked to the states of convergence and accommodation of the eyes (see Peli, 1999).

It is clear from the previous discussion that virtual reality is by no means a novelty if we consider that pictures provide indirect access to a space other than the one occupied by the visual display. However, the increasing power of cameras and computers has added a new dimension to both virtual reality and remote vision—the visual display of current information that can be rapidly updated. Not only does this offer the opportunity to have apparently moving pictures in real time, but it also allows the viewer to interact, and control, the sequence of scenes displayed visually. The advantages of such systems are obvious for explorations of scenes that are inaccessible otherwise (like the surface of planets) or are dangerous (like the inner workings of nuclear power stations). They also permit the exploration of virtual environments. Remote vision is now much closer to home, as it is used in a variety of situations with which we might come into contact. One of these is endoscopic surgery, which will be discussed in pages 255–258.

Working with computer-generated displays

For over 50 years, an increasing proportion of the pictures seen by human observers have been those created every 15–20 ms on cathode ray tubes. Television images are ubiquitous, but until the very recent advent of interactive television they have been passive in the same way as painted pictures or photographs. They are observed, but not altered by the observer. Images generated by personal computers are normally interacted with, and play an important part in, both work and leisure. Much employment now depends on being able to work with information presented under computer control on various sorts of VDU. These can be based on a number of technologies, and the range will no doubt increase. However, VDUs employing the same cathode ray tube as the domestic television are so commonly encountered that they seem likely to remain the basis of working with computers for some time to come. Certainly, most of what is known about vision with VDUs is based on studies with these devices, and the discussion that follows will therefore be largely confined to them. Any account of perception with a current technology is likely to be outdated very quickly. Nevertheless, a theme running through this book is the need to bear in mind the characteristics and

limitations of the human visual system, no matter what the source of stimulation to which it is exposed. The best aim for technological advance is to match the properties of devices, which we can determine, to those of the visual system, which are essentially constant and a reflection of the natural environment in which they evolved.

There is a considerable literature relating to the problems of working with VDUs, extending back to the early days of interactive computing (Gould, 1968). The main aim of the early studies was to establish acceptable values for properties such as the contrast, colour, luminance, polarity, and resolution of the display. The information displayed was almost entirely confined to text, and it was only in the 1970s that computer systems began to have the capability of displaying more complex images that could represent moving objects and scenes. The growth of the computer games industry undoubtedly played a part in this development, and there continues to be very rapid change in the graphical capacities of computers.

Images displayed on a VDU are created by causing some of the phosphor dots with which the screen is covered to emit light (in some systems the dots are replaced by small vertical strips). The perception of colour is generated by replacing the single dots of a monochrome display with groups of dots in which each has different wavelength emission properties, normally corresponding to the visible red, green, and blue. Each dot in the group can be activated independently, thus building up an image which appears to have areas of colour. The emission of light is stimulated by a beam of electrons (the cathode ray of the cathode ray tube), which is scanned across the screen by a magnetic field. The pattern of scanning can vary, but typically proceeds from one top corner of the screen, across successive lower rows of dots. The phosphor dots emit light only very briefly when stimulated by the beam, typically decaying to 1% of peak luminance in around 0.5 ms. Thus the screen is actually blank for around 90% of the time, and the apparent continuity of the displayed image is the result of integrative processes in the visual system. The time taken to completely redraw the screen determines the refresh rate, which is the maximum speed at which new information can be displayed. In television systems, alternate rows are scanned from the top to the bottom of the screen, and the beam then returns to the top to scan the interleaved rows. This is known as interlacing, since only half the image is redrawn in each pass. Interlacing helps to reduce the effects of flicker when the refresh rate is low, but it also reduces the rate at which the screen is fully updated. If the refresh rate is determined by the frequency of the mains alternating current (50 Hz in Europe, 60 Hz in the USA) then a new interlaced image is fully redrawn 25 or 30 times per second. With computer-controlled VDUs the electron beam may be driven at a higher rate than in a mains-governed television, and 120 Hz is not uncommon as an option. It is worth noting that all display devices have a refresh rate, although in the case of some, like the flat panel displays found on laptop computers, it is very high and flicker is not an issue. No matter what the technology, the human user is presented with a

series of static images, which may be seen to represent motion if they succeed one another fast enough to create a perception of apparent movement.

The rate at which information is displayed by a computer system depends on various factors. All systems that transmit information have a limit on their bandwidth, which is the amount of information that can be carried in a given time. The overall graphics speed of a computer system is limited by the component that has the lowest bandwidth. The speed of the processor and the complexity of the calculations it performs will limit how much information can be updated between refresh cycles. There may also be limitations imposed by the graphics system that prepares signals in a suitable form for the display device. A VDU displays an image that is computed as a matrix of points, or pixels. The number of pixels defines the resolution of the image, and this has been increasing rapidly in recent years. Whereas personal computers in the early 1980s typically displayed monochrome text images made up of 320 by 240 pixels, values of 1024 by 960 (or higher) are not now uncommon, in a palette of thousands or even millions of colours.

The goal is to present images that convey sufficient information for the task in hand, that are convincingly realistic representations and that give a perception of smooth rather than discontinuous movement. Realism and continuity of movement depend on sufficient spatial and temporal resolution. A highly detailed image requires a display with a large number of pixels, and smooth movement requires small differences between each successive image frame presented with sufficient frequency. These characteristics are important for perceived realism, but they place great demands on the processor and other components of the graphics system. If the image is to be updated fast enough to give rise to acceptable perceived quality, then there will usually need to be a compromise between resolution, colour and the computational task if a human user is to interact with the system in real time. One outcome is often to reduce the number of calculations to be performed by computing or storing the images in advance or defining represented objects in terms of blocks or polygons. In the latter case, internal detail is restricted, so that in effect fewer pixels have to be recalculated in a given time. Another approach is to process the image in order to remove any redundant or irrelevant information. There are many such compression or encoding algorithms, and the best can reduce the transmitted information by a factor of a hundred or more. Feynman (1999) provides the most lucid account both of the mathematical principles of encoding and of the general principles underlying computation. Since there is some inevitable loss of image quality as a result, a key requirement is to ensure that any degradation is not readily perceived by the user.

Interestingly, the principles underlying information compression in computers and other communication systems can also be shown to be operating in the transmission of information in the sensory systems of animals. For example, as discussed in Chapter 3, the visual system transmits the pattern of stimulation on the retina by means of an optic nerve with around 1% of the number of rods and cones. Cells in the visual pathway with spatially extended receptive fields combine the input of many receptors, and signal the presence of a particular pattern of stimulation, not the stimulation itself. As a result, spatial and temporal change is detected and enhanced but areas of constant stimulation are not, since their presence is conveyed by the absence of signals from change or pattern detectors.

In general, we are still some way from the goal of fully realistic computer imagery that can be altered as a consequence of an observer's movements in the same way as retinal images arising from the natural environment. The processing power needed for this is very great, and although it will almost certainly be achieved eventually as a result of market demand, the systems we have at present hardly warrant the term virtual reality.

Reading text from a screen

Perhaps the most commonly encountered image on a computer screen consists largely or only of text. Text processing has been at the heart of interactive computing from its inception, to the extent that the preparation of documents by any other means is becoming increasingly uncommon in the more developed economies. It is perhaps therefore surprising that problems with reading text on computer-driven VDUs have been reported and studied from the earliest stages of development but the solutions have not been found. Although this work is of obvious practical importance, it also sheds light on fundamental visual processes, such as the control of saccadic eye movements (see Kennedy, Radach, Heller, & Pynte, 2000). The basic finding is that people read text on VDUs more slowly than on paper, and make more mistakes. For example, proof-reading can be slower and less accurate with a VDU compared to paper presentation of text. Reading from a VDU can also give rise to greater levels of reported fatigue or "eye strain", a subjective phenomenon commonly associated with prolonged work with VDUs. The difficulty of drawing clear general conclusions is however shown by studies that report only some or even none of these effects, and the difficulty of attributing effects to the orientation of the screen or the contrast, polarity, or resolution of the characters. Dillon (1992) provides a review of many studies relating to this field. However there is one factor for which there is good evidence of interference with efficient reading. This factor is the flickering, or more correctly, the intermittency of the visual stimulation. Although a display may have a refresh rate well above the point at which flickering is perceived (i.e., over around 70 Hz), there are measurable detrimental effects on performance. These are not confined to reading, but can include guidance of a mouse device or fingerprint identification. It appears that an intermittently illuminated screen may interfere with control of the saccadic eye movements that are involved in reading fluently and in visual search. The reasons for this are not yet fully established, but saccades seem to fall short of their intended position and this may happen even with refresh rates as high as 120 Hz (Kennedy, Brysbaert, & Murray, 1997).

While the effects of intermittent illumination on working with computers are still not agreed or fully understood, there is a great deal of evidence from other lines of investigation. Flickering light sources are common in the form of fluorescent lighting and domestic television, and Wilkins (1995) has documented the consequences in the home and workplace. These include reports of fatigue, headaches, and lack of ability to concentrate, and in extreme cases attacks of photosensitive epilepsy. The latter may be triggered by intermittent illumination, and occurs with varying severity in around 1% of the population. Wilkins (1995) has pointed out, however, that many of the other effects of intermittent illumination may be considered as mild versions of the same syndrome. He has also drawn the connection with patterns that are spatially intermittent. Inspection of repetitive striped patterns may have similar effects to repetitive flashed light, and people with a strong sensitivity to the latter may also find difficulty in looking at the former. The possibility exists that some of the problems with reading that are attributed to dyslexia may be caused by a heightened sensitivity to the striped patterns formed by lines of text, whether they are presented on paper or a VDU.

Endoscopic imagery

There is a tendency to consider that new developments in technology will impose novel theories to address them. We do not consider that this is the case for vision. There are novel demands on the perceiver, but these can be treated theoretically within the same framework we have adopted for dealing with everyday tasks, like crossing the road. Accordingly, we can use the concepts of frames of reference to address the problems that arise with remote vision. The principal issue is that the normal links between vision and action are disrupted because skilled manipulation, which is necessarily geocentric, is based upon visual information that is not.

Any visual-motor task requires a match between the coordinate systems operating in both vision and motor control. This issue is of particular importance for skilled tasks upon which life itself can depend, like surgery. Typically when normal perceptual-motor relations are modified in some way it is assumed that a new motor skill is required. Insufficient attention has been paid to acquiring new perceptual skills which will enable the established motor patterns to be expressed. This situation has been brought sharply into focus with the application of remote vision to surgery. Open surgery maintains equivalence between visual and motor coordinate systems because there is no additional interface between the visual and the motor. Increasing numbers of operations are now conducted by remote vision: Cameras and surgical instruments are inserted into the patient and the surgeon manipulates the instruments using visual feedback from VDUs. This is referred to as endoscopic surgery, minimal access surgery, or minimal invasive therapy. With these procedures coordinate systems for vision and motor control are dissociated and the visual-motor tasks are much more demanding and fatiguing.

This is probably because of the enormous neural computation required to bring the coordinate systems into register. That is, the images on the VDU have to be remapped into three-dimensional coordinates that are appropriate to the manipulation of the unseen instruments within the patient. The question is how can this best be done? Is the remapping easier from two-dimensional or stereoscopic displays?

Two-dimensional displays utilise monocular, or pictorial cues, as described in Chapter 4. They include occlusion, height in the field, relative size, shading, and motion parallax. These cues are relational or patterncentric—that is, they provide information about whether one represented object is nearer to or farther from another. Binocular cues are retinal disparities and convergence; a geometrically equivalent source to horizontal disparity is motion parallax (if the head moves from side to side). By far the most attention has been paid to stereopsis from horizontal retinal disparity, almost to the exclusion of other non-monocular cues (see Reinhardt-Rutland, Annett, & Gifford, 1999). This is due largely to the ease with which retinal disparity can be manipulated using a stereoscope. In fact it has divorced the study of depth perception from depth itself, by providing a paired two-dimensional surrogate for it. Horizontal disparity also provides relative depth information.

As we argued in Chapter 4, rather than classifying cues as binocular or monocular, it is more instructive to divide them into egocentric and relational. Egocentric cues provide information for the distance that an object is from the observer; relational cues signal distance with respect to other objects, whether they are nearer or farther from them, not how near or how far. Likely sources of egocentric distance are convergence, and vertical disparity; all the others indicate distance relative to other objects. Vertical disparity relates to the differences in vertical dimensions of an object projected to each eye. Wheatstone (1852) himself showed that the depth seen with a given horizontal disparity varies inversely with the convergence of the eyes (see Chapter 4).

In normal viewing, distance or depth is overspecified: Many cues are brought to bear on resolving it, and we rarely make errors of distance perception when active in the natural environment. Endoscopic surgery involves visual environments that are anything but natural, but the normal three-dimensional motor behaviours apply to it. One important point to bear in mind is that while there are two-dimensional displays there is no two-dimensional vision! All perception is three-dimensional; even when we look at a two-dimensional screen it is perceived at an egocentric distance. Similarly, if we look at a stereo display, the depth seen will depend on its distance from us—provided either by convergence or monocular cues. The term three-dimensional for a display system is usually a misnomer, since the two images will be projected within a frame that is clearly seen as flat. In this case they are pseudo-three-dimensional at best. The theoretical distinction we should be examining is that between egocentric and relational depth, not two-dimensional and stereoscopic displays.

Many studies in visual science have pitted monocular and binocular cues against one another in order to determine which prevails. When there is conflict between monocular and stereoscopic cues in displays it has generally been found that the monocular were dominant (see Howard & Rogers, 1995). This observation can be traced back to the earliest work on stereoscopic and pseudoscopic vision: Wheatstone (1852) devised a pseudoscope, which reversed the disparities in the two eyes, and noted how difficult it was to see objects pseudoscopically because of the competing monocular cues. The message from such studies is that stereo might not be as powerful a source of depth as has been supposed—especially if it conflicts with monocular cues. However, the practicalities of endoscopic surgery do not allow the study of single cues in isolation, and so the comparisons are more difficult to design and to evaluate. There are many constraints that are operating on the imaging system as well as on the surgeon.

If we accept that the displays convey relative distance information how can the remapping be achieved? There must be some anchoring information available in the image to make the conversion possible. That is, some feature of the display is required to rescale all others for both size and depth. The most likely of these is the familiar size of the instruments imaged, and knowledge of the dimensions of the anatomical structures imaged. Even though the instruments will in all probability be seen in a different location and at a different size they can still be used to rescale the sizes of other structures in the display. Another possibility (in the tradition of British empiricism described in Chapter 2) is to use the motor system to calibrate the ambiguous visual array. Moving the displayed instruments in some familiar manner and noting their translation across the display could act as an anchor for spatial scale. This possibility is unlikely to be reliable because the instruments (which have long extensions and constrained pivot points) are seen rather than the hand itself.

Various depth cues will operate irrespective of the type of display; of these occlusion is probably the most powerful. Stereo might be useful if it is in correspondence with the anchoring information (such as instrument size). However, with a moving camera there is a basic difference between the changes of pictorial and disparity information. Projected size is linearly related to distance, but disparity operates on an inverse square law. That is, halving the distance between camera and instrument doubles the projected size of the instrument, whereas it would quadruple the disparity. This can provide a problem for a moving stereo system, and would place even further demands on the remapping of the displayed image. There have been many studies comparing two-dimensional and stereoscopic displays (see Taffinder, Smith, Huber, Russell, & Darzi 1999), but any advantages associated with the latter are not startling; whether these small advantages are still present with moving cameras remains to be determined.

In short, if the scaling of monocular and stereo signals is not matched, then the addition of stereo might be detrimental to visual scaling and thence to motor control. That is, the cues should act in harmony whether the displays are two-dimensional or stereoscopic; the likelihood of disharmony is greater for stereoscopic than two-dimensional displays. Matching stereo with some monocular reference (like an instrument) is nontrivial when both the cameras and the instrument can move, not to mention movements of the surgeon.

It might seem that a virtual solution to endoscopic surgery would be ideal—to have two cameras separated by the distance of the eyes (and changing in convergence as the eyes do) with their images delivered to the two eyes independently (stereoscopically). Even this would not be free of constraints since the surgeon's head would need to be fixed in space—because of the limitations on camera movement—and the cameras themselves would not move (other than to vary convergence). But such an arrangement could well be counterproductive because it would be as if the eyes were in the body of the patient rather than attached to the body of the surgeon.

If it is accepted that endoscopic surgery involves artificial displays that cannot, in principle, mirror natural vision then we must seek the best artificial system that enables remapping of the displayed image onto the three-dimensional manipulations of the instruments. The critical requirement of endoscopic surgery is the coordination of action with vision, so that skilled manipulations can still be made under visual guidance. This raises empirical questions that can be resolved, but they should be tackled with the theoretical issues of spatial perception in mind.

This chapter has covered a wide range of topics, but they are all connected by the need to understand what is involved in perceiving images that represent objects or environmental events. The representation may be quite direct and seemingly obvious, as in a photograph, or indirect and symbolic, as with text. We have sought to demonstrate that in all cases, the perception of images may give an illusory impression of simplicity. Their perception depends on the visual processes that we bring to bear on any pattern of optical stimulation, but the outcome depends on the complex relationship between the image and the natural world. The need to understand this relationship is most acute if the perceiver is to carry out some form of manipulation; that is, when vision guides action. If we are to design images so as to permit accurate manipulations, then we need to know how they are formed and how the visual system responds to the image itself as well as to what is represented.

In the following and final chapter, we will summarise the ideas developed throughout the book and draw some conclusions about the general principles that emerge from an emphasis on vision as a basis for action.

8 Summary and conclusions

The study of perception has a long history, as long as the history of science itself. The framework for science and for the study of perception was outlined by Greek philosophers, but we have concentrated upon the advances made in the modern era, following the scientific revolution in the seventeenth century. Our current theories of perception have been shaped by ideas in physics, art, physiology, biology, philosophy, psychology, and more recently computer science. Physics contributed an understanding of the nature of light and of the laws of optical transmission in air and in the eye. The former led to a recognition that vision is not due to the emission of energy from the eye, and the latter made it possible to understand how objects in the external world were represented as images on the retinal surface. The laws of optics were also employed in artistic representation: The formation of an image on a transparent screen at a fixed distance in front of the eye will produce a picture in linear perspective; if the screen is considered to lie at the back of the eye then a similar pattern will be produced (though inverted and reversed with respect to the external picture). When this similarity between image formation in the eye, in cameras, and in art was appreciated the problem of perception was thought of in terms of extracting information from a two-dimensional image. The retinal image was conceived in terms of a static picture, which has had profound effects upon both theory and experiment. It has meant that pictorial representations of objects could be considered as adequate experimental substitutes for the objects themselves, and that the dynamic aspects of vision could be too readily ignored. Because our eyes are in constant motion, the retinal image is an abstraction, not actually present in the eye unless a scene is viewed for a very brief interval, too short for the eyes to move. Anatomists examined the structure of the retina and of the optic nerves. Physiologists conjectured how the brain could distinguish between neural signals arising from different sense organs.

Towards the end of the nineteenth century specific cortical regions were found that received neural signals from the different sense organs. The biological perspective, following Darwin's theory, placed humans in a closer relationship to other animals and so added to the relevance of experiments on animal perception to interpretations of human perception. It emphasised developmental processes in both behaviour and perception; and it also examined instinctive and learned behaviours in more detail. Issues of innate and learned processes in perception have provided constant conflict within philosophy. On the one hand the nativists argued that certain aspects of perception (like space and time) were inborn, on the other the empiricists proposed that we derive our knowledge of the world through the senses and we learn to perceive spatial attributes by a process of association. These distinctions remain with us and have permeated psychological theories generally. Psychology has provided the study of perception with its basic experimental methodologies. It was the harnessing of psychophysical methods and the invention of a novel one for studying consciousness (analytic introspection) that led to the formation of psychology as an independent discipline. The psychophysical methods have stood the test of time (with constant improvements), but analytic introspection has fared less well: Its demise saw the emergence of Gestalt and behaviourist psychologies in the early part of the twentieth century, with the former showing more concern with perceptual matters than the latter.

Gestalt theory drew upon facts of magnetic and electrical fields in physics and speculated about similar field influences in the brain. That is, it considered that both perception and its underlying physiology were modelled on organising principles that could not be reduced to the operations of simplified elements. The Gestalt psychologists emphasised the holistic aspects of perception rather than the analytic: They did not believe that perception could be explained by reducing either stimuli or responses to their simplest levels. This contrast between holistic and analytic approaches to perception is one that remains in theories of perception. Ironically, the subsequent advances in the neurophysiology of vision have been based on precisely the reductionist ideas that the Gestalt psychologists rejected. The detailed study of the structure and function of nerve cells has suggested the ways in which complex patterns of light striking the retina are analysed in terms of simplified features that they contain. Thus, cortical cells could be excited by chromatic or spatio-temporal changes in the pattern of light falling over particular regions of the retina. Thus features of the stimulus (like retinal location, contour orientation, direction of motion, and colour) are thought to be extracted by single cells in the visual cortex of higher mammals, and they are preferentially processed at subsequent cortical sites. The presence of such feature detectors and cortical maps has been related to certain simple phenomena like visual aftereffects and illusions. However, the range of phenomena that has been successfully interpreted in neurophysiological terms remains limited. The more recent developments in modelling the behaviour of neural nets, derived from computer science, may provide a basis for returning to a more holistic approach to perception. Such networks have capacities for learning that are not localised in particular units, but that are a property of the net as a whole.

We know much more about the visual neurophysiology of cats and monkeys when presented with simple patterns than we do of humans. On the other hand, we have a great body of knowledge about human perception under similar simplified circumstances. In recent years this has been extended by the use of patterns of parallel lines called gratings. It seems as though such patterns are processed at early stages in vision, and there is evidence that spatial frequency is another stimulus dimension that is extracted by some single cortical cells. This has been a case of psychophysical experiments with human subjects leading to the neurophysiological search for a specific class of detectors in monkey visual cortex.

We still do not know how these feature detectors are involved in perception generally. This is largely because in almost all the neurophysiological experiments that are conducted with experimental animals the eye muscles are paralysed to avoid any eye movements during the presentation of stimuli. In our terms these studies are concerned with stimulus processing at the retinocentric level. That is, the representation of features like contour orientation, spatial frequency, direction of motion, and colour is with respect to the retinal coordinate system alone. Such a representation is unlikely to be adequate for vision in an animal with moving eyes, because retinocentric displacements could be a consequence of object movement or eye movement.

Perception of objects in the world involves seeing where they are, when they occur and what they are. That is, we need to determine their location, whether they are moving, and to recognise them. These characteristics are defined relative to a frame of reference, so that statements about an object's motion, for example, are typically made with respect to the surface of the earth. Perception of object characteristics needs to conform to the frame of reference within which behaviour takes place, which will also normally be the surface of the earth. Such perceptions can be termed geocentric. An active perceiver, whether human or animal, must recover the geocentric properties of objects, despite self motion. We have described the frames of reference relative to which information can be represented, and from which geocentric information can be derived. The first, retinocentric, level is the one that is studied by neurophysiologists: Information is coded in terms of the coordinate system of the retina. Retinocentric information describes image characteristics with respect to retinal coordinates, but it is not necessarily localised in the retina. The fact that a response occurs in the visual cortex, or elsewhere, need not preclude it from being retinocentric in character. The term retinocentric expresses the nature of the information, and not its anatomical site.

This level is essential for vision but it cannot serve as a basis for object perception because we have two eyes and both of them move. The next frame of reference uses an integrated binocular signal from the two eyes together with their movements to provide an egocentric frame of reference, the origin of which lies between the eyes. We perceive the directions of objects with respect to the egocentre. Visual direction alone would not enable us to locate objects in space; in order to do this we also need to determine the distance objects are away from us. There are many sources of information for the relative distances between objects—which is nearer or further—but these need to be anchored by information for egocentric distance before objects can be adequately located in space. If information for the observer's own movements is incorporated, then objects will be represented in the geocentric frame of reference. When we have derived a geocentric representation of objects, we are in a position to behave appropriately with respect to them. The operation of these frames of reference can be more fully illustrated in the context of motion perception.

Perceiving whether, and to what extent, an object is moving depends on many factors. Consideration of retinal stimulation alone cannot account for geocentric visual perception. Many other sensory systems are involved in the recovery of the location and movement of objects in space. For example, information from the vestibular system is used to determine accelerations of the head in three dimensions, and this is essential if the pattern of retinal change arising from a head movement is to be interpreted unambiguously. The integration of these sensory systems constitutes visual perception, and it would be wrong to suppose that visual perception can be understood solely in terms of light reaching the eye. Figure 6.1 (see page 219) summarised the process of recovering geocentric movement. Initial registration of retinocentric motion in each eye gives rise to a single binocular (cyclopean) retinocentric signal. This expresses motion with respect to a point located between the eyes. Since the two eyes move by equal amounts when version occurs, a single signal for eye movement can be combined with the binocular retinocentric signal to give an egocentric representation. This carries information for changes in angular direction with respect to the observer, despite movements of the eyes. It will correctly express changes in object direction, but will only represent the position of objects in the environment if the observer is stationary. If the observer's head moves then the eyes necessarily move too. This causes displacement of the retinal image, in a way which cannot be interpreted unless the extent of self motion and the distance of the object are known. Scaling the egocentric information by perceived distance gives the three-dimensional location of objects with respect to the observer. This can be corrected for the effects of self movement, since both are expressed in terms of three-dimensional displacements, to produce a geocentric representation of the movement of objects in the environment.

We can generate a geocentric representation of space and motion under the conditions described previously, although they are rarely encountered in the natural environment. Objects are seldom seen in isolation; other background objects will be in view, and they might undergo different transformations relative to the observer. Moving objects are seen in the context of others that are typically supported on the ground plane and remain in a fixed position with respect to it. Thus, there is another frame of reference that is of vital significance to perception and visual-motor control generally. It concerns the location and motion of one part of a visual scene with respect to others. Since it refers to visual pattern interactions we have called it a patterncentric frame of reference. Thus, if one object moves with respect to others (that remain in the same spatial relations with respect to one another) then the object is seen to be moving. This is the situation that obtains almost all the time in our interaction with the world. For example, cars are seen as moving because the features surrounding them, like trees and buildings, remain in the same relation to one another. The trees and buildings provide a patterncentric frame of reference relative to which the displacements of the car are assigned. Stars, on the other hand, are not so firmly anchored in perceptual space: They can appear to be stationary or to move, depending upon their visible background. They appear stationary on a cloudless night, but can seem to move when clouds pass by them. This indicates the manner in which the patterncentric process operates: When the stars are seen behind moving clouds they appear to move in the opposite direction to the clouds. This is called induced motion, and it reflects the influence of a larger visual pattern on the visibility of parts enclosed within it. The clouds provide a patterncentric frame of reference, and are treated as stationary, whereas the displacement of the stars with respect to them is treated as motion. Under almost all normal conditions the patterncentric frame of reference will correspond to that operating geocentrically and it will cooperate with the uniform system, in the manner represented in Figure 8.1.

The model incorporates all the features present in Figure 6.1 and adds to it the effects of a patterned background. In order to accommodate the known physiological properties of cortical cells (Chapter 3) together with the psychophysical evidence from motion interactions (Chapter 5) the patterncentric mechanisms are both monocular and binocular. That is, the patterncentric signals are derived monocularly and then are combined to provide a binocular patterncentric signal. The latter is determined by the purely monocular patterncentric signals as well as by their logical combination through AND and OR operations. The evidence for these derives from experiments on induced motion and motion aftereffects, and is described in greater detail in Wade and Swanston (1996).

Under almost all natural conditions the patterncentric frame of reference will correspond to the geocentric. However, they can be separated in the laboratory by removing or manipulating the visible background. The examples of induced motion given earlier and in Chapter 5 involved isolating and moving visible backgrounds. Our sensitivity to relational motion is far more acute than that for uniform motion, as was indicated in Chapter 5. Induced motion is also the phenomenon exploited in many video games, where a central pattern (like a car) appears to move in the opposite direction to the moving background. Such induced motion is rarely complete because the monitor on which the motion is presented is both visible and in the same position relative to other objects (like the walls of the room).

At this level of analysis, the nature of the information required for a geocentric representation is defined, rather than its sources. The concern is with

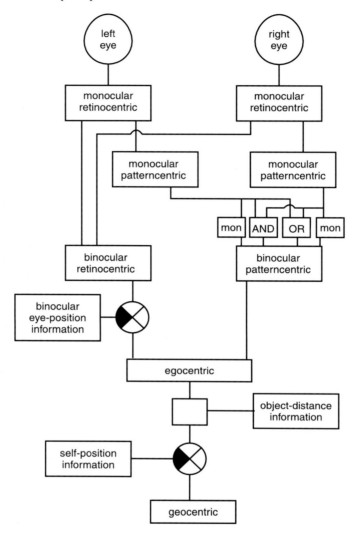

Figure 8.1 Schematic diagram of spatial representation in the presence of a patterned background. All the features of the uniform model (Figure 6.1)
are present, with the addition of patterncentric signals for the location
and motion of one visible object with respect to others. The patterncentric signals are extracted monocularly and combined
independently of the retinocentric signals. The logical AND and OR
operators reflect the processes involved in both stereopsis and binocular single vision. The binocular patterncentric signals are integrated with the eye-position compensated retinocentric signals at the
egocentric level. Perceived distance and body position operate on the
egocentric signals in the manner described for Figure 6.1, to yield a
geocentric representation of object location and motion. (After Wade
& Swanston, 1996).

the rules and relationships that permit a geocentric representation of the external world by an observer who can move in the environment, and whose sense organs can move with respect to the body. A geocentric representation is required for effective action in the environment, since it conveys information which is independent of the observer's movements. A geocentric representation has the properties required for perceptual constancies, such as size, shape, and location. It will not change despite changes in viewing distance or angle of regard. It will therefore provide a basis for object recognition, since objects are represented in a manner which is consistent even when the conditions of observation change. If a geocentric representation is stored in memory, it can be matched to the same object when encountered on a subsequent occasion, because it is independent of the observer and the circumstances of observation.

There may of course be errors in the process of recovering a geocentric description. Relational motions, eye movements, self movements, or distance may not be accurately detected, and image displacements on the retina may be more or less than the signal to which they give rise. If so, then the perception of shape, size, or movement may no longer accord with their physical dimensions, and object recognition may fail. The model shown in Figure 8.1 is a description of the steps needed to achieve geocentric perception; in practice these may be carried out more or less successfully.

Geocentric representations may be employed to carry out tasks that are expressed in terms of other coordinate systems. For example, someone may be asked to state the direction of an object with respect to their head, or some other part of their body. Alternatively, it may be necessary to judge the location of one object with respect to another. These tasks can be accomplished on the basis of geocentric information. Although the required frame of reference is no longer explicit, it can be recovered when needed if information about the articulation of the eyes, head, and body is preserved. It is important to distinguish the frame of reference used to describe an activity, from that which determines an observer's spatial perception.

All perception is necessarily geocentric, but it may not seem so under restricted laboratory conditions. Stimuli may be exposed for intervals too short for the eyes to move during their presentation. If very briefly exposed stimuli are used, eye movements will not take place, and perception will correspond to the egocentric level. It might be thought that in this case perception would be retinocentric, but binocular combination is unavoidable, even when one eye is covered or non-functional. Egocentric directions and movements are always based upon binocular signals, at least in humans and other species with overlapping monocular visual fields. If the observer remains stationary, then the importance of perceived distance and perceived self motion in spatial vision will not be appreciated. A high proportion of studies of human spatial perception incorporate restrictions that eliminate one or more of these factors.

Although this discussion has been expressed in terms of the fundamental requirements for human perception, it is interesting to consider the similarities, and differences, that may apply to other species. Few animals have large overlapping binocular fields of view, and some have more than two eyes. In some crustaceans and insects, eyes are mounted on the end of flexible stalks which can move in three dimensions relatively independently of the rest of the body. Despite these complications, it is still necessary to obtain a geocentric representation of the world. Even a cursory examination of animal behaviour shows that most actions require information about the location in space of salient objects like predators, prey, mates, or offspring. Although we have considerable knowledge about the physiology of vision in many species, we know much less about the logic of the perceptual processes they serve. One point at any rate is clear: Geocentric perception is not necessarily based on knowledge of the world expressed in linguistic symbols. If this were so, only humans and perhaps the higher primates would be able to act effectively in the natural environment. Of course, a geocentric representation may be achieved in quite different ways by different species, just as a given arithmetical problem may have a number of equally valid routes to the correct answer. Nevertheless, the underlying requirements are the same; to obtain from the senses information which is capable of guiding the activities required for survival.

The role of cognitive processes in perception has been exceptionally difficult to establish. To an extent, this has become a matter of theoretical dispute. Those who have followed Gibson's approach have regarded perception as wholly independent of cognition, and determined entirely by a direct response to patterns of stimulation without any intervening process. By contrast, others have claimed that perception is akin to high-level cognitive processes such as problem solving and hypothesis formation. What we see would then be determined at least as much by what we know as by what is there to be seen. It is in the context of arbitrary stimuli, like pictures and written script, that the cognitive approaches to perception are at their strongest. We learn to attach significance to certain shapes that formerly were of no importance to us. However such learning processes are not confined to humans. Pigeons can discriminate between letters of the alphabet, and many artificial seeing machines can carry out industrial inspection tasks. Our metaphorical guide dog is also able to learn the significance of initially arbitrary objects and act on them, like stopping in front of overhanging barriers that it, but not a human, could walk under.

The goal of this book has been to concentrate on the functions that a perceptual system must perform, and to show how the understanding of these has developed in the modern era. It is clear that many of the theoretical issues defined in the eighteenth and nineteenth centuries are still not resolved, and they persist despite great advances in the twentieth century in techniques for manipulating visual stimulation. Nevertheless, vision is an endlessly fascinating object of study, drawing as it does on such diverse disciplines for insight and advance. Even if the final goal is not in sight, the journey is worth the effort.

References

Addams, R. (1834). An account of a peculiar optical phænomenon seen after having looked at a moving body. *London and Edinburgh Philosophical Magazine and Journal of Science, 5*, 373–374.

Aleksander, I. (1983). Emergent intelligent properties of progressively structured pattern recognition nets. *Pattern Recognition Letters, 1*, 375–384.

Ash, M.G. (1995). *Gestalt psychology in German culture 1890–1967: Holism and the quest for objectivity*. Cambridge, UK: Cambridge University Press.

Attneave, F. (1954). Some informational aspects of visual perception. *Psychological Review, 61*, 183–193.

Aubert, H. (1865). *Physiologie der Netzhaut*. Breslau: Morgenstern.

Barlow, H.B. (1972). Single units and sensation: A neuron doctrine for perceptual psychology? *Perception, 1*, 371–394.

Barlow, H.B., & Mollon, J.D. (Eds.). (1982). *The senses*. Cambridge, UK: Cambridge University Press.

Bartlett, F.C. (1932). *Remembering: A study in experimental and social psychology*. Cambridge, UK: Cambridge University Press.

Bartlett, F.C. (1958). *Thinking: An experimental and social study*. London: Allen & Unwin.

Berkeley, G. (1709). *An essay towards a new theory of vision*. Dublin, Ireland: Pepyat.

Biederman, I. (1987). Recognition by components: A theory of human image understanding. *Psychological Review, 94*, 115–147.

Biederman, I. (2000). Recognizing depth-rotated objects: A review of recent research and theory. *Spatial Vision, 13*, 241–253.

Biederman, I., & Cooper, E.E. (1991). Priming contour-deleted images: Evidence for intermediate representations in visual object recognition. *Cognitive Psychology, 23*, 393–419.

Blakemore, C. (1973). The baffled brain. In R.L. Gregory & E.H. Gombrich (Eds.) *Illusion in nature and art*, pp. 9–47. London: Duckworth.

Blakemore, C. (Ed.). (1990). *Vision: Coding and efficiency*. Cambridge, UK: Cambridge University Press.

Boring, E.G. (1942). *Sensation and perception in the history of experimental psychology*. New York: Appleton-Century-Crofts.

Braddick, O.J. (1974). A short-range process in apparent motion. *Vision Research, 14*, 519–527.

Brewster, D. (1849). Account of a new stereoscope. *Report of the British Association, Transaction of the Sections*, pp. 6–7.

Broadbent, D.E. (1958). *Perception and communication*. London: Pergamon Press.

Bruce, V. (1988). *Recognising faces*. London: Lawrence Erlbaum Associates Ltd.

Bruce, V., Green, P.R., & Georgeson, M. (1996). *Visual perception: Physiology, psychology and ecology* (3rd ed.). Hove, UK: Lawrence Erlbaum Associates Ltd.

Brunswik, E. (1956). *Perception and the representative design of psychological experiments*. Berkeley, CA: University of California Press.

Brunswik, E. & Reiter, L. (1937). Eindrucks – Charaktere Schematisierer Gesichte. *Zeitschrift für Psychologie, 142*, 67–134.

Burton, H.E. (1945). The optics of Euclid. *Journal of the Optical Society of America, 35*, 357–372.

Cavanagh, P. (1991). Short-range vs long-range motion: Not a valid distinction. *Spatial Vision, 5*, 303–309.

Cavanagh, P. (1992). Attention-based motion perception. *Science, 257*, 1563–1565.

Coren, S., Ward, L.M., & Enns, J.T. (1999). *Sensation and perception* (5th ed.). Fort Worth, TX: Harcourt Brace.

Cornsweet, T.N. (1970). *Visual perception*. New York: Academic Press.

Craik, K.J.W. (1966). *The nature of psychology: A selection of papers, essays and other writings by the late Kenneth J.W. Craik* (S. L. Sherwood, Ed.). Cambridge, UK: Cambridge University Press.

Crombie, A.C. (1964). Kepler: De Modo visionis. In *Mélange Alexandre Koyré I. L'aventure de la science* (pp. 135–172). Paris: Hermann.

Cutting, J.E. (1986). *Perception with an eye for motion*. Cambridge, MA: MIT Press.

Darwin, C. (1859). *The origin of species by means of natural selection or the preservation of favoured races in the struggle for life*. London: Murray.

Darwin, C. (1872). *The expression of the emotions in man and animals*. London: Murray.

Dember, W.N. (1964). *Visual perception: The nineteenth century*. New York: Wiley.

Descartes, R. (1902). *La dioptrique*. In C. Adam & P. Tannery (Eds.), *Oeuvres de Descartes*, Vol. VI. Paris: Cerf. (Original work published 1637)

Descartes, R. (1965). *Discourse on method, optics, geometry, and meteorology* (P.J. Olscamp, Trans). New York: Bobbs-Merrill.

Descartes, R. (1972). *Treatise of man* (T.S. Hall, Trans). Cambridge, MA: Harvard University Press.

Dillon, A. (1992). Reading from paper versus screens: A critical review of the empirical literature. *Ergonomics, 35*, 1297–1326.

Edgerton, S.Y. (1975). *The Renaissance rediscovery of linear perspective*. New York: Basic Books.

Ellis, W.D. (Ed.) (1938). *A source book of Gestalt psychology*. London: Routledge & Kegan Paul.

Epstein, W. (Ed.). (1977). *Stability and constancy in visual perception: Mechanisms and processes*. New York: Wiley.

Ernst, B. (1976). *The magic mirror of M.C. Escher*. New York: Ballantine.

Fancher, R.E. (1996). *Pioneers of psychology* (3rd ed.). New York: Norton.

Farah, M.J. (2000). *The cognitive neuroscience of vision*. Oxford, UK: Blackwell.

Farah, M.J. & Ratcliff, G. (Eds.). (1994) *Neuropsychology of high-level vision*. Hillside, NJ: Lawrence Erlbaum Associates Inc.

Fechner, G.T. (1860). *Elements der Psychophysik*. Leipzig: Breitkopf & Härtel.

Fechner, G.T. (1966). *Elements of psychophysics, Vol. 1.* (H.E. Adler, Trans.). New York: Holt, Rinehart and Winston.

Feynman, R.P. (1999). *Lectures on computation.* London: Penguin.

Finger, S. (1994). *Origins of neuroscience: A history of explorations into brain function.* New York: Oxford University Press.

Frackowiak, R.S.J., Friston, K.J., Frith, C.D., Dolan, R.J., & Mazziotta, J.C. (1997). *Human brain function.* London: Academic Press.

Frisby, J.P. (1979). *Seeing: Illusion, brain and mind.* London: Oxford University Press.

Gardner, H. (1987). *The mind's new science: A history of the cognitive revolution.* New York: Basic Books.

Gescheider, G.A. (1997). *Psychophysics: Method, theory, and application* (3rd ed.). Mahwah, NJ: Lawrence Erlbaum Associates Inc.

Gibson, J.J. (1950). *Perception of the visual world.* Boston: Houghton Mifflin.

Gibson, J.J. (1966). *The senses considered as perceptual systems.* Boston: Houghton Mifflin.

Gibson, J.J. (1979). *The ecological approach to visual perception.* Boston: Houghton Mifflin.

Gilchrist, A.L. (1977). Perceived lightness depends on perceived spatial arrangement. *Science, 195,* 185–187.

Goethe, J.W. (1840). *Theory of colours* (C.L. Eastlake, Trans.). London: Murray.

Gogel, W.C. (1969). The sensing of retinal size. *Vision Research, 9,* 1079–1094.

Gogel, W.C. (1973). Absolute notion parallax and the specific distance tendency. *Perception and Psychophysics, 13,* 284–292.

Gogel, W.C. (1978). The adjacency principle in visual perception. *Scientific American, 238,* 126–139.

Gogel, W.C. (1982). Analysis of the perception of motion concomitant with lateral motion of the head. *Perception and Psychophysics, 32,* 241–250.

Gogel, W.C. (1990). A theory of phenomenal geometry and its applications. *Perception and Psychophysics, 48,* 105–123.

Gogel, W.C. (1993). The analysis of perceived space. In S.C. Masin (Ed.), *Foundations of perceptual theory* (pp. 113–182). Amsterdam: Elsevier.

Gogel, W.C., & Mershon, D.H. (1968). The perception of size in a distorted room. *Perception and Psychophysics, 4,* 26–28.

Goldstein, E.B. (1999). *Sensation and perception* (5th ed.). Pacific Grove, CA: Brooks/Cole.

Gombrich, E.H. (1960). *Art and illusion: A study in the psychology of pictorial representation.* London: Phaidon.

Gordon, I.E. (1997). *Theories of visual perception* (2nd ed.). London: Wiley.

Gould, J.D. (1968). Visual factors in the design of computer-controlled CRT displays. *Human Factors, 10,* 359–376.

Green, D.M. & Swets, J.A. (1966). *Signal detection theory and psychophysics.* New York: Wiley.

Gregory, R.L. (1997). *Eye and brain* (5th ed.). Oxford, UK: Oxford University Press.

Gregory, R.L., Harris J., Heard, P., & Rose, D. (Eds.). (1995). *The artful eye.* Oxford, UK: Oxford University Press.

Grimaldi, F.M. (1665). *Physico-mathesis de lumine, coloribis et iride.* Bologna: Bernia.

Gross, C.G. (1998). *Brain, vision, memory: Tales in the history of neuroscience.* Cambridge, MA: MIT Press.

Hagen, M.A. (1986). *Varieties of realism: Geometries of representational art.* New York: Cambridge University Press.

Hammond, J.H. (1981). *The camera obscura: A chronicle*. Bristol, UK: Hilger.

Harris, J. (1775). *A treatise of optics: Containing elements of the science: In two books*. London: White.

Hebb, D.O. (1949). *The organisation of behaviour*. New York: Wiley.

Helmholtz, H. von (2000). *Treatise on physiological optics, Vols. I–III* (J.P.C. Southall, Trans.). Bristol, UK: Thoemmes.

Hering, E. (1942). *Spatial sense and movement of the eye* (A. Radde, Trans.). Baltimore: American Academy of Science. (Original work published 1868)

Howard, I.P. (1982). *Human visual orientation*. London: Wiley.

Howard, I.P. (1993). Spatial vision within egocentric and exocentric frames of reference. In S.R. Ellis, M. Kaiser, & A.J. Grunwald (Eds.), *Pictorial communication in virtual and real environments* (2nd ed. pp. 338–358). London: Taylor & Francis.

Howard, I.P. & Rogers, B.J. (1995). *Binocular vision and stereopsis*. New York: Oxford University Press.

Hubel, D.H. (1995). *Eye, brain, and vision*. New York: Scientific American Library.

Hubel, D.H. & Wiesel, T.N. (1959). Receptive fields of single neurones in the cat's striate cortex. *Journal of Physiology, 148*, 574–591.

Humphreys, G.W., & Riddoch, M.J. (1994). Visual object processing in normality and pathology: Implications for rehabilitation. In M.J. Riddoch & G.W. Humphreys (Eds.), *Cognitive neuropsychology and cognitive rehabilitation*. Hove, UK: Lawrence Erlbaum Associates Ltd.

Ittelson, W.H. (1952). *The Ames demonstrations in perception*. Princeton, NJ: Princeton University Press.

James, W. (1890). *Principles of psychology, Vol. 1*. New York: Holt.

Johansson, G. (1973). Visual perception of biological motion and a model for its analysis. *Perception and Psychophysics, 14*, 201–211.

Johansson, G. (1975). Visual motion perception. *Scientific American, 232* (June), 76–89.

Julesz, B. (1970). *Foundations of cyclopean perception*. Chicago: University of Chicago Press.

Kandel, E.R., & Schwartz, J.H. (Eds.). (1985). *Principles of neural science* (2nd ed.). New York: Elsevier.

Kandel, E.R., Schwartz, J.H., & Jessel, T.M. (Eds.). (2000). *Principles of neural science* (4th ed.). New York: McGraw-Hill.

Kaufman, L. (1974). *Sight and mind*. Oxford, UK: Oxford University Press.

Kemp, M. (1990). *The science of art: Optical themes in western art from Brunelleschi to Seurat*. Hartford, CT: Yale University Press.

Kennedy, A., Brysbaert, M., & Murray, W.S. (1997). Intermittent illumination, visual inspection and reading. *Quarterly Journal of Experimental Psychology, 51A*, 135–151.

Kennedy, A., Radach, R., Heller, D., & Pynte, J. (2000). *Reading as a perceptual process*. Amsterdam: Elsevier.

Kepler, J. (1604). *Ad Vitellionem Paralipomena*. Frankfurt, Germany: Marinium and Aubrii.

Kepler, J. (1611). *Dioptrice*. Augsburg, Germany: Franci.

Kirby, J. (1755). *Dr. Brook Taylor's method of perspective made easy, both in theory and practice. In two books* (2nd ed.). Ipswich, UK: Author.

Köhler, W., & Wallach, H. (1944). Figural after-effects: An investigation of visual processes. *Proceedings of the American Philosophical Society, 88*, 269–357.

Kozlowski, L.T., & Cutting, J.E. (1977). Recognizing the sex of a walker from a dynamic point-light display. *Perception and Psychophysics, 21*, 575–580.

Land, E.H. (1977). The retinex theory of color vision. *Scientific American, 237*(6), 108–128.

Land, M., Mennie, N., & Rusted, J. (1999). The roles of vision and eye movements in the control of activities of daily living. *Perception, 28*, 1311–1328.

Lennie, P. (1998). Single units and visual cortical organization. *Perception, 27*, 889–935.

Leonardo da Vinci (1721). *A treatise of painting*. London: Senex & Taylor.

Lindberg, D.C. (1976). *Theories of vision from Al-Kindi to Kepler*. Chicago: University of Chicago Press.

Lindberg, D.C. (1992). *The beginnings of Western science*. Chicago: University of Chicago Press.

Locke, J. (1975). *An essay concerning human understanding*. Oxford, UK: Clarendon Press. (Original work published 1690)

Mach, E. (1865). Über die Wirkung der räumlichen Vertheilung des Lichtreizes auf die Netzhaut. *Sitzungsberichte der mathematisch-naturwissenschaftlichen Classe der kaiserlichen Akademie der Wissenschaften, 52*, 303–322.

Mach, E. (1866). Über die physiologische Wirkung raümlich vertheilter Lichtreize. (Dritte Abhandlung). *Sitzungsberichte der mathematisch-naturwissenschaftlichen Classe der kaiserlichen Akademie der Wissenschaften, 54*, 393–408.

Marr, D. (1982). *Vision*. San Francisco: Freeman.

Marr, D. and Nishihara, H.K. (1978). Representation and recognition of the spatial organisation of three-dimensional shapes. *Proceedings of the Royal Society of London*, B200, 269–299.

Mather, G., & Murdoch, L. (1994). Gender discrimination in biological motion displays based on dynamic cues. *Proceedings of the Royal Society of London, B258*, 273–279.

Mather, G., Verstraten, F., & Anstis, S. (Eds.). (1998). *The motion after-effect: A modern perspective*. Cambridge, MA: MIT Press.

May, M.T. (1968). *Galen: On the usefulness of the parts of the body*. Ithaca, NY: Cornell University Press.

Michaels, C.F., & Carello, C. (1981). *Direct perception*. Englewood Cliffs, NJ: Prentice-Hall.

Millodot, M. (2000). *Dictionary of optometry and visual science* (5th ed.). London: Butterworth-Heinemann Medical.

Milner, A.D., & Goodale, M.A. (1995). *The visual brain in action*, Oxford, UK: Oxford University Press.

Mollon, J.D. (1989). "Tho' she kneel'd in that place where they grew . . ." The uses and origins of primate colour vision. *Journal of Experimental Biology, 146*, 21–38.

Molyneux, W. (1692). *Dioptrica nova. A treatise of dioptricks in two parts*. London: Tooke.

Morgan, M.J. (1977). *Molyneux's question: Vision, touch and the philosophy of perception*. Cambridge, UK: Cambridge University Press.

Müller, J. (1840). *Elements of Physiology*. Vol. 1. (2nd edn, W. Baly, Trans.). London: Taylor & Walton.

Müller, J. (1843). *Elements of Physiology*. Vol. 2. (2nd edn, W. Baly, Trans.). London: Taylor & Walton.

Necker, L.A. (1832). Observations on some remarkable phenomena in Switzerland: and an optical phenomenon which occurs on viewing a figure of a crystal or geometrical solid. *London and Edinburgh. Philosophical Magazine and Journal of Science, 1,* 329–337.

Newton, I. (1672). A letter of Mr. Isaac Newton . . . containing his new theory about light and colours. *Philosophical Transactions of the Royal Society, 7,* 3075–3087.

Newton, I. (1704). *Opticks: Or, a treatise of the reflections, refractions, inflections and colours of light.* London: Smith & Walford.

Nishida, S., & Ashida, H. (2000). A hierarchical structure of motion system revealed by interocular transfer of flicker motion aftereffects. *Vision Research, 40,* 265–278.

Ono, H. (1981). On Wells' (1792) law of visual direction. *Perception and Psychophysics, 32,* 201–210.

Ono, H. (1990). Binocular visual directions of an object when seen as single or double. In D. Regan (Ed.), *Vision and visual dysfunction: Vol. 9. Binocular vision* (pp. 1–18). New York: Macmillan.

Palmer, S.E. (1999). *Vision science: Photons to phenomenology.* Cambridge, MA: MIT Press.

Papathomas, T.V., Chubb, C., Gorea, A., & Kowler, E. (Eds.). (1995). *Early vision and beyond.* Cambridge, MA: MIT Press.

Park, D. (1997). *The fire within the eye: A historical essay on the nature and meaning of light.* Princeton, NJ: Princeton University Press.

Parker, D.M., & Deregowski, J. (1990). *Perception and artistic style.* Amsterdam: North-Holland.

Parkin, A.J. (1996). *Explorations of cognitive neuropsychology.* Oxford, UK: Blackwell.

Peli, E. (1999). Optometric and perceptual issues with head-mounted displays. In P. Mouroulis (Ed.), *Visual instrumentation: Optical design and engineering principles* (pp. 205–276). NewYork: McGraw-Hill.

Perret, D.I., Hietanen, J.K., Oram, M.W., & Benson, P.J. (1992). Organisation and function of cells responsive to faces in the temporal cortex. *Philosophical Transactions of the Royal Society, B335,* 23–30.

Pirenne, M.H. (1970). *Optics, painting and photography.* Cambridge, UK: Cambridge University Press.

Platter, F. (1583). *De corporis humani structur et usu.* Basel: König.

Pliny. (1940). *Natural history: Vol. 3. Books VIII–XI* (H. Rackham, Trans.) London: Heinemann.

Polyak, S. (1957). *The vertebrate visual system.* Chicago: University of Chicago Press.

Posner, M.I., & Raichle, M.E. (1997). *Images of mind.* New York: Scientific American Library.

Post, R.B., & Leibowitz, H.W. (1985). A revised analysis of the role of efference in motion perception. *Perception, 14,* 631–643.

Pylyshyn, Z. (1999). Is vision contiguous with cognition? The case for cognitive impenetrability of visual perception. *Behavioral and Brain Sciences, 22,* 341–423.

Quinlan, P.T. (1991). *Connectionism and psychology: A psychological perspective on new connectionist research.* London: Harvester Wheatsheaf.

Ratliff, F. (1965). *Mach bands: Quantitative studies on neural networks in the retina.* San Francisco: Holden-Day.

Reed, E., & Jones, R. (Eds.) (1982). *Reasons for realism: Selected essays of James J. Gibson.* Hillsdale, NJ: Lawrence Erlbaum Associates Inc.

Reid, T. (1764). *An inquiry into the human mind: On the principles of common sense.* Edinburgh, UK: Millar, Kincaid & Bell.

Reinhardt-Rutland, A.H., Annett, J.M., & Gifford, M. (1999). Depth perception and indirect viewing: Reflections on minimally invasive surgery. *International Journal of Cognitive Ergonomics, 3*, 77–90.

Rock, I. (1984). *Perception.* San Francisco: Freeman.

Rock, I. (Ed.). (1997). *Indirect perception.* Cambridge, MA: MIT Press.

Ronchi, V. (1970). *The nature of light: An historical survey* (V. Barocas, Trans.). London: Heinemann.

Rose, D. (1999). The historical roots of the theories of local signs and labelled lines. *Perception, 28*, 675–685.

Rosenblatt, F. (1959). Two theorems of statistical separability in the perceptron. In *The mechanisations of thought processes* (pp. 421–456). London: Her Majesty's Stationery Office.

Rubin, E. (1915). *Synsoplevede figurer.* Copenhagen: Gyldendalske.

Runeson, S., & Frykholm, G. (1981). Visual perception of lifted weights. *Journal of Experimental Psychology: Human Perception and Performance, 7*, 733–740.

Sabra, A.I. (Trans. & Ed.). (1989). *The optics of Ibn Al-Haytham: Books I–III. On direct vision.* London: Warburg Institute.

Sacks, O. (1985). *The man who mistook his wife for a hat.* London: Duckworth.

Saito, A. (Ed.). (2000). *Bartlett, culture and cognition.* Hove, UK: Psychology Press.

Scheiner, C. (1619). *Oculus hoc est: Fundamentum opticum.* Innsbruck, Austria: Agricola.

Sekuler, R., & Blake, R. (1994). *Perception* (3rd ed.). New York: McGraw-Hill.

Selfridge, O.G. (1959). Pandemonium: a paradigm for learning. In *The mechanisation of thought processes* (pp. 513–526). London: Her Majesty's Stationery Office.

Selfridge, O.G. & Neisser, U. (1960). Pattern recognition by machine. *Scientific American, 203*, 60–68.

Slater, A. (Ed.). (1998). *Perceptual developments: Visual, auditory, and speech perception in infancy.* Hove, UK: Psychology Press.

Smith, A.M. (1996). *Ptolemy's theory of visual perception: An English translation of the* Optics *with introduction and commentary.* Philadelphia: American Philosophical Society.

Smith, A.M. (1998). Ptolemy, Alhazen, and Kepler and the problem of optical images. *Arabic Sciences and Philosophy, 8*, 9–44.

Springer, S.P., & Deutsch, G. (1997). *Left brain right brain: Perspectives from cognitive neuroscience* (5th ed.). New York: Freeman.

Stevens, S.S. (1975). *Psychophysics.* New York: Wiley.

Swanston, M.T. (1979). The effects of verbal meaning and response categorisation on the fragmentation of steadily fixated lines. *Perception, 4*, 45–48.

Swanston, M.T. (1994). Frames of reference and motion aftereffects. *Perception, 24*, 1257–1264.

Swanston, M.T., & Gogel, W.C. (1986). Perceived size and motion in depth from optical expansion. *Perception and Psychophysics, 39*, 309–326.

Swanston, M.T. & Wade, N.J. (1994). A peculiar optical phænomenon. *Perception, 23*, 1107–1110.

Taffinder, N., Smith, S.G.T., Huber, J., Russell, R.C.G., & Darzi, A. (1999). The effect of a second-generation 3D endoscope on the laproscopic precision of novices and experienced surgeons. *Surgical Endoscopy, 13*, 1087–1092.

Tarr, M.J. & Bülthoff, H.H. (Eds.). (1999). *Object recognition in man, monkey, and machine*. Cambridge, MA: MIT Press.

Tovée, M.J. (1996). *An introduction to the visual system*. Cambridge, UK: Cambridge University Press.

Treisman, A. (1988). Features and objects: The fourteenth Bartlett Memorial Lecture. *Quarterly Journal of Experimental Psychology, 40A*, 201–237.

Turner, R.S. (1994). *In the eye's mind: Vision and the Helmholtz–Hering controversy*. Princeton, NJ: Princeton University Press.

Tyler, C.W., & Clarke, M.B. (1990). The autostereogram. *Proceedings of the International Society for Optical Engineering, 1256*, 182–197.

Ullman, S. (1979). *The interpretation of visual motion*. Cambridge, MA: MIT Press.

Ullman, S. (1996). *High-level vision: Object recognition and visual cognition*. Cambridge, MA: MIT Press.

Ungeleider, L.G., & Mishkin, M. (1982). Two cortical visual systems. In D.J. Ingle, M.A. Goodale, & R.J.W. Mansfield (Eds.), *Analysis of visual behavior* (pp. 549–586). Cambridge, MA: MIT Press.

Vernon, M.D. (1970). *Perception through experience*. London: Methuen.

Vesalius, A. (1543). *De humani corporis fabrica libri septem*. Basel, Switzerland: Oporini.

Vital-Durand, F., Atkinson, J., & Braddick, O.J. (Eds.). (1996). *Infant vision*. Oxford, UK: Oxford University Press.

Wade, N. (1982). *The art and science of visual illusions*. London: Routledge & Kegan Paul.

Wade, N. (1990). *Visual allusions: Pictures of perception*. London: Lawrence Erlbaum Associates Ltd.

Wade, N. (1995). *Psychologists in word and image*. Cambridge, MA: MIT Press.

Wade, N.J. (1983). *Brewster and Wheatstone on vision*. London: Academic Press.

Wade, N.J. (1987). On the late invention of the stereoscope. *Perception, 16*, 785–818.

Wade, N.J. (1992). The representation of orientation in vision. *Australian Journal of Psychology, 44*, 139–145.

Wade, N.J. (1994). Hermann von Helmholtz (1821–1894). *Perception, 23*, 981–989.

Wade, N.J. (1998). *A natural history of vision*. Cambridge, MA: MIT Press.

Wade, N.J. (2000). Porterfield and Wells on the motion of our eyes. *Perception, 29*, 221–239.

Wade, N.J., & Brožek, J. (2001). *Purkinje's vision: The dawning of neuroscience*. Mahwah, NJ: Lawrence Erlbaum Associates Inc.

Wade, N.J., & Bruce, V. (2001). Surveying the seen: 100 years of British vision. *British Journal of Psychology, 92*, 79–112.

Wade, N.J., & Heller, D. (1997). Scopes of perception: The experimental manipulation of space and time. *Psychological Research, 60*, 227–237.

Wade, N.J., & Hughes, P. (1999). Fooling the eyes: *Trompe l'oeil* and reverse perspective. *Perception, 28*, 1115–1119.

Wade, N.J., Ono, H., & Lillakas, L. (2001). Leonardo da Vinci's struggles with representations of reality. *Leonardo, 34*, 231–235.

Wade, N.J., Spillmann, L., & Swanston, M.T. (1996). Visual motion aftereffects: Critical adaptation and test conditions. *Vision Research, 36*, 2167–2175.

Wade, N.J., & Swanston, M.T. (1987). The representation of nonuniform motion: Induced movement. *Perception, 16*, 555–571.

Wade, N.J., & Swanston, M.T. (1996). A general model for the perception of space and motion. *Perception, 25*, 187–194.

Wade, N.J., Swanston, M.T., & de Weert, C.M.M. (1993). On interocular transfer of the motion aftereffect. *Perception, 22*, 1365–1380.

Wallach, H. (1976). *On perception*. Chicago: Quadrangle.

Wallach, H., & O'Connell, D.N. (1953). The kinetic depth effect. *Journal of Experimental Psychology, 45*, 205–217.

Walsh, V., & Cowey, A. (1998). Magnetic stimulation studies of visual cognition. *Trends in Cognitive Sciences, 2*, 103–110.

Wandell, B.A. (1995). *Foundations of vision*. Sunderland, MA: Sinauer Associates.

Wasserman, G.S. (1978). *Color vision: An historical introduction*. New York: Wiley.

Watson, J.B. (1913). Psychology as the behaviorist views it. *Psychological Review, 20*, 158–177.

Watson, R.I. (1968). *The great psychologists: From Aristotle to Freud* (2nd ed.)., Philadelphia: J.B. Lippincott.

Watson, R.I. (1979). *Basic writings in the history of psychology*. New York: Oxford University Press.

Weiskrantz, L. (1990). Outlooks for blindsight: Explicit methodologies for implicit processes. *Proceedings of the Royal Society (London), B239*, 247–278.

Werblin, F.S. (1976). The control of sensitivity in the retina. In R. Held & W. Richards (Eds.), *Recent progress in perception*. San Francisco: Freeman.

Wertheim, A. (1994). Motion perception during self-motion: The direct versus inferential controversy revisited. *Behavioral and Brain Sciences, 17*, 293–311.

Wertheimer, M. (1922). Untersuchungen zur Lehre von der Gestalt. I. Prinzipielle Bemerkungen. *Psychologische Forschung, 1*, 47–58.

Wertheimer, M. (1923). Untersuchungen zur Lehre von der Gestalt. II. *Psychologische Forschung, 4*, 301–350.

Wertheimer, M. (1938). Gestalt theory. In W.D. Ellis (Ed.) *A source book of Gestalt psychology* (pp. 1–11). New York: The Humanities Press.

Wheatstone, C. (1838). Contributions to the physiology of vision—Part the first. On some remarkable, and hitherto unobserved, phenomena of binocular vision. *Philosophical Transactions of the Royal Society, 128*, 371–394.

Wheatstone, C. (1852). Contributions to the physiology of vision—Part the second. On some remarkable, and hitherto unobserved, phenomena of binocular vision. *Philosophical Transactions of the Royal Society, 142*, 1–17.

Wickens, C.D. (1999). Frames of reference for navigation. In D. Gopher & A. Koriat (Eds.), *Attention and performance XVII* (pp. 113–144). Cambridge, MA: MIT Press.

Wilkes, A.L., & Wade, N.J. (1997). Bain on neural networks. *Brain and Cognition, 33*, 295–305.

Wilkins, A.J. (1995). *Visual stress*. Oxford, UK: Oxford University Press.

Willats, J. (1997). *Art and representation*. Princeton, NJ: Princeton University Press.

Wittreich, W.J. (1959). Visual perception and personality. *Scientific American, 200*(4), 56–75.

Young, T. (1793). Observations on vision. *Philosophical Transactions of the Royal Society, 83*, 169–181.

Young, T. (1801). On the mechanism of the eye. *Philosophical Transactions of the Royal Society, 91*, 23–88.

Young, T. (1802). On the theory of lights and colours. *Philosophical Transactions of the Royal Society, 92*, 12–48.

Zeki, S. (1993). *A vision of the brain*. London: Blackwell.

Zeki, S. (1999). *Inner vision: An exploration of art and the brain*. Oxford, UK: Oxford University Press.

Name index

Numbers in **boldface** indicate pages on which portraits can be found

Subject index

Entries in **boldface** indicate chapter subsections